C# Programming Cookbook

Quick fixes to your common C# programming problems, with a focus on C# 6.0

Dirk Strauss

BIRMINGHAM - MUMBAI

C# Programming Cookbook

First published: July 2016

Production reference: 1210716

Published by Packt Publishing Ltd.
Livery Place
35 Livery Street
Birmingham B3 2PB, UK.

ISBN 978-1-78646-730-0

www.packtpub.com

Credits

Author
Dirk Strauss

Reviewer
Fabio Claudio Ferracchiati

Commissioning Editor
Edward Gordon

Acquisition Editor
Nitin Dasan

Content Development Editor
Zeeyan Pinheiro

Technical Editor
Kunal Chaudhari

Copy Editor
Karuna Narayan

Project Coordinator
Izzat Contractor

Proofreader
Safis Editing

Indexer
Rekha Nair

Graphics
Jason Monteiro

Production Coordinator
Melwyn Dsa

Cover Work
Melwyn Dsa

About the Author

Dirk Strauss is a software developer and Microsoft .NET MVP from South Africa with over 13 years of programming experience. He has extensive experience in SYSPRO Customization, an ERP system, with C# and web development as his main focus.

He works for Evolution Software, but in all fairness, he doesn't really like to call it working at all. According to him, when you're having fun and loving what you do with incredibly inspirational individuals, you will not work a day in your life.

Acknowledgements

Firstly, I would like to thank my mom for giving me the opportunities I had in life. Without your support, love, and sacrifice, I would not be where I am today. You made do with less so that I could have more. As I grow older, with kids of my own, I now realize the depth and breadth of your love and dearly appreciate it all.

I would also like to thank all of the educators at the Nelson Mandela Metropolitan University who are shaping the future IT professionals for an increasingly complex technological world. I specifically want to thank Professor Reinhardt A. Botha and Dr. Johan Van Niekerk. Their passion for information technology and their dedication to their students had a huge impact on me and made me the IT person I am today.

Throughout my career, I have met many people, had many colleagues, and dealt with more clients than I can probably remember. There is, however, a colleague and dear friend that has remained steadfast and resolute in his friendship, support, and mentorship. Vincent Van Zyl formed a big part of my early career and gave me a friendly nudge in the right direction when I was trying to find my way within a technology that was new to me. He was, and still is, a mentor and confidant in my professional life. He possesses a gentle spirit and a friendly nature that sets an example and truly makes the world a better place to live in. He loves his wife more than any man I have ever met and I am honored to know him, utterly humbled to call him a colleague, and incredibly blessed to have him as a friend.

Last but by no means least, I'd like to thank my wife and children. It would seem like such a cliché to thank you for putting up with me during the weekends and evenings that I spent working on this book, as this is a common theme that almost all authors thank their families for. The reality is that you all went above and beyond what was needed for me to complete this book. You guys expressed a profound understanding of what this project meant to me, which was so evident in the way your actions and sacrifices made a difference. Adele, you are my wingman, my comrade of can-do, and my rock throughout some grueling times. From the little things you did, such as supplying copious amounts of coffee in the cold evenings with an accuracy that made me wonder if you could read my mind, to the more important things, such as being mommy and daddy to our kids, fills me with an appreciation and gratitude that I will probably never be able to repay. I saw it all, I appreciate it all, and I love you all the more for it.

To my daughter Irénéé (pops) and my son Tristan (squeak), while you are still too young to read this now, you will be able to one day. I want to thank you for making do with a little less daddy time and for being patient and understanding when daddy could not play. You kids make me a better man and inspire me to face challenges in all aspects of my life with a determination and resolve I see in your eyes every day. You teach me more about life and all that is good by just being who you are. Your dreams are my dreams come true and there is nothing in this existence of ours that can separate me from the love I have for you. I therefore dedicate this book to Adele, Irénéé, and Tristan.

About the Reviewer

Fabio Claudio Ferracchiati is a senior consultant and a senior analyst/developer using Microsoft technologies. He works for Blu Arancio (www.bluarancio.com). He is a Microsoft Certified Solution Developer for .NET, Microsoft Certified Application Developer for .NET, and Microsoft Certified Professional. He is also a prolific author and technical reviewer. Over the last ten years, he's written articles for Italian and international magazines and coauthored more than 10 books on a variety of computer topics.

www.PacktPub.com

eBooks, discount offers, and more

Did you know that Packt offers eBook versions of every book published, with PDF and ePub files available? You can upgrade to the eBook version at www.PacktPub.com and as a print book customer, you are entitled to a discount on the eBook copy. Get in touch with us at customercare@packtpub.com for more details.

At www.PacktPub.com, you can also read a collection of free technical articles, sign up for a range of free newsletters and receive exclusive discounts and offers on Packt books and eBooks.

https://www2.packtpub.com/books/subscription/packtlib

Do you need instant solutions to your IT questions? PacktLib is Packt's online digital book library. Here, you can search, access, and read Packt's entire library of books.

Why Subscribe?

- ► Fully searchable across every book published by Packt
- ► Copy and paste, print, and bookmark content
- ► On demand and accessible via a web browser

Table of Contents

Preface

Visual Studio 2015 brings a lot to the developer's toolset when it comes to creating world-class applications across a variety of platforms. The new language features in C# 6.0 provide developers with easier ways to perform familiar tasks. This book will show you the beauty of C#, which when combined with the power of Visual Studio, makes you a very formidable developer capable of meeting a variety of programming challenges head on.

Many of the chapters in this book will provide you with just enough to jumpstart your understanding of the topics discussed. Irrespective of your skill level, when it comes to programming with C#, this book provides something for everyone.

What this book covers

Chapter 1, New Features in C# 6.0, introduces you to the new features available in C# 6.0.

Chapter 2, Classes and Generics, covers classes and generics, which form the building blocks of modern day applications. You will learn what they are and how to use them more effectively.

Chapter 3, Object-Oriented Programming in C#, covers OOP, which is why we do what we do in the way we do it. We will discuss the fundamentals when it comes to this concept.

Chapter 4, Composing Event-Based Programs Using Reactive Extensions, helps you make your applications more responsive using Rx and leveraging the power of providing real-time data.

Chapter 5, Create Microservices on Azure Service Fabric, shows how you can break away from the traditional approach to developing applications. Instead of one single monolithic application, microservices break an application up into smaller bits that can function on their own.

Chapter 6, Making Apps Responsive with Asynchronous Programming, covers using asynchronous programming to never let your application lock up because it is waiting for a long running task to complete.

Chapter 7, High Performance Programming Using Parallel and Multithreading in C#, demonstrates how you can make good use of the performance provided by today's multicore CPUs.

Chapter 8, Code Contracts, deals with writing robust code that will validate the correctness of data being passed to a method. We will also cover code contracts, which allow developers to write better code.

Chapter 9, Regular Expressions, covers regex, which is a technology that is baked into the .NET Framework and is often overlooked in most books. Understanding it better will go a long way toward adding value to your skillset.

Chapter 10, Choosing and Using a Source Control Strategy, delves into the different strategies that different developers in different situations require when it comes to using source control.

Chapter 11, Creating a Mobile Application in Visual Studio, discusses what you can do with Visual Studio, which has made it possible to make developing mobile applications across multiple platforms within reach for practically any developer.

Chapter 12, Writing Secure Code and Debugging in Visual Studio, emphasizes how being able to write more secure code will set your application apart from others. Being able to debug like a boss will set you apart from the rest.

Chapter 13, Creating a Web Application in Azure, demonstrates just how easy it is to create a web application in Azure.

What you need for this book

To complete the code samples in this book, you will need a copy of Visual Studio 2015 or later. Most other required components can be installed via NuGet.

Who this book is for

This book is aimed at developers who have basic familiarity with C# programming and know the VS 2015 environment.

Sections

In this book, you will find several headings that appear frequently (Getting ready, How to do it, How it works, There's more, and See also).

To give clear instructions on how to complete a recipe, we use these sections as follows:

Getting ready

This section tells you what to expect in the recipe, and describes how to set up any software or any preliminary settings required for the recipe.

How to do it...

This section contains the steps required to follow the recipe.

How it works...

This section usually consists of a detailed explanation of what happened in the previous section.

There's more...

This section consists of additional information about the recipe in order to make the reader more knowledgeable about the recipe.

See also

This section provides helpful links to other useful information for the recipe.

Conventions

In this book, you will find a number of text styles that distinguish between different kinds of information. Here are some examples of these styles and an explanation of their meaning.

Code words in text, database table names, folder names, filenames, file extensions, pathnames, dummy URLs, user input, and Twitter handles are shown as follows: "Add a class called `CSharpSix`. Add a property to this class called `FavoriteFeature`."

A block of code is set as follows:

```
public class CSharpSix
{
    public string FavoriteFeature { get; set; }
}
```

Any command-line input or output is written as follows:

```
PM> Install-Package System.Reactive.Windows.Forms
```

New terms and **important words** are shown in bold. Words that you see on the screen, for example, in menus or dialog boxes, appear in the text like this: "Start Visual Studio 2015 and click on the **File** menu. Then, click on **New** and then select **Project**."

> Warnings or important notes appear in a box like this.

> Tips and tricks appear like this.

Reader feedback

Feedback from our readers is always welcome. Let us know what you think about this book—what you liked or disliked. Reader feedback is important for us as it helps us develop titles that you will really get the most out of.

To send us general feedback, simply e-mail `feedback@packtpub.com`, and mention the book's title in the subject of your message.

If there is a topic that you have expertise in and you are interested in either writing or contributing to a book, see our author guide at `www.packtpub.com/authors`.

Customer support

Now that you are the proud owner of a Packt book, we have a number of things to help you to get the most from your purchase.

Downloading the example code

You can download the example code files for this book from your account at `http://www.packtpub.com`. If you purchased this book elsewhere, you can visit `http://www.packtpub.com/support` and register to have the files e-mailed directly to you.

You can download the code files by following these steps:

1. Log in or register to our website using your e-mail address and password.
2. Hover the mouse pointer on the **SUPPORT** tab at the top.
3. Click on **Code Downloads & Errata**.
4. Enter the name of the book in the **Search** box.

5. Select the book for which you're looking to download the code files.

6. Choose from the drop-down menu where you purchased this book from.

7. Click on **Code Download**.

You can also download the code files by clicking on the **Code Files** button on the book's webpage at the Packt Publishing website. This page can be accessed by entering the book's name in the **Search** box. Please note that you need to be logged in to your Packt account.

Once the file is downloaded, please make sure that you unzip or extract the folder using the latest version of:

- ► WinRAR / 7-Zip for Windows
- ► Zipeg / iZip / UnRarX for Mac
- ► 7-Zip / PeaZip for Linux

The code bundle for the book is also hosted on GitHub at `https://github.com/PacktPublishing/C#-Programming-Cookbook`. We also have other code bundles from our rich catalog of books and videos available at `https://github.com/PacktPublishing/`. Check them out!

Downloading the color images of this book

We also provide you with a PDF file that has color images of the screenshots/diagrams used in this book. The color images will help you better understand the changes in the output. You can download this file from `http://www.packtpub.com/sites/default/files/downloads/C#ProgrammingCookbook_ColorImages.pdf`.

Errata

Although we have taken every care to ensure the accuracy of our content, mistakes do happen. If you find a mistake in one of our books—maybe a mistake in the text or the code—we would be grateful if you could report this to us. By doing so, you can save other readers from frustration and help us improve subsequent versions of this book. If you find any errata, please report them by visiting `http://www.packtpub.com/submit-errata`, selecting your book, clicking on the **Errata Submission Form** link, and entering the details of your errata. Once your errata are verified, your submission will be accepted and the errata will be uploaded to our website or added to any list of existing errata under the Errata section of that title.

To view the previously submitted errata, go to `https://www.packtpub.com/books/content/support` and enter the name of the book in the search field. The required information will appear under the **Errata** section.

Piracy

Piracy of copyrighted material on the Internet is an ongoing problem across all media. At Packt, we take the protection of our copyright and licenses very seriously. If you come across any illegal copies of our works in any form on the Internet, please provide us with the location address or website name immediately so that we can pursue a remedy.

Please contact us at `copyright@packtpub.com` with a link to the suspected pirated material.

We appreciate your help in protecting our authors and our ability to bring you valuable content.

Questions

If you have a problem with any aspect of this book, you can contact us at `questions@packtpub.com`, and we will do our best to address the problem.

1
New Features in C# 6.0

In this chapter, we will cover the following recipes with regard to the new features of C# 6.0:

- Creating your Visual Studio project
- String interpolation
- Null-conditional operator
- Initializers for auto-implemented properties and getter-only auto properties
- Index initializers
- The `nameof` expressions
- Expression-bodied functions and properties
- Using `static`
- Exception filters
- Using `await` operator in `catch` and `finally` blocks

Introduction

C# as a programming language first appeared in 2000. Its development team is led by the prominent Danish software engineer Anders Hejlsberg. He is the lead architect of C# and core developer of TypeScript. The C# programming language is simple to use, and this book will deal with C# 6.0, which was released on 20 July, 2015.

Knowing what new language features are available in C# 6.0 will not only make you a more effective developer, but will also allow you to implement the latest and best practices in the software that you create. A little-known fact is that C# was actually called **C-like Object Oriented Language** (**Cool**) before its release at Microsoft's *Professional Developers Conference* in July 2000, but was changed to C# at the time of its release.

The name might have changed, but C# remains a very cool language to learn and use. This chapter will take you through the new features of C# 6.0 and illustrate how to effectively use these features in you daily programming tasks.

Creating your Visual Studio project

The Visual Studio project that you will create will be used to add the classes that contain the code samples in each recipe of this book. The project will be a simple console application that will call into static classes that do the work of illustrating the recipe code and outputting the results (if any) to the console window.

Getting ready

To step through the recipes in this book, you will need a copy of Visual Studio 2015. If you do not have a copy of Visual Studio 2015, you can download a free copy of Visual Studio 2015 Community from `https://www.visualstudio.com/en-us/products/visual-studio-community-vs.aspx`.

You can also compare editions of Visual Studio 2015 by navigating to `https://www.visualstudio.com/en-us/products/compare-visual-studio-2015-products-vs.aspx`.

After you have downloaded and installed Visual Studio 2015, create a new console application that will contain the recipes illustrated in this book.

How to do it...

1. Start Visual Studio 2015 and click on the **File** menu. Then, click on **New** and then select **Project**. You can also use the *Ctrl + Shift + N* keyboard shortcut:

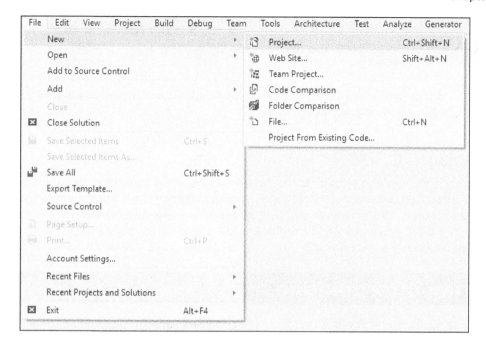

2. From the **New Project** dialog screen, select **Console Application**, which can be found by going to **Installed | Templates | Visual C# | Windows | Classic Desktop** in the tree view to the left. You can call your console application `CodeSamples`:

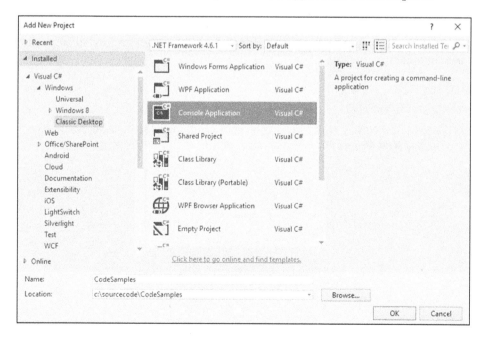

You will notice that the selected framework is **.NET Framework 4.6.1**, which is selected by default. Leave this framework selected when creating your project.

3. Visual Studio now creates your console application, which we will use to create all the code samples needed for this book.

How it works...

This console application will form the base of the recipes in this book. Each recipe can be individually added to this console application. A recipe, therefore, can function on its own without the need to create a previous recipe. You can also easily separate any custom code you might want to add and experiment with. It is also recommended that you play around with the code by adding classes of your own.

String interpolation

String interpolation is a very easy and precise way to inject variable values into a string. An interpolated string expression looks at contained expressions. It then replaces those expressions with the `ToString` representations of the expressions' results.

Getting ready

Create a new class to test your code. We will use the example of reading the current exchange rate for a specific currency to illustrate how string interpolation can be used to output strings to the user interface.

How to do it...

1. Create a new class by right-clicking on your solution, selecting **Add,** and then selecting **New Project** from the context menu:

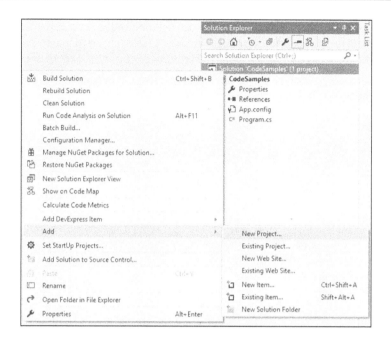

2. From the **Add New Project** dialog screen, select **Class Library** from the installed templates and call your class Chapter1:

3. Your new class library will be added to your solution with a default name of `Class1.cs`, which I renamed to `Recipes.cs` in order to distinguish the code properly. You can, however, rename your class to whatever you like if that makes more sense to you.

4. To rename your class, simply click on the class name in **Solution Explorer** and select **Rename** from the context menu:

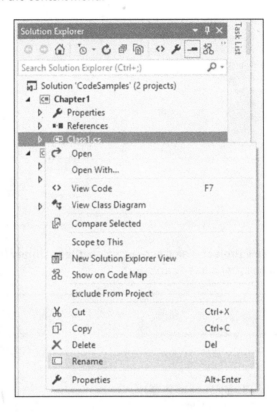

5. Visual Studio will ask you to confirm a rename of all references to the **Class1** code element in the project. Just click on **Yes**:

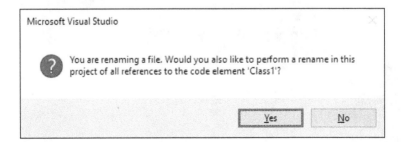

6. The class that is created now needs to be made static using the `static` keyword. Also, rename the class name in code to `Recipe1StringInterpolation`:

```
namespace Chapter1
{
    public static class Recipe1StringInterpolation
    {

    }
}
```

> Note that static classes, therefore, do not need to be instantiated and will be sealed classes by default. This means that they cannot be inherited further. In practice, you would normally define helper or utility classes as static. These are classes that will be used often by your application to, for example, parse dates or perform calculations. The use of the `static` keyword here is simply to illustrate the specific new features of C# 6.0 within a class that can easily and quickly be called from the console application. The static class in reality would most likely not be a good fit for all the examples illustrated.

7. Inside your class, add a property to contain the base currency:

```
public static string BaseCurrency { get; private set; }
```

8. Next, include a dummy method to return the exchange rate:

```
private static decimal PreformConversion(string toCurrency)
{
    decimal rate = 0.0m;

    if (BaseCurrency.Equals("ZAR"))
    {
        switch (toCurrency)
        {
            case "USD":
                rate = 16.3040m;
                break;
            default:
                rate = 1.0m;
                break;
        }
    }

    return rate;
}
```

9. The last method to add is the method that will return the interpolated string expression:

```
public static string ReadExchangeRate(string
fromCurrencyCode, string toCurrencyCode)
{
    BaseCurrency = fromCurrencyCode;
    decimal conversion = PreformConversion(toCurrencyCode);
    return $"1 {toCurrencyCode} = {conversion}
{fromCurrencyCode} ";
}
```

10. You now need to hook up the class you created to your console application. You therefore need to add a reference to the class from the console application. Right-click on **References** in your `CodeSamples` project and select **Add Reference...**:

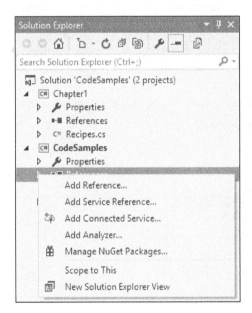

11. From the **Reference Manager** dialog that pops up, select the `Chapter1` solution to add it as a reference. Then, click on the **OK** button:

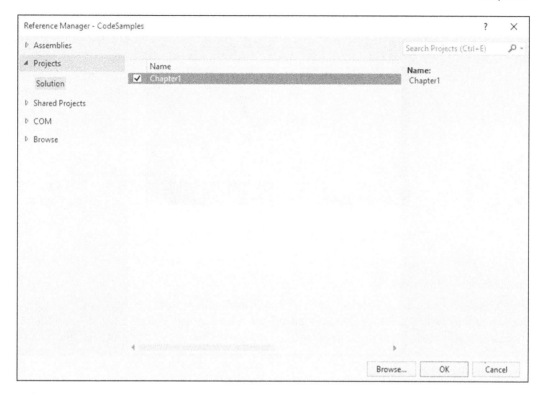

12. In your `CodeSamples` project, double-click on the `Program.cs` file and add the following code to the `Main` method:

```
string RandDollarExchangeRate =
Chapter1.Recipe1StringInterpolation.ReadExchangeRate("ZAR",
"USD");
Console.WriteLine("The current Rand / Dollar exchange rate
is:");
Console.WriteLine(RandDollarExchangeRate);
Console.Read();
```

13. To see the result, run your application and see the output in the console application:

14. The interpolated string expression is output as `1 USD = 16,3040 ZAR`.

How it works...

The console application passes the currency codes for South African Rand and US Dollar to the static class by calling the following line of code:
`Chapter1.Recipe1StringInterpolation.ReadExchangeRate("ZAR", "USD");`

This class is static and, as mentioned previously, does not need to be instantiated. The `ReadExchangeRate` method then reads the exchange rate and formats it into a suitable string using string interpolation. You will notice that the interpolated string expression is written as `$"1 {toCurrencyCode} = {conversion} {fromCurrencyCode} ";`.

The `toCurrencyCode`, `conversion`, and `fromCurrencyCode` variables are expressed directly inside the string expression. This is a much easier way of formatting strings because you can do away with `String.Format`, used in the previous versions of C#. Previously, the same expression would have been written as `String.Format("1 {0} = {1} {2} ", toCurrencyCode, conversion, fromCurrencyCode);`.

As you can see, the interpolated string expression is much easier to read and write. In reality though, string interpolation is merely syntactical sugar because the compiler treats the expression like `String.Format` anyway. You might be wondering how you would express a curly bracket when using string interpolation. To do this, you can simply use a double curly bracket in your expression. If you need to express the exchange rate as `{16,3040}`, you would need to express it as `$"{{{conversion}}}";`.

You can also format your string right there inside the interpolated string expression. If you returned the `$"The date is {DateTime.Now}";` expression, the output would be `The date is 2016/01/10 3:04:48 PM`. You can go ahead and modify the expression to format the date using a colon, followed by the format to use. Change the code to `$"The date is {DateTime.Now : MMMM dd, yyyy}";`. The output will be formatted and result in `The date is January 5, 2016`.

Another great tip is that you can express a condition in the string expression. Consider the following line of code that determines whether a year is a leap year or not:

```
$"The year {DateTime.Now.Year}
{(DateTime.IsLeapYear(DateTime.Now.Year) ? " is " : " is not ")} a
leap year.";
```

We can use the ternary ? operator one step further. Consider the following line of code:

```
$"There {(StudentCount > 1 ? "are " : "is ")}{StudentCount}
student{(StudentCount > 1 ? "s" : "")} in the list."
```

As the colon is used to denote formatting, we have to wrap the conditional part of the expression in parenthesis. String interpolation is a very nice way to express strings in code that is easy to read and understand.

Null-conditional operator

The worst thing that a developer can do is not check for null in code. This means that there is no reference to an object, in other words, there is a null. Reference-type variables have a default value of null. Value types, on the other hand, cannot be null. In C# 2, developers were introduced to the nullable type. To effectively make sure that objects are not null, developers usually write sometimes elaborate if statements to check whether objects are null or not. C# 6.0 made this process very easy with the introduction of the null-conditional operator.

It is expressed by writing ?. and is called the question-dot operator. The question is written after the instance, right before calling the property via the dot. An easy way to think of the null-conditional operator is to remember that if the left-hand side of the operator is null, the whole expression is null. If the left-hand side is not null, the property is invoked and becomes the result of the operation. To really see the power of the null-conditional operator is to see it in action.

Getting ready

We will create another class that will illustrate the use of the null-conditional operator. The method will call a Student class to return a count of students in the resulting list. We will check to see whether the Student class is valid before returning the student count.

How to do it...

1. Create another class called `Recipe2NullConditionalOperator` beneath the last class you wrote in the *Creating your Visual Studio project* recipe:

```
public static class Recipe2NullConditionalOperator
{

}
```

2. Add a method called `GetStudents` to the class and add the following code to it:

```
public static int GetStudents()
{
    List<Student> students = new List<Student>();
    Student st = new Student();

    st.FirstName = "Dirk";
    st.LastName = "Strauss";
    st.JobTitle = "";
    st.Age = 19;
    st.StudentNumber = "20323742";
    students.Add(st);

    st.FirstName = "Bob";
    st.LastName = "Healey";
    st.JobTitle = "Lab Assistant";
    st.Age = 21;
    st.StudentNumber = "21457896";
    students.Add(st);

    return students?.Count() ?? 0;
}
```

3. Next, add a third class to your code called `Student` with the following properties:

```
public class Student
{
    public string StudentNumber { get; set; }
    public string FirstName { get; set; }
    public string LastName { get; set; }
    public int Age { get; set; }
    public string JobTitle { get; set; }
}
```

4. Our `Student` class will be the object we will call from our `GetStudents` method. In the `Program.cs` file, add the following code:

```
int StudentCount =
Chapter1.Recipe2NullConditionalOperator.GetStudents();
            if (StudentCount >= 1)
                Console.WriteLine($"There {(StudentCount >
1 ? "are " : "is ")}{StudentCount} student{(StudentCount >
1 ? "s" : "")} in the list.");
            else
                Console.WriteLine($"There were
{StudentCount} students contained in the list.");
            Console.Read();
```

5. Running the console application will result in the application telling us that there are two students contained in the list. This is expected, because we added two `Student` objects to our `List<Student>` class:

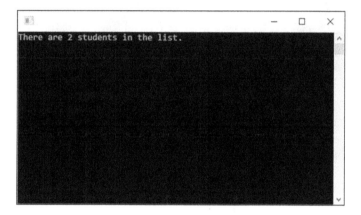

6. To see the null-conditional operator in action, modify the code in your `GetStudents` method to set the `students` variable to null. Your code should look like this:

```
public static int GetStudents()
{
    List<Student> students = new List<Student>();
    Student st = new Student();

    st.FirstName = "Dirk";
    st.LastName = "Strauss";
    st.JobTitle = "";
    st.Age = 19;
    st.StudentNumber = "20323742";
    students.Add(st);
```

```
st.FirstName = "Bob";
st.LastName = "Healey";
st.JobTitle = "Lab Assistant";
st.Age = 21;
st.StudentNumber = "21457896";
students.Add(st);

students = null;
return students?.Count() ?? 0;
}
```

7. Run the console application again, and see how the output has changed:

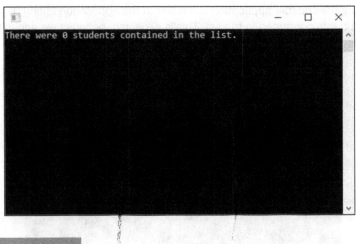

How it works...

Consider the code we used in the `return` statement:

```
return students?.Count() ?? 0;
```

We told the compiler to check whether the `List<Student>` class' variable `students` is null. We did this by adding ? after the `students` object. If the `students` object is not null, we use the dot operator, and the `Count()` property becomes the result of the statement.

If the `students` object however is null, then we return zero. This way of checking for null makes all that `if (students != null)` code unnecessary. The null check sort of fades into the background and makes it much easier to express and read null checks (not to mention less code).

If we had to change the `return` statement to a regular `Count()` method without the null-conditional operator, we would see an `ArgumentNullException was unhandled` error:

```
return students.Count();
```

Calling `Count()` on the `students` object without using the null-conditional operator breaks the code. The null-conditional operator is an exciting addition to the C# language because it makes writing code to check for null a lot easier. Less code is better code.

Initializers for auto-implemented properties and getter-only auto properties

The release of C# 6.0 saw two enhancements made to auto-implemented properties. You can now initialize auto-implemented properties inline, and you can also define them without a setter.

Getting ready

To illustrate how to implement these two new enhancements to auto-implemented properties, we will create another class that calculates the sales price after discount for a given barcode and discount type.

How to do it...

1. Start off by creating a static class called `Recipe3AutoImplementedProperties` and add the `DiscountType` enumerator to the class, along with the auto-implemented properties. You will then initialize those auto-implemented properties with default values:

```
public static class Recipe3AutoImplementedProperties
{
    public enum DiscountType { Sale, Clearout, None }
    private static int SaleDiscountPercent { get; } = 20;
    private static int ClearoutDiscountPercent { get; } =
    35;
    public static decimal ShelfPrice { get; set; } = 100;
    public static decimal SalePrice { get; set; } = 100;
}
```

2. The next step is to add the method to calculate the sales price of an item linked to the barcode supplied to the method:

```
public static void CalculateSalePrice(string barCode, DiscountType
discount)
{
    decimal shelfPrice = GetPriceFromBarcode(barCode);

    if (discount == DiscountType.Sale)
        SalePrice = (shelfPrice == 0 ?
        ShelfPrice.CalculateSalePrice(SaleDiscountPercent) :
        shelfPrice.CalculateSalePrice(SaleDiscountPercent));
```

```
    if (discount == DiscountType.Clearout)
     SalePrice = (shelfPrice == 0 ?
     ShelfPrice.CalculateSalePrice(ClearoutDiscountPercent):
     shelfPrice.CalculateSalePrice(ClearoutDiscountPercent));

    if (discount == DiscountType.None)
       SalePrice = (shelfPrice == 0 ? ShelfPrice :shelfPrice);
}
```

3. In order to simulate a database lookup to find the selling price of a barcode, create another method to return a price for a given barcode:

```
private static decimal GetPriceFromBarcode(string barCode)
{
    switch (barCode)
    {
        case "123450":
            return 19.95m;
        case "123451":
            return 7.55m;
        case "123452":
            return 59.99m;
        case "123453":
            return 93.99m;
        default:
            return 0;
    }
}
```

4. Finally, we will create an extension method class to calculate the sale price after the discount has been applied:

```
public static class ExtensionMethods
{
    public static decimal CalculateSalePrice(this decimal
    shelfPrice, int discountPercent)
    {
        decimal discountValue = (shelfPrice / 100) *
        discountPercent;
        return shelfPrice - discountValue;
    }
}
```

Extension methods are static methods by default and allow you to extend your code's functionality (extend existing types) without having to modify the original type. You can now have an extension methods class in your solution where you add helpful code. A nice example of using an extension method is to calculate the financial year for a given date. Extension methods are differentiated from other static methods using the `this` keyword in the method signature. In the preceding example, the compiler knows that this is an extension method for the decimal class by looking at the type it extends.

5.   Replace the code of your `Progam.cs` file and run the program:

```
string BarCode = String.Empty;

BarCode = "123450";
Chapter1.Recipe3AutoImplementedProperties.CalculateSalePric
e(BarCode,
Chapter1.Recipe3AutoImplementedProperties.DiscountType.Sale
);
Console.WriteLine(Chapter1.Recipe3AutoImplementedProperties
.SalePrice);
```

6.   The sales price is calculated after applying the sale discount and returned to the console application:

How it works...

If you look at the auto-implemented properties again, you would notice that we have two getter-only auto-implemented properties. All four auto-implemented properties have been initialized with default values. The `SaleDiscountPercent` and `ClearoutDiscountPercent` properties are read-only. This ensures that the discount values can't be modified in any way.

You will also notice that if the shelf price returned from the `GetPriceFromBarcode` method is zero, then the default `ShelfPrice` property value is used in determining the discount price. If no discount is applied, the `CalculateSalePrice` method simply returns the barcode price. If no price is determined from the barcode, the default `ShelfPrice` property value is returned.

Auto-implemented property initializers and getter-only auto-implemented properties are great to cut down on unnecessary `if else` statements. It also makes the code implementing the properties more readable because the intent can be contained in the property itself by initializing it.

Look at what happens if we try to set the `SaleDiscountPercent` or `ClearoutDiscountPercent` property to a different value:

```
public static void CalculateSalePrice(string barCode, DiscountType discount)
{
    decimal shelfPrice = GetPriceFromBarcode(barCode);

    if (discount == DiscountType.Sale)
        SalePrice = (shelfPrice == 0 ? ShelfPrice.CalculateSalePrice(SaleDiscountPercent) : shelfPrice.CalculateSalePrice(SaleDiscountPercent));

    if (discount == DiscountType.Clearout)
        SalePrice = (shelfPrice == 0 ? ShelfPrice.CalculateSalePrice(ClearoutDiscountPercent) : shelfPrice.CalculateSalePrice(ClearoutDiscountPercent));

    if (discount == DiscountType.None)
        SalePrice = (shelfPrice == 0 ? ShelfPrice : shelfPrice);

    SalePrice = 200;
    ShelfPrice = 200;
    SaleDiscountPercent = 75;
    ClearoutDiscountPercent = 95;
}
```

```
int Recipe3AutoImplementedProperties.ClearoutDiscountPercent { get; }

Property or indexer 'Recipe3AutoImplementedProperties.ClearoutDiscountPercent' cannot be assigned to -- it is read only
```

Visual Studio will emit an error for the getter-only properties because using the `get` keyword, we can only read from this property, not assign a value to it.

Index initializers

You need to remember that C# 6.0 does not introduce big new concepts, but small features designed to make your code cleaner and easier to read and understand. With index initializers, this is not an exception. You can now initialize the indices of newly created objects. This means you do not have to use separate statements to initialize the indexes.

Getting ready

The change here is subtle. We will create a method to return the day of the week based on an integer. We will also create a method to return the start of the financial year and salary increase month, and then set the salary increase month to a different value than the default. Finally we will use properties to return a specific type of species to the console window.

How to do it...

1. Start off by creating a new class called `Recipe4IndexInitializers` and add a second class called `Month` to your code. The `Month` class simply contains two auto-implemented properties that have been initialized. `StartFinancialYearMonth` has been set to month two (February), and `SalaryIncreaseMonth` has been set to month three (March):

```
public static class Recipe4IndexInitializers
{

}

public class Month
{
    public int StartFinancialYearMonth { get; set; } = 2;
    public int SalaryIncreaseMonth { get; set; } = 3;
}
```

2. Go ahead and add a method called `ReturnWeekDay` that takes an integer for the day number as a parameter, to the `Recipe4IndexInitializers` class:

```
public static string ReturnWeekDay(int dayNumber)
{
    Dictionary<int, string> day = new Dictionary<int,
    string>
    {
        [1] = "Monday",
        [2] = "Tuesday",
        [3] = "Wednesday",
        [4] = "Thursday",
        [5] = "Friday",
        [6] = "Saturday",
        [7] = "Sunday"
    };

    return day[dayNumber];
}
```

3. For the second example, add a method called `ReturnFinancialAndBonusMonth` to the `Recipe4IndexInitializers` class:

```
public static List<int> ReturnFinancialAndBonusMonth()
{
    Month currentMonth = new Month();
    int[] array = new[] {
    currentMonth.StartFinancialYearMonth,
    currentMonth.SalaryIncreaseMonth };
    return new List<int>(array) { [1] = 2 };
}
```

4. Finally, add several auto-implemented properties to the class to contain species and a method called `DetermineSpecies` to the `Recipe4IndexInitializers` class. Your code should look like this:

```
public static string Human { get; set; } = "Homo sapiens";
public static string Sloth { get; set; } = "Choloepus
hoffmanni";
public static string Rabbit { get; set; } = "Oryctolagus
cuniculus";
public static string Mouse { get; set; } = "Mus musculus";
public static string Hedgehog { get; set; } = "Erinaceus
europaeus";
public static string Dolphin { get; set; } = "Tursiops
truncatus";
public static string Dog { get; set; } = "Canis lupus
familiaris";

public static void DetermineSpecies()
{
    Dictionary<string, string> Species =  new
    Dictionary<string, string>
    {
        [Human] = Human + " : Additional species
        information",
        [Rabbit] = Rabbit + " : Additional species
        information",
        [Sloth] = Sloth + " : Additional species
        information",
        [Mouse] = Mouse + " : Additional species
        information",
        [Hedgehog] = Hedgehog + " : Additional species
        information",
        [Dolphin] = Dolphin + " : Additional species
        information",
        [Dog] = Dog + " : Additional species information"
    };

    Console.WriteLine(Species[Human]);
}
```

5. In your console application, add the following code to call the code in the `Recipe4IndexInitializers` class:

```
int DayNumber = 3;
string DayOfWeek =
Chapter1.Recipe4IndexInitializers.ReturnWeekDay(DayNumber);
```

```
Console.WriteLine($"Day {DayNumber} is {DayOfWeek}");

List<int> FinancialAndBonusMonth =
Chapter1.Recipe4IndexInitializers.ReturnFinancialAndBonusMo
nth();
Console.WriteLine("Financial Year Start month and Salary
Increase Months are:");
for (int i = 0; i < FinancialAndBonusMonth.Count(); i++)
{
    Console.Write(i == 0 ?
    FinancialAndBonusMonth[i].ToString() + " and " :
    FinancialAndBonusMonth[i].ToString());
}

Console.WriteLine();
Chapter1.Recipe4IndexInitializers.DetermineSpecies();
Console.Read();
```

6. Once you have added all your code, run your application. The output will look like this:

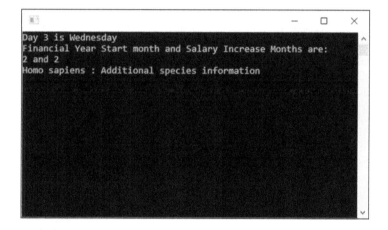

How it works...

The first method `ReturnWeekDay` created a `Dictionary<int, string>` object. You can see how the indices are initialized with the day names. If we now pass the day integer to the method, we can return the day name by referencing the index.

> The reason for not using a zero-based index in `ReturnWeekDay` is because the first day of the week is associated to the numerical value 1.

In the second example, we called a method called `ReturnFinancialAndBonusMonth` that creates an array to hold the financial year start month and the salary increase month. Both properties of the `Month` class are initialized to 2 and 3, respectively. You can see that we are overriding the value of the `SalaryIncreaseMonth` property and setting it to 2. It is done in the following line of code:

```
return new List<int>(array) { [1] = 2 };
```

The last example uses the `Human`, `Rabbit`, `Sloth`, `Mouse`, `Hedgehog`, `Dolphin`, and `Dog` properties to return the correct index value of the `Species` object.

The nameof expressions

The `nameof` expressions are particularly nice. You can now provide a string that names an object in code. This is especially handy if you are throwing exceptions. You can now see which variable caused the exception. In the past, developers had to rely on messy string literals in their code. This was particularly error prone and vulnerable to spelling errors. Another problem was that any code refactoring might miss a string literal, and then that code becomes obsolete and broken.

The `nameof` expressions have come to save the day. The compiler will see that you are referencing the name of a specific variable and correctly convert it to a string. `nameof` expressions, therefore, also stay in sync with any refactoring you may do.

Getting ready

We will use the same code example that we wrote in the *String interpolation* recipe from this chapter, with a few small changes. We will create a `Student` object and add students to it. We will then return that object to the console and output the student count.

How to do it...

1. Create a class called `Recipe5NameofExpression`. Add an auto-implemented property to this class called `StudentCount`:

```
public static class Recipe5NameofExpression
{
    public static int StudentCount { get; set; } = 0;
}
```

2. Next, we need to add the `GetStudents` method, which returns a `List<Student>` object. The method contains a `try/catch` statement and will throw `ArgumentNullException()`:

```
public static List<Student> GetStudents()
{
```

```
List<Student> students = new List<Student>();
try
{
    Student st = new Student();

    st.FirstName = "Dirk";
    st.LastName = "Strauss";
    st.JobTitle = "";
    st.Age = 19;
    st.StudentNumber = "20323742";
    students.Add(st);

    st.FirstName = "Bob";
    st.LastName = "Healey";
    st.JobTitle = "Lab Assistant";
    st.Age = 21;
    st.StudentNumber = "21457896";
    students.Add(st);

    //students = null;

    StudentCount = students.Count();

    return students;
}
catch (Exception ex)
{
    throw new ArgumentNullException(nameof(students));
}
}
```

 In reality, we would not simply return `ArgumentNullException` off the bat like that. This is simply being used to illustrate the concept of the `nameof` expression as used in `ArgumentNullException`.

3. In the console application, we will add code that returns the `List<Student>` object and reports how many students were contained in the list by outputting the `StudentCount` property value to the console window:

```
try
{
    List<Chapter1.Student> StudentList =
    Chapter1.Recipe5NameofExpression.GetStudents();
```

```
        Console.WriteLine($"There are
        {Chapter1.Recipe5NameofExpression.StudentCount}
        students");
    }
    catch (Exception ex)
    {
        Console.WriteLine(ex.Message);
    }
    finally
    {
        Console.Read();
    }
```

How it works...

Running the console application with the code as is will call the `GetStudents()` method. This will then create the `List<Student>` object and add two `Student` objects to it. The `StudentCount` property is set equal to the count of the `List<Student>` object. The `GetStudents()` method then returns the result to the console application, which then reads the `StudentCount` property and displays it in the console output:

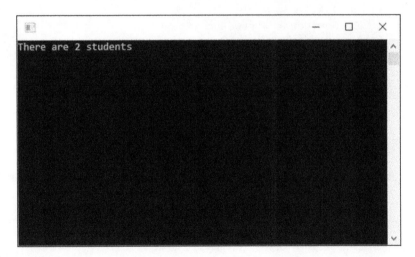

If we now went ahead and modified the code in the `GetStudents()` method to set the `students` variable to `null` right before we called `students.Count()`, an exception would be thrown. The exception is caught in `catch`, and this is where we use the `nameof` expression to display a string literal of the `students` variable:

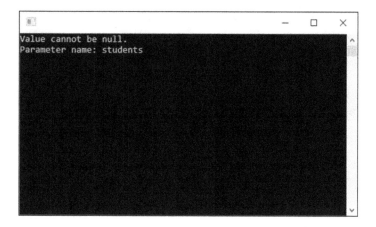

```
Value cannot be null.
Parameter name: students
```

Using the `nameof` expression, we can ensure that the expression stays in sync with refactoring actions such as renaming the `students` variable:

```
2 references
public static class Recipe5NameofExpression
{
    2 references
    public static int StudentCount { get; set; } = 0;
    1 reference
    public static List<Student> GetStudents()
    {
        List<Student> students = new List<Student>();
        try
        {
            Student st = new Student();

            st.FirstName = "Dirk";
            st.LastName = "Strauss";
            st.JobTitle = "";
            st.Age = 19;
            st.StudentNumber = "20323742";
            students.Add(st);

            st.FirstName = "Bob";
            st.LastName = "Healey";
            st.JobTitle = "Lab Assistant";
            st.Age = 21;
            st.StudentNumber = "21457896";
            students.Add(st);

            students = null;

            StudentCount = students.Count();

            return students;
        }
        catch (Exception ex)
        {
            throw new ArgumentNullException(nameof(students));
        }
    }
}
```

Rename: students ✕

Modify any highlighted location to begin renaming.

☐ Include comments
☐ Include strings

☐ Preview changes

Rename will update 7 references in 1 file.

Apply

If we had written the code in the `catch` statement using a string literal, we would not have had the code updated automatically when we renamed the `students` variable. The `nameof` expression effectively allowed developers to stop writing `throw new ArgumentNullException("students");`, which will not be affected by refactoring actions.

Another benefit of using a `nameof` expression in your code is that it involves no runtime cost, because the code containing the string literal is generated at compile time.

Modify the code in the console application slightly to make it look like this:

```
List<Chapter1.Student> StudentList =
Chapter1.Recipe5NameofExpression.GetStudents();

int iStudentCount = Chapter1.Recipe5NameofExpression.StudentCount;
Console.WriteLine($"The value of the
{ nameof(Chapter1.Recipe5NameofExpression.StudentCount)} property
is {iStudentCount}");
```

When you run your console application now, you can see that the `nameof` expression has been used to create the string literal of the `StudentCount` property:

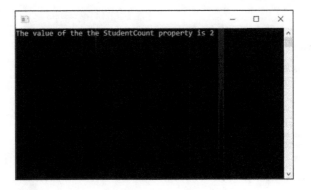

 Ensure that you have commented out the `students = null;` line of code in the `GetStudents()` method; otherwise, you will still receive the null exception.

You can also use the `nameof` expression with enumerators. Add the following code to your class. We are basically creating an enumerator called `Course`. In the `SetCourse()` method, we set a course based on a course ID:

```
public enum Course { InformationTechnology = 1, Statistics = 2,
AppliedSciences = 3 }
public static string SelectedCourse { get; set; }
public static void SetCourse(int iCourseID)
{
```

```
Course course = (Course)iCourseID;
switch (course)
{
    case Course.InformationTechnology:
        SelectedCourse = nameof(Course.InformationTechnology);
        break;
    case Course.Statistics:
        SelectedCourse = nameof(Course.InformationTechnology);
        break;
    case Course.AppliedSciences:
        SelectedCourse = nameof(Course.InformationTechnology);
        break;
    default:
        SelectedCourse = "InvalidCourse";
        break;
}
}
```

We then use a `switch` statement to select the course defined by the course ID parameter and set the `SelectedCourse` property equal to the `nameof` expression of the enumerator. Add the following code to your console application:

```
Chapter1.Recipe5NameofExpression.SetCourse(1);
Console.WriteLine($"The selected course is
{ Chapter1.Recipe5NameofExpression.SelectedCourse}");
```

Running the console application will result in the string representation of the selected enumerator value:

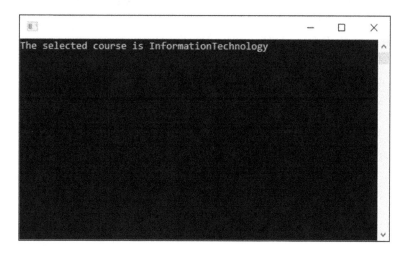

The `nameof` expression is a very good way of keeping your code in sync when dealing with the string literals of objects in C# 6.0.

Expression-bodied functions and properties

As the name suggests, expression-bodied functions and properties allow methods and properties to have a body that is an expression instead of a statement. You will notice that expression-bodied members look a lot like lambda expressions, because they are inspired by lambda expressions.

Getting ready

To truly appreciate expression-bodied functions and properties, we need to look at the way code had to be written previously. We will create a class to calculate the sale price of an item, and the class will contain two public methods. One will set a shelf price, and the other will return a message displaying the calculated sale price.

How to do it...

1. Create a class called `Recipe6ExpressionBodiedFunctionMembers` and add two private auto-implemented properties to hold the sale discount percent and the shelf price:

```
public static class Recipe6ExpressionBodiedFunctionMembers
{
    private static int SaleDiscountPercent { get; } = 20;
    private static decimal ShelfPrice { get; set; } = 100;
}
```

2. If you haven't done so in an earlier recipe, add the extension method class to calculate the sale price of an item:

```
public static class ExtensionMethods
{
    public static decimal CalculateSalePrice(this decimal
    shelfPrice, int discountPercent)
    {
        decimal discountValue = (shelfPrice / 100) *
        discountPercent;
        return shelfPrice - discountValue;
    }
}
```

3. We will now add a calculated property to the class. This calculated property uses the extension method on the `ShelfPrice` property to get the sale price:

```
private static decimal GetCalculatedSalePrice
{
    get { return
Math.Round(ShelfPrice.CalculateSalePrice(SaleDiscountPercen
    t) ,2); }
}
```

4. Finally, add two methods to your class to set the shelf price and another to return a message with the sale price:

```
public static void SetShelfPrice(decimal shelfPrice)
{
    ShelfPrice = shelfPrice;
}


public static string ReturnMessage(string barCode)
{
    return $"The sale price for barcode {barCode} is
    {GetCalculatedSalePrice}";
}
```

5. To see the result of the code, add the following code to your console application:

```
string BarCode = "12345113";
decimal ShelfPrice = 56.99m;
Chapter1.Recipe6ExpressionBodiedFunctionMembers.SetShelfPri
ce(ShelfPrice);              Console.WriteLine(Chapter1.
Recipe6ExpressionBodiedFunctionM
embers.ReturnMessage(BarCode));
Console.Read();
```

How it works...

Running your application produces the message displaying the calculated sale price:

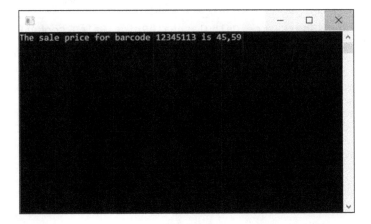

 Here, we are just supplying the bar code in the output message. However, in a live system, the shelf price would be looked up from a data store for the specific bar code.

Looking back at our class, we can see that it is somewhat bulky. We have a calculated property that returns a sale price and two methods with a single `return` statement. One sets the shelf price, while the other gets a message containing the sale price. This is where expression-bodied function members come into play. Modify your code in the `Recipe6ExpressionBodiedFunctionMembers` class to make it look like this:

```csharp
public static class Recipe6ExpressionBodiedFunctionMembers
{
    private static int SaleDiscountPercent { get; } = 20;
    private static decimal ShelfPrice { get; set; } = 100;

    private static decimal GetCalculatedSalePrice => Math.
Round(ShelfPrice.CalculateSalePrice(SaleDiscountPercent));

    public static void SetShelfPrice(decimal shelfPrice) => ShelfPrice
= shelfPrice;

    public static string ReturnMessage(string barCode) => $"The sale
price for barcode {barCode} is {GetCalculatedSalePrice}";
}
```

What we are left with is a terse class that does exactly the same as the code we wrote before. There is less code, it is easier to read, and it looks much cleaner. You will notice the use of the lambda => operator. For the GetCalculatedSalePrice computed property, the get keyword is missing. This became implied when we changed the computed property body to an expression.

One point to remember though is that expression-bodied function members do not work with constructors.

Using static

C# 6.0 introduces a new kind of using statement that now refers to types instead of namespaces. This means that the static members of the type are then directly put into scope. What this means for your code is evident in the condensed result of this recipe.

Getting ready

We will create a class called Recipe7UsingStatic that will determine the sale price of an item depending on the day of the week. If it is Friday, we want to apply the sale discount to the item. On any other day, we will sell the item at the shelf price.

How to do it...

1. Start by creating a Recipe7UsingStatic class that contains two auto-implemented properties and an enumerator for the day of the week:

```
public static class Recipe7UsingStatic
{
    public enum TheDayOfWeek
    {
        Monday, Tuesday, Wednesday, Thursday, Friday, Saturday, Sunday
    }

    private static int SaleDiscountPercent { get; } = 20;
    private static decimal ShelfPrice { get; set; } = 100;
}
```

2. We will now add a computed property and two methods to our Recipe7UsingStatic class. One method will set the shelf price and the other will get the sale price:

```
private static decimal GetCalculatedSalePrice
{
    get { return
    Math.Round(ShelfPrice.CalculateSalePrice
    (SaleDiscountPercen t), 2); }
```

```
    }

    public static void SetShelfPrice(decimal shelfPrice)
    {
        ShelfPrice = shelfPrice;
    }

    public static decimal GetSalePrice(TheDayOfWeek dayOfWeek)
    {
        return dayOfWeek == TheDayOfWeek.Friday ?
GetCalculatedSalePrice : ShelfPrice;
    }
```

3. In the console application, we will add the code to define the day of the week, set the shelf price, and then get the sale price. The sale price is then written out to the console application:

```
decimal ShelfPrice = 56.99m;

Chapter1.Recipe7UsingStatic.TheDayOfWeek weekday =
Chapter1.Recipe7UsingStatic.TheDayOfWeek.Friday;
Chapter1.Recipe7UsingStatic.SetShelfPrice(ShelfPrice);
Console.WriteLine(Chapter1.Recipe7UsingStatic.GetSalePrice(
weekday));
Console.Read();
```

How it works...

Run your console application and see that the sale price is calculated correctly and output to the console application:

Now, let's have a closer look at the code. In particular, look at the `GetCalculatedSalePrice` computed property. It uses the `Math.Round` function to round the sale price to two decimals:

```
private static decimal GetCalculatedSalePrice
{
    get { return
    Math.Round(ShelfPrice.CalculateSalePrice
    (SaleDiscountPercent), 2); }
}
```

The `Math` class is in reality a static class that contains a collection of functions that you can use throughout your code to perform different mathematical calculations. So, go ahead and add the following `using` statement at the top of your `Recipes.cs` file:

```
using static System.Math;
```

We can now change our computed `GetCalculatedSalePrice` property to omit the `Math` class name:

```
private static decimal GetCalculatedSalePrice
{
    get { return Round(ShelfPrice.CalculateSalePrice(SaleDiscountPerc
ent), 2); }
}
```

This is really a fantastic enhancement. Look at the following lines of code:

```
Math.Sqrt(64);
Math.Tan(64);
Math.Pow(8, 2);
```

Because of this enhancement, the preceding lines of code can simply be written as follows:

```
Sqrt(64);
Tan(64);
Pow(8, 2);
```

There is, however, more to using the `static` keyword's functionality. We are using static classes for all the recipes in this chapter. We can, therefore, also implement the `using static` statement for our own custom static classes. Add the following `using` statements to the top of the console application's `Program` class:

```
using static Chapter1.Recipe7UsingStatic;
using static Chapter1.Recipe7UsingStatic.TheDayOfWeek;
using static System.Console;
```

You will notice that we have included the enumerator in the `using static` statements. This is equally fantastic, because Friday is clearly a day of the week, and the enumerator doesn't need to be called fully, as in the old console application code. By adding the `using static` statements, the code in our console application can be changed as follows:

```
TheDayOfWeek weekday = Friday;
SetShelfPrice(ShelfPrice);
WriteLine(GetSalePrice(weekday));
Read();
```

This is where the real benefit of the `using static` statements become evident. It means less code and makes your code more readable. To recap the idea behind C# 6.0, it didn't introduce big new concepts but many small features to make your code cleaner and your intent easier to understand. The `using static` feature does exactly this.

Exception filters

Exception filters have been around for some time. **Visual Basic.NET** (**VB.NET**) and F# devs have had this functionality for a while. Luckily for us, it has now been introduced in C# 6.0. Exception filters do more than what meets the eye. At first glance, it looks as if exception filters merely specify a condition when an exception needs to be caught. This is, after all, what the name "exception filter" implies. Upon closer inspection, however, we see that exception filters act as more than just syntactical sugar.

Getting ready

We will create a new class called `Recipe8ExceptionFilters` and call a method that reads an XML file. The file read logic is determined by a Boolean flag being set to `true`. Imagine here that there is some other database flag that when set, also sets our Boolean flag to `true`, and thus, our application knows to read the given XML file.

How to do it...

1. Create a class called `Recipe8ExceptionFilters` that contains two methods. One method reads the XML file, and the second method logs any exception errors:

```
public static class Recipe8ExceptionFilters
{
    public static void ReadXMLFile(string fileName)
    {
        try
        {
            bool blnReadFileFlag = true;
            if (blnReadFileFlag)
            {
```

```
            File.ReadAllLines(fileName);
        }
    }
    catch (Exception ex)
    {
        Log(ex);
        throw;
    }
}

private static void Log(Exception e)
{
    /* Log the error */
}
}
```

2. In the console application, add the following code to call the `ReadXMLFile` method, passing it the file name to read:

```
string File = @"c:\temp\XmlFile.xml";
Chapter1.Recipe8ExceptionFilters.ReadXMLFile(File);
```

How it works...

If we had to run our application now, we would obviously receive an error (this is assuming that you actually don't have a file called `XMLFile.xml` in your `temp` folder). Visual Studio will break on the `throw` statement:

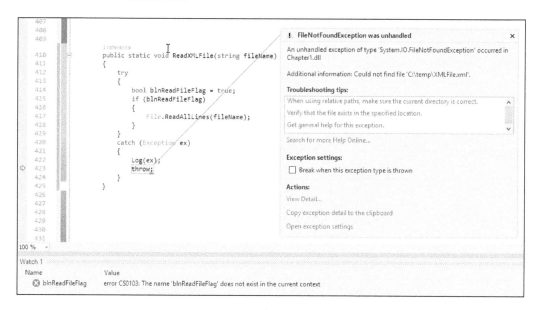

You need to add the correct namespace using `System.IO` at the top of your code file.

The `Log(ex)` method has logged the exception, but have a look at the **Watch1** window. We have no idea what the value of `blnReadFileFlag` is. When an exception is caught, the stack is unwound (adding overhead to your code) to whatever the actual catch block is. Therefore, the state of the stack before the exception happened is lost. Modify your `ReadXMLFile` and `Log` methods as follows to include an exception filter:

```csharp
public static void ReadXMLFile(string fileName)
{
    try
    {
        bool blnReadFileFlag = true;
        if (blnReadFileFlag)
        {
            File.ReadAllLines(fileName);
        }
    }
    catch (Exception ex) when (Log(ex))
    {

    }
}

private static bool Log(Exception e)
{
    /* Log the error */
    return false;
}
```

When you run your console application again, Visual Studio will break on the actual line of code that caused the exception:

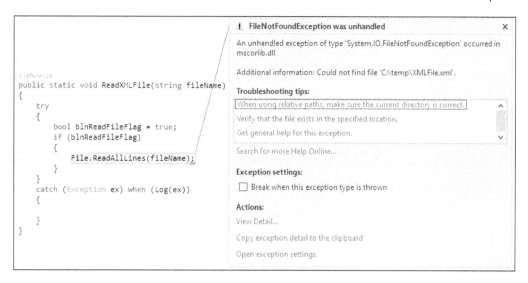

More importantly, the value of `blnReadFileFlag` is still in scope. This is because exception filters can see the state of the stack at the point where the exception occurred instead of where the exception was handled. Looking at the **Locals** window in Visual Studio, you will see that the variables are still in scope at the point where the exception occurred:

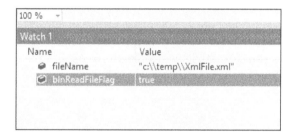

Imagine being able to view the exception information in a log file with all the local variable values available. Another interesting point to note is the `return false` statement in the `Log(ex)` method. Using this method to log the error and return `false` will allow the application to continue and have the exception handled elsewhere. As you know, catching `Exception ex` will catch everything. By returning `false`, the exception filter doesn't run into the `catch` statement, and more specific `catch` exceptions (for example, `catch (FileNotFoundException ex)` after our `catch (Exception ex)` statement) can be used to handle specific errors. Normally, when catching exceptions, `FileNotFoundException` will never be caught in the following code example:

```
catch (Exception ex)
{

}
```

```
catch (FileNotFoundException ex)
{

}
```

This is because the order of the exceptions being caught is wrong. Traditionally, developers must catch exceptions in their order of specificity, which means that `FileNotFoundException` is more specific than `Exception` and must therefore be placed before `catch (Exception ex)`. With exception filters that call a false returning method, we can inspect and log an exception accurately:

```
catch (Exception ex) when (Log(ex))
{

}
catch (FileNotFoundException ex)
{

}
```

The preceding code will catch all exceptions, and in doing so log the exception accurately but not step into the exception handler because the `Log(ex)` method returns `false`.

Another implementation of exception filters is that they can allow developers to retry code in the event of a failure. You might not specifically want to catch the first exception, but implement a type of timeout element to your method. When the error counter has reached the maximum iterations, you can catch and handle the exception. You can see an example of catching an exception based on a `try` clauses' count here:

```
public static void TryReadXMLFile(string fileName)
{
    bool blnFileRead = false;
    do
    {
        int iTryCount = 0;
        try
        {
            bool blnReadFileFlag = true;
            if (blnReadFileFlag)
                File.ReadAllLines(fileName);
        }
        catch (Exception ex) when (RetryRead(ex, iTryCount++) == true)
        {

        }
    } while (!blnFileRead);
```

```
    }

    private static bool RetryRead(Exception e, int tryCount)
    {
        bool blnThrowEx = tryCount <= 10 ? blnThrowEx = false : blnThrowEx
    = true;
        /* Log the error if blnThrowEx = false */
        return blnThrowEx;
    }
```

Exception filtering is a very useful and extremely powerful way to handle exceptions in your code. The behind-the-scenes workings of exception filters are not as immediately obvious as one might imagine, but here lies the actual power of exception filters.

Using await operator in catch and finally blocks

Finally, in C# 6.0, you can now use the `await` keyword in the `catch` and `finally` blocks. Previously, developers had to resort to all sorts of strange workarounds to achieve what is now easily achievable in C# 6.0. There really is not much more to it than the following.

Getting ready

We will create another class that will simulate the deletion of a file. An exception is thrown, and the `catch` block is then executed along with the `finally` statement. In both the `catch` and `finally` clauses, we will delay and await a task for 3 seconds. Then, we will output this delay to the console application window.

How to do it...

1. Create a class called `Recipe9AwaitInCatchFinally` and add a method called `FileRunAsync()` to the class with the following code. Make sure that the file does not exist in the path given to the `filePath` variable:

```
public static class Recipe9AwaitInCatchFinally
{
    public static void FileRunAsync()
    {
        string filePath = @"c:\temp\XmlFile.xml";
        RemoveFileAcync(filePath);
        ReadLine();
    }
}
```

2. Then, add another method called `RemoveFileAcync()` to the class that takes a file path as a parameter. Include `try catch` in this method and add the code that will attempt to read the file at the path supplied:

```
public static async void RemoveFileAcync(string filepath)
{
    try
    {
        WriteLine("Read file");
        File.ReadAllLines(filepath);
    }
    catch (Exception ex)
    {

    }
    finally
    {

    }
}
```

3. In the `catch` clause, add the following code to simulate a process that takes a few seconds to complete:

```
WriteLine($"Exception - wait 3 seconds
{DateTime.Now.ToString("hh:MM:ss tt")}");
await Task.Delay(3000);
WriteLine($"Exception - Print
{DateTime.Now.ToString("hh:MM:ss tt")}");
WriteLine(ex.Message);
```

4. In the `finally` clause, add another delay that simulates a task which also takes a few seconds to complete:

```
WriteLine($"Finally - wait 3 seconds
{DateTime.Now.ToString("hh:MM:ss tt")}");
await Task.Delay(3000);
WriteLine($"Finally - completed
{DateTime.Now.ToString("hh:MM:ss tt")}");
```

5. In the console application, simply add a call to the `FileRunAsync()` method in the `Recipe9AwaitInCatchFinally` class:

```
Chapter1.Recipe9AwaitInCatchFinally.FileRunAsync();
```

How it works...

After adding the code, run the console application and have a look at the output:

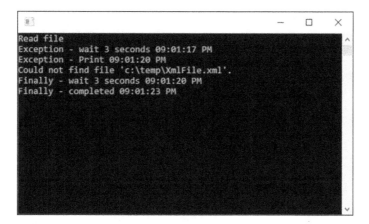

```
Read file
Exception - wait 3 seconds 09:01:17 PM
Exception - Print 09:01:20 PM
Could not find file 'c:\temp\XmlFile.xml'.
Finally - wait 3 seconds 09:01:20 PM
Finally - completed 09:01:23 PM
```

You will notice that the exception thrown was a "file not found" exception. In `catch`, the code stopped for 3 seconds while the task was delayed. The same is evident for the code in the `finally` clause. It too was delayed for 3 seconds while the task was delayed.

This means that now, in your C# 6.0 applications, you can, for example, await in the `catch` clause while an exception log message is written to the log. You can do the same thing in the `finally` clause while closing database connections to dispose of other objects.

The process of how the compiler does this is rather complicated. You, however, don't need to worry about how this functionality is achieved. All you need to do is know that the `await` keyword is now available to you as a developer for use in the `catch` and `finally` blocks.

Detailed steps to download the code bundle are mentioned in the Preface of this book. Please have a look. The code bundle for the book is also hosted on GitHub at `https://github.com/PacktPublishing/C#-Programming-Cookbook`. We also have other code bundles from our rich catalog of books and videos available at `https://github.com/PacktPublishing/`. Check them out!

2
Classes and Generics

Classes form the building blocks of software development and are essential in building good code. In this chapter, we will be looking at classes and generics and why we need to use them. The recipes we will be covering are going to be as follows:

- ▶ Creating and implementing an abstract class
- ▶ Creating and implementing an interface
- ▶ Creating and using a generic class or method
- ▶ Creating and using a generic interface

Introduction

As you probably know, classes are simply containers for related methods and properties to describe some object in your software. An object is an instance of a specific class and, sometimes, mimics real-world things. When thinking of a car, you might create a vehicle class that contains certain attributes (properties) that all vehicles contain, such as automatic or manual transmission, wheel count (not all vehicles have only four wheels), or fuel type.

When we create an instance of the vehicle class, we can create a car object, an SUV object, and so on. Here lies the power of classes, which is to describe the world around us and translate it into a programming language that a compiler can understand.

Creating and implementing an abstract class

Many developers have heard about abstract classes, but their implementation is a mystery. How can you as a developer identify an abstract class and decide when to use one? The definition is quite a simple one actually. Once you understand this fundamental definition of an abstract class, when and why to use one becomes obvious.

Imagine for a moment that you are developing an application that manages the animals in a cat sanctuary. The cat sanctuary rehabilitates lions, tigers, jaguars, leopards, cheetahs, pumas, and even domestic cats. The common noun that describes all these animals is the word *cat*. You can, therefore, safely assume that the abstraction of all these animals is a cat, and thus, this word identifies our abstract class. You would then create an abstract class called `Cat`.

However, you need to keep in mind that you will never ever create an instance of the abstract class `Cat`. All the classes that inherit from the abstract class also share some functionality. This means that you will create a `Lion` class and a `Tiger` class that inherit from the abstract class `Cat`. In other words, the inherited classes are a kind of cat. Both classes share functionality in the form of `Sleep()`, `Eat()`, `Hunt()`, and various other methods. In this way, we can ensure that inherited classes all contain this common functionality.

Getting ready

Let's go ahead and create our abstract class for cat. We will then use it to inherit from and create other objects to define different types of cats.

How to do it...

1. In the Visual Studio **Solution Explorer**, right-click on the solution, click on **Add**, and then click on **New Project**. Select **Class Library** option to add a new class library project to your solution and call it `Chapter2`:

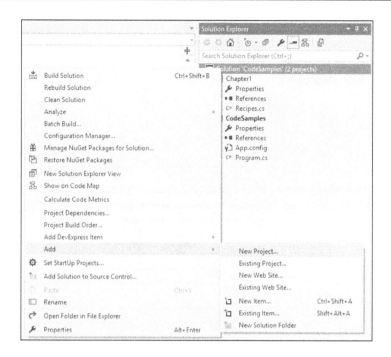

2. A class library project called Chapter2 is added to your solution. Go ahead and right-click on the default class called Class1.cs that was added to your Chapter2 project and rename it to Recipes.cs:

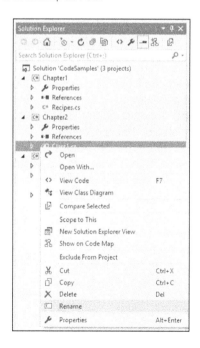

3. Once you have done this, your code should resemble the following code listing. You can see that the default class has been renamed to `Recipes` and that it exists in the `Chapter2` namespace:

```
namespace Chapter2
{
    public class Recipes
    {
    }
}
```

4. We will now change the default class `Recipes` to an abstract class called `Cat`. To do this, add the `abstract` keyword to the class and change the name from `Recipes` to `Cat`. We are now ready to describe the `Cat` abstract class:

```
namespace Chapter2
{
    public abstract class Cat
    {
    }
}
```

> The `abstract` keyword indicates to us that the object it is applied to has no implementation. When used in a class declaration, it basically tells the compiler that the class is to be used as a base class. This means that no instance of the class can be created. The only way in which implementation of the abstract class happens is when it is implemented by derived classes that inherit from the base class.

5. Add three methods to the abstract class called `Eat()`, `Hunt()`, and `Sleep()`. You will notice that these methods don't contain a body (curly braces). This is because they have been defined as abstract. As with abstract classes, the abstract methods contained within the abstract class contain no implementation. These three methods basically describe functionality that is common to all cats. All cats must eat, hunt, and sleep. Therefore, to ensure that all classes that inherit from the `Cat` abstract class contain this functionality, it is added to the abstract class. These methods are then implemented in the derived classes, which we will see in the upcoming steps:

```
public abstract class Cat
{
    public abstract void Eat();
    public abstract void Hunt();
    public abstract void Sleep();
}
```

6. We want to define two types of cat. The first type of cat we want to define is a lion. For this, we create a `Lion` class:

```
public class Lion
{

}
```

7. At this point in time, the `Lion` class is simply an ordinary class and does not contain any common functionality defined in the `Cat` abstract class. To inherit from the `Cat` abstract class, we need to add `: Cat` after the `Lion` class name. The colon indicates that the `Lion` class inherits from the `Cat` abstract class. The `Lion` class is therefore a derived class of the `Cat` abstract class:

```
public class Lion : Cat
{

}
```

As soon as you specify that the `Lion` class inherits from the `Cat` class, Visual Studio will show you an error. This is expected, because we have told the compiler that the `Lion` class needs to inherit all the features of the `Cat` abstract class, but we have not actually added these features to the `Lion` class. The derived class is said to override the methods in the abstract class, and needs to specifically be written with the `override` keyword.

8. If you hover over the red squiggly line underlining the `Lion` class, Visual Studio will offer an explanation for the error via the lightbulb feature. As you can see, Visual Studio is telling you that while you have defined the class to be inheriting from the abstract class, you have not implemented any of the abstract members of the `Cat` class:

You can, therefore, see that using abstract classes is a fantastic way to enforce specific functionality within your system. If you define abstract members in an abstract class, the derived classes that inherit from that abstract class must implement those members; otherwise, your code will not compile. This can be used to enforce standards and practices adopted by your company, or to simply allow other developers to implement certain best practices as they use your base class for their derived classes. With the advent of the Visual Studio 2015 feature code analyzers, this can ensure a consistent development effort by the team.

9. To implement these members that Visual Studio is warning us about, place your mouse cursor on the Lion class name and hit *Ctrl + .* (period). You can also click on the **Show potential fixes** link in the lightbulb popup. Visual Studio will give you a small heads up, displaying the changes it will make to your code. You can preview these changes by clicking on the **Preview changes** link, as well as fix all occurrences in the document, project, or solution by clicking on the appropriate link:

```
0 references
public class Lion : Cat
{
      💡 ▾
}           Implement Abstract Class  ▸  ⊗ CS0534 'Lion' does not implement inherited abstract member
                                          'Cat.Sleep()'
                                       ...
                                       {
                                           public override void Eat()
                                           {
                                               throw new NotImplementedException();
                                           }

                                           public override void Hunt()
                                           {
                                               throw new NotImplementedException();
                                           }

                                           public override void Sleep()
                                           {
                                               throw new NotImplementedException();
                                           }
                                       }
                                       ...

                                       Preview changes
                                       Fix all occurrences in: Document | Project | Solution
```

After Visual Studio has added the changes displayed in the suggestions window, your Lion class will be correct and will look like the code listed in the following step.

10. You will notice that Visual Studio automatically adds a `NotImplementedException` exception with the following line of code in each overridden method: `throw new NotImplementedException();`:

```
public class Lion : Cat
{
    public override void Eat()
    {
        throw new NotImplementedException();
    }

    public override void Hunt()
    {
        throw new NotImplementedException();
    }

    public override void Sleep()
    {
        throw new NotImplementedException();
    }
}
```

 This is the default behavior of Visual Studio when overriding methods in the base class. Basically, if you had to instantiate the `Lion` class without writing any implementation in the overridden methods, a runtime exception would be generated. The idea of inheriting from our abstract class was to extend it and implement common functionality. This is where we need to implement that functionality, and this is the reason there is no implementation in the abstract class. The abstract class just tells us that the following methods need to be implemented. The derived class does the actual implementation.

11. Go ahead and add some implementation to the overridden methods of the `Lion` class. First, add the `using static` statement for the `Console.WriteLine` method to the top of your class file:

```
using static System.Console;
```

12. Then, add the implemented code for the methods, as follows:

```
public override void Eat()
{
    WriteLine($"The {LionColor} lion eats.");
}

public override void Hunt()
{
    WriteLine($"The {LionColor} lion hunts.");
}
```

```
        }

        public override void Sleep()
        {
            WriteLine($"The {LionColor} lion sleeps.");
        }
```

13. Next, we will create another class called `Tiger` that also derives from the abstract class `Cat`. Follow step 7 to step 12 to create the `Tiger` class and inherit the `Cat` abstract class:

```
public class Tiger : Cat
{
    public override void Eat()
    {
        throw new NotImplementedException();
    }

    public override void Hunt()
    {
        throw new NotImplementedException();
    }

    public override void Sleep()
    {
        throw new NotImplementedException();
    }
}
```

14. Add the same implementation for the `Tiger` class, as follows:

```
public override void Eat()
{
    WriteLine($"The {TigerColor} tiger eats.");
}

public override void Hunt()
{
    WriteLine($"The {TigerColor} tiger hunts.");
}

public override void Sleep()
{
    WriteLine($"The {TigerColor} tiger sleeps.");
}
```

15. For our `Lion` class, add an enumerator for `ColorSpectrum` and a property called `LionColor`. It is here that the implementations of the `Lion` and `Tiger` classes will differ. While they both must implement the common functionality specified in the abstract class, namely `Eat()`, `Hunt()`, and `Sleep()`, only the lion can have a color of either brown or white in its available range of colors:

```
public enum ColorSpectrum { Brown, White }
public string LionColor { get; set; }
```

16. Next, add the `Lion()` constructor in our `Lion` class. This will allow us to specify a color for the lions in the cat sanctuary. The constructor also takes as parameter a variable of the `ColorSpectrum` enumerator type:

```
public Lion(ColorSpectrum color)
{
    LionColor = color.ToString();
}
```

17. Slightly similar to this, but quite different in color, the `Tiger` class can only have a `ColorSpectrum` enumeration that defines tigers as being orange, white, gold, blue (yes, you actually get a blue tiger), or black. Add the `ColorSpectrum` enumerator to the `Tiger` class, as well as a property called `TigerColor`:

```
public enum ColorSpectrum { Orange, White, Gold, Blue,
Black }
public string TigerColor { get; set; }
```

18. Finally, we will create a `Tiger()` constructor for our `Tiger` class to set the colors of tigers in the cat sanctuary to the valid colors that tigers are found in. By doing this, we are separating certain functionality specific only to tigers and lions in their respective classes, while all the common functionality is contained in the abstract class `Cat`:

```
public Tiger(ColorSpectrum color)
{
    TigerColor = color.ToString();
}
```

19. To see the class in action, we first need to add a reference to our `Chapter2.cs` class file. Right-click on **References** in the console application project:

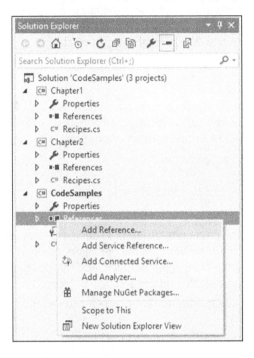

20. The **Reference Manager** window will open for the `CodeSamples` project. Select `Chapter2` and click on the **OK** button. Then, add the `using Chapter2;` statement:

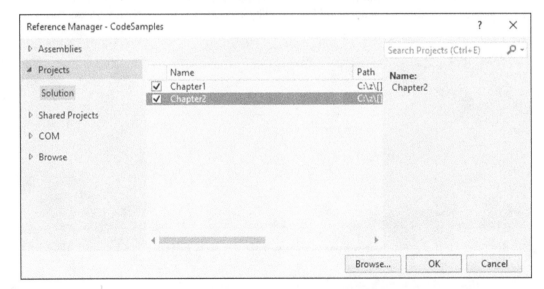

21. We now need to instantiate the `Lion` and `Tiger` classes. You will see that we set the respective cat's color from the constructor:

```
Lion lion = new Lion(Lion.ColorSpectrum.White);
lion.Hunt();
lion.Eat();
lion.Sleep();

Tiger tiger = new Tiger(Tiger.ColorSpectrum.Blue);
tiger.Hunt();
tiger.Eat();
tiger.Sleep();

Console.ReadLine();
```

22. When you run your console application, you see that the methods are called in sequence:

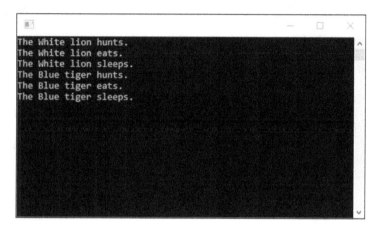

How it works...

While the example illustrated earlier is a rather simplistic one, the theory is sound. The abstract class takes collective functionality across all cats and groups so that it can be shared inside each derived class. No implementation exists in the abstract class; it only defines what needs to happen. Think of abstract classes as a type of blueprint for classes that inherit from the abstract class.

While the content of the implementation is up to you, the abstract class requires that you add the abstract methods it defines. From here on, you can create a solid foundation for similar classes in your applications that are supposed to share functionality. This is the goal of inheritance. Let's recap the features of an abstract class:

▶ You can't instantiate an abstract class with the `new` keyword.

▶ You can only add abstract methods and accessors to an abstract class.

▶ You can never modify an abstract class as `sealed`. The `sealed` modifiers prevents inheritance, while abstract requires inheritance.

▶ Any class derived from your abstract class must include the implementations of the abstract methods that were inherited from the abstract class.

▶ Because abstract methods inside the abstract class have no implementation, they don't contain a body either.

Creating and implementing an interface

For many developers, interfaces are confusing and their purpose not clearly understood. Interfaces are actually quite easy to get to grips with once you understand the concept that defines an interface.

Interfaces act like verbs. So, for example, if we had to create two classes called `Lion` and `Tiger` that derive from the `Cat` abstract class, the interface would describe some sort of action. Lions and tigers can roar (but not purr). We can then create an interface called `IRoarable`. If we had to derive a class called `Cheetah` from our abstract class `Cat`, we would not be able to use the `IRoarable` interface, because cheetahs purr. We would need to create an `IPurrable` interface.

Getting ready

Creating an interface is very similar to creating an abstract class. The difference is that the interface is describing what the class can do, in the case of the `Cheetah` class, by implementing `IPurrable`.

How to do it...

1. If you haven't already done so in the previous recipe, create an abstract class called
    `Cat`:

    ```
    public abstract class Cat
    {
        public abstract void Eat();
        public abstract void Hunt();
        public abstract void Sleep();
    }
    ```

2. Next, add a class called `Cheetah` that inherits from the `Cat` abstract class:

    ```
    public class Cheetah : Cat
    {

    }
    ```

3. As soon as you inherit from the `Cat` abstract class, Visual Studio will show you a
    warning via the lightbulb feature. As you inherited from the abstract class `Cat`, you
    have to implement the abstract members within the abstract class in your derived
    class `Cheetah`:

    ```
    0 references
    public class Cheetah : Cat
    {
    }
    ```

    class Chapter2.Cheetah

    'Cheetah' does not implement inherited abstract member 'Cat.Sleep()'

    'Cheetah' does not implement inherited abstract member 'Cat.Hunt()'

    'Cheetah' does not implement inherited abstract member 'Cat.Eat()'

    Show potential fixes (Ctrl+.)

4. This is easily fixable by typing *Ctrl +.* (period) and fixing all occurrences in the document. You can also do this for the project or solution. For our purpose, we only select the **Document** link at the bottom of the lightbulb suggestions. Visual Studio will automatically add the abstract methods defined in the abstract class to implement inside your Cheetah class:

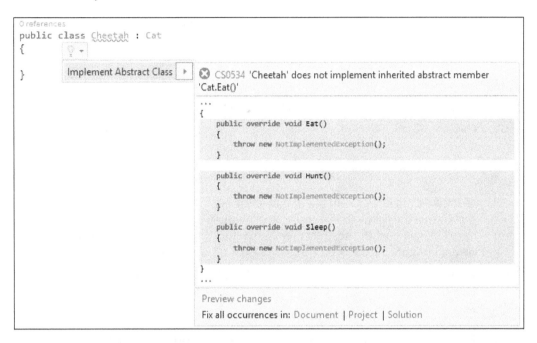

5. You will notice that Visual Studio adds just the methods you need to override but will throw NotImplementedException if you try to use the class as is. The reason for using an abstract class is to implement the functionality defined in the abstract class Cat in the derived class Cheetah. Not doing so contravenes the rules for using abstract classes:

```
public class Cheetah : Cat
{
    public override void Eat()
    {
        throw new NotImplementedException();
    }

    public override void Hunt()
    {
        throw new NotImplementedException();
    }

    public override void Sleep()
```

```
    {
        throw new NotImplementedException();
    }
}
```

6. To add some implementation, modify your Cheetah class as follows. The implementation in the overridden methods is simple, but this validates the rule of writing some sort of implementation in the overridden methods:

```
public class Cheetah : Cat
{
    public override void Eat()
    {
        WriteLine($"The cheetah eats.");
    }

    public override void Hunt()
    {
        WriteLine($"The cheetah hunts.");
    }

    public override void Sleep()
    {
        WriteLine($"The cheetah sleeps.");
    }
}
```

 You will notice that the following WriteLine method is used without the Console class. This is because we are using a new feature in C# 6.0 that allows developers to bring static classes into scope by adding the using static System.Console; statement to the top of your class file.

7. Create an interface called IPurrable that will be implemented on the Cheetah class. A common naming convention for interfaces dictates that the interface name should be prefixed with a capital I:

```
interface IPurrable
{

}
```

8. Next, we will add a method to the interface that any class implementing the interface must implement. You will notice that the interface's `SoftPurr` method contains no implementation at all. It however specifies that we will need to pass this method an integer value for the decibel that the `Cheetah` class will purr at:

```
interface IPurrable
{
    void SoftPurr(int decibel);
}
```

9. The next step is to implement the `IPurrable` interface on the `Cheetah` class. To do this, we need to add the `IPurrable` interface name after the `Cat` abstract class name. If the `Cheetah` class did not inherit from the abstract class, then the interface name would simply follow after the colon:

```
public class Cheetah : Cat, IPurrable
{
    public override void Eat()
    {
        WriteLine($"The cheetah eats.");
    }

    public override void Hunt()
    {
        WriteLine($"The cheetah hunts.");
    }

    public override void Sleep()
    {
        WriteLine($"The cheetah sleeps.");
    }
}
```

10. After specifying that the `Cheetah` class implements the `IPurrable` interface, Visual Studio once again displays a warning via the lightbulb feature. It is warning us that the `Cheetah` class does not implement the `SoftPurr` method defined in the interface `IPurrable`:

```
0 references
public class Cheetah : Cat, IPurrable
{
    3 references
    public override void Eat()
    {
        WriteLine($"The cheetah eats.");
    }

    3 references
    public override void Hunt()
    {
        WriteLine($"The cheetah hunts.");
    }
}
```

11. As we did earlier, we can let Visual Studio suggest possible fixes for the problems encountered by typing *Ctrl + .* (period). Visual Studio suggests that the interface can be implemented implicitly or explicitly:

```
public class Cheetah : Cat, IPurrable
{
    3 references
    public override voi  Implement interface            ▶   ⊗ CS0535 'Cheetah' does not implement interface member
    {                     Implement interface explicitly        'IPurrable.SoftPurr(int)'
        WriteLine($"The ...                                  ...
    }                                                        }

    3 references                                        public void SoftPurr(int decibel)
    public override void Hunt()                         {
    {                                                       throw new NotImplementedException();
        WriteLine($"The cheetah hunts.");               }
    }                                                 }
                                                        ...
    3 references                                        Preview changes
    public override void Sleep()
    {                                                   Fix all occurrences in: Document | Project | Solution
        WriteLine($"The cheetah sleeps.");
    }
}
```

12. Knowing when to use an implicit or explicit implementation is also quite easy. We first need to know when using one over the other would be preferred. Let's start off by implementing the `SoftPurr` method implicitly by selecting the first option in the lightbulb suggestion. You will see that by selecting to implement the `SoftPurr` method defined in the `IPurrable` interface implicitly, adds it as if it were part of the `Cheetah` class:

```
public class Cheetah : Cat, IPurrable
{
    public void SoftPurr(int decibel)
    {
        throw new NotImplementedException();
    }

    public override void Eat()
    {
```

```
        WriteLine($"The cheetah eats.");
    }

    public override void Hunt()
    {
        WriteLine($"The cheetah hunts.");
    }

    public override void Sleep()
    {
        WriteLine($"The cheetah sleeps.");
    }
}
```

13. If we look at the SoftPurr method, it looks like a normal method inside the
Cheetah class. This would be fine unless our Cheetah class already contains a
property called SoftPurr. Go ahead and add a property called SoftPurr to your
Cheetah class:

```
public class Cheetah : Cat, IPurrable
{
    public int SoftPurr { get; set; }

    public void SoftPurr(int decibel)
    {
        throw new NotImplementedException();
    }

    public override void Eat()
    {
        WriteLine($"The cheetah eats.");
    }

    public override void Hunt()
    {
        WriteLine($"The cheetah hunts.");
    }

    public override void Sleep()
    {
        WriteLine($"The cheetah sleeps.");
    }
}
```

14. Visual Studio immediately displays a warning by telling us that the `Cheetah` class already contains a definition for `SoftPurr`:

```
0 references
public class Cheetah : Cat, IPurrable
{
    0 references
    public int SoftPurr { get; set; }
    1 reference
    public void SoftPurr(int decibel)
    {
        throw new    ⊘  void Cheetah.SoftPurr(int decibel)

    }                    The type 'Cheetah' already contains a definition for 'SoftPurr'

    3 references
    public override void Eat()
    {
        WriteLine($"The cheetah eats.");
    }
}
```

15. It is here that the use of an explicit implementation becomes evident. This specifies that the `SoftPurr` method is a member of the implementation defined in the `IPurrable` interface:

```
public class Cheetah : Cat, IPurrable
{
                        🔧 ▾
    3 references
    public override void  Implement interface              ⊗ CS0535 'Cheetah' does not implement interface member
    {                                                         'IPurrable.SoftPurr(int)'
                          Implement interface explicitly  ▸
        WriteLine($"The ...                                   ...
    }                                                         }

    3 references                                              void IPurrable.SoftPurr(int decibel)
    public override void Hunt()                               {
    {                                                             throw new NotImplementedException();
        WriteLine($"The cheetah hunts.");                     }
    }                                                       }
                                                              ...
    3 references                                            ──────────────────────────────────────────
    public override void Sleep()                            Preview changes
    {                                                       Fix all occurrences in: Document | Project | Solution
        WriteLine($"The cheetah sleeps.");
    }
}
```

16. Therefore, selecting the second option to implement the interface explicitly will add the `SoftPurr` method to your `Cheetah` class as follows:

```
public class Cheetah : Cat, IPurrable
{
    public int SoftPurr { get; set; }

    void IPurrable.SoftPurr(int decibel)
    {
        throw new NotImplementedException();
```

```
    }

        public override void Eat()
        {
            WriteLine($"The cheetah eats.");
        }

        public override void Hunt()
        {
            WriteLine($"The cheetah hunts.");
        }

        public override void Sleep()
        {
            WriteLine($"The cheetah sleeps.");
        }
    }
```

The compiler now knows that this is an interface that is being implemented and is therefore a valid line of code.

17. For the purpose of this book, let's just use the implicit implementation. Let's write some implementation for the `SoftPurr` method and use the new `nameof` keyword in C# 6.0, as well as the interpolated string for the output. Also, remove the `SoftPurr` property added earlier:

```
public void SoftPurr(int decibel)
{
    WriteLine($"The {nameof(Cheetah)} purrs at {decibel}
    decibels.");
}
```

18. Heading over to our console application, we can call our `Cheetah` class as follows:

```
Cheetah cheetah = new Cheetah();
cheetah.Hunt();
cheetah.Eat();
cheetah.Sleep();
cheetah.SoftPurr(60);
Console.ReadLine();
```

19. Running the application will produce the following output:

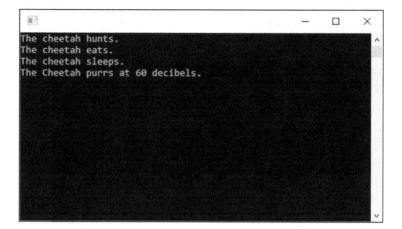

How it works...

So, you might be wondering what the difference between an abstract class and an interface is. It basically comes down to where you want your implementation. If you need to share functionality between derived classes, then an abstract class is the best fit for your needs. In other words, we had specific things that were common to all cats (lions, tigers, and cheetahs) such as hunting, eating, and sleeping. This is then best used within an abstract class.

If your implementation is specific to a class or several classes (but not all classes), then your best course of action would be to use an interface. In this case, the `IPurrable` interface can be applied to several classes (for example, cheetahs and domestic cats) but can't be applied to all cats (such as lions and tigers), because not all cats can purr.

Knowing this difference and where you need to place your implementation will aid you in deciding whether you need to use an abstract class or an interface.

Creating and using a generic class or method

Generics is a very interesting way of writing code. Instead of specifying the data type of the elements in the code at design time, you can actually delay the specification of those elements until they are used in code. This basically means that your class or method can work with any data type.

Getting ready

We will start off by writing a generic class that can take any data type as a parameter in its constructor and do something with it.

How to do it...

1. Declaring a generic class is actually very easy. All that we need to do is create the class with the generic type parameter <T>:

```
public class PerformAction<T>
{

}
```

 The generic type parameter is basically a placeholder for a specific type that will need to be defined when the class of variable is instantiated. This means that the generic class PerformAction<T> can never just be used without specifying the type argument inside angle brackets when instantiating the class.

2. Next, create a private variable of the generic type parameter T. This will hold the value we pass to the generic class:

```
public class PerformAction<T>
{
    private T _value;
}
```

3. We now need to add a constructor to the generic class. The constructor will take as parameter a value of type T. The private variable _value will be set to the parameter passed to the constructor:

```
public class PerformAction<T>
{
    private T _value;

    public PerformAction(T value)
    {
        _value = value;
    }
}
```

4. Finally, to complete our generic class, create a void return method called `IdentifyDataType()`. All that this is going to do is tell us what data type we passed to the generic class. We can find the type of the variable using `GetType()`:

```
public class PerformAction<T>
{
    private T _value;

    public PerformAction(T value)
    {
        _value = value;
    }

    public void IdentifyDataType()
    {
        WriteLine($"The data type of the supplied variable
        is {_value.GetType()}");
    }
}
```

5. To see the true beauty of our generic class in action, instantiate the generic class in the console application and specify different data type arguments inside the angle brackets of each new instantiation:

```
PerformAction<int> iAction = new PerformAction<int>(21);
iAction.IdentifyDataType();

PerformAction<decimal> dAction = new
PerformAction<decimal>(21.55m);
dAction.IdentifyDataType();

PerformAction<string> sAction = new
PerformAction<string>("Hello Generics");
sAction.IdentifyDataType();

Console.ReadLine();
```

6. Running your console application will output the given data types that you instantiated the generic class with each time:

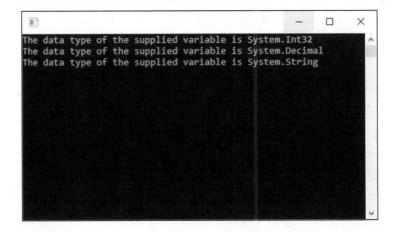

```
The data type of the supplied variable is System.Int32
The data type of the supplied variable is System.Decimal
The data type of the supplied variable is System.String
```

We have used the exact same class but let it perform with three very different data types. This kind of flexibility is a very powerful feature in your code.

Another feature of C# is that you can constrain the generic types implemented:

1. We can do this by telling the compiler that only types that implement the `IDisposable` interface can be used with the generic class. Change your generic class by adding `where T : IDisposable` to it. Your generic class should now look like this:

```csharp
public class PerformAction<T> where T : IDisposable
{
    private T _value;

    public PerformAction(T value)
    {
        _value = value;
    }

    public void IdentifyDataType()
    {
        WriteLine($"The data type of the supplied variable is {_
value.GetType()}");
    }
}
```

2. Go back to the console application and have a look at the previous instantiations of the generic class:

```
PerformAction<int> iAction = new PerformAction<int>(21);
iAction.IdentifyDataType();

PerformAction<decimal> dAction = new PerformAction<decimal>(21.55m);
dAction.IdentifyDataType();

PerformAction<string> sAction = new PerformAction<string>("Hello Generics");
sAction.IdentifyDataType();
```

Visual Studio will tell you that the types underlined by the red squiggly lines do not implement `IDisposable` and therefore can't be supplied to the `PerformAction` generic class.

3. Comment out those lines of code and add the following instantiation to your console application:

```
DataSet dsData = new DataSet();
PerformAction<DataSet> oAction = new
PerformAction<DataSet>(dsData);
oAction.IdentifyDataType();
```

 Note that for this to work, you might need to add `using System.Data;` to your code file. This is needed so that you can declare a `DataSet`.

4. As you might know, a `DataSet` type implements `IDisposable`, and therefore, it is a valid type to pass to our generic class. Go ahead and run the console application:

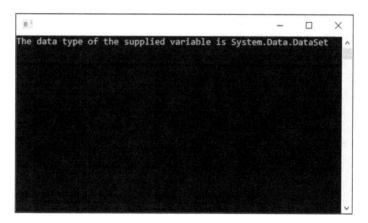

The `DataSet` type is valid, and the generic class performs as expected, identifying the type of the parameter passed to the constructor.

But what about generic methods? Well, just like generic classes, generic methods also do not specify their type at design time. It is only known when the method is called. Let's have a look at the following implementation of generic methods:

1. Let's go ahead and create a new helper class called `MyHelperClass`:

```
public class MyHelperClass
{
}
```

2. Inside this helper class, we will create a generic method called `InspectType`. What is interesting about this generic method is that it can return multiple types because the return type is also marked with the generic type parameter. Your generic method does not have to return anything. It can also be declared as `void`:

```
public class MyHelperClass
{
    public T InspectType<T>(T value)
    {

    }
}
```

3. To illustrate that this generic method can return multiple types, we will output the type passed to the generic method to the console window and then return that type and display it in the console application. You will notice that you need to cast the return type as `(T)` when returning it:

```
public class MyHelperClass
{
    public T InspectType<T>(T value)
    {
        WriteLine($"The data type of the supplied parameter
        is {value.GetType()}");

        return (T)value;
    }
}
```

4. In the console application, go ahead and create an enumerator called `MyEnum`. The generic method can also accept enumerators:

```
public enum MyEnum { Value1, Value2, Value3 }
```

5. After creating the enumerator, add the following code to the console application. We are instantiating and calling the `oHelper` class and passing different values to it:

```
MyHelperClass oHelper = new MyHelperClass();
var intExample = oHelper.InspectType(25);
Console.WriteLine($"An example of this type is
{intExample}");

var decExample = oHelper.InspectType(11.78m);
Console.WriteLine($"An example of this type is
{decExample}");

var strExample = oHelper.InspectType("Hello Generics");
Console.WriteLine($"An example of this type is
{strExample}");

var enmExample = oHelper.InspectType(MyEnum.Value2);
Console.WriteLine($"An example of this type is
{enmExample}");

Console.ReadLine();
```

6. If you run the console application, you will see that the generic method correctly identifies the type of the parameter passed to it and then returns that type to the calling code in the console application:

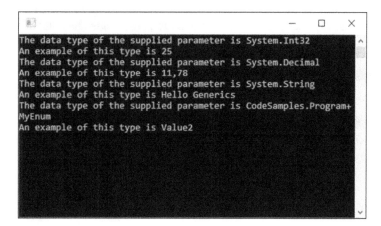

Generic methods can be used in a multitude of situations. This is however only an introduction to generic classes and methods. It is recommended that you do further research to learn how to implement generics in your code appropriately.

How it works...

At the heart of generics lies the ability to reuse a single class or method. It allows developers to essentially not repeat similar code throughout their code base. This conforms well to the **Don't Repeat Yourself** (**DRY**) principle. This design principle states that a specific bit of logic should be represented in code only once.

Using generic classes also allows developers to create a class that is type safe when compiling. Type safe basically means that the developer can be assured of the type of the object and can use the class in a specific way without experiencing any unexpected behavior. Therefore, the compiler takes over the burden of type safety.

Generics also allow developers to write less code because code can be reused, and less code also performs better.

Creating and using a generic interface

Generic interfaces work in much the same way as the previous examples in generics. Let's assume that we want to find the properties of certain classes in our code, but we can't be sure how many classes we will need to inspect. A generic interface could come in very handy here.

Getting ready

We need to inspect several classes for their properties. To do this, we will create a generic interface that will return a list of all the properties found for a class as a list of strings.

How to do it...

Let's take a look at the following implementation of the generic interface as follows:

1. Go ahead and create a generic interface called `IListClassProperties<T>`. The interface will define a method that needs to be used called `GetPropertyList()` that simply uses a LINQ query to return a `List<string>` object:

```
interface IListClassProperties<T>
{
    List<string> GetPropertyList();
}
```

2. Next, create a generic class called `InspectClass<T>`. Let the generic class implement the `IListClassProperties<T>` interface created in the previous step:

```
public class InspectClass<T> : IListClassProperties<T>
{

}
```

3. As usual, Visual Studio will highlight that the interface member `GetPropertyList()` has not been implemented in the `InspectClass<T>` generic class:

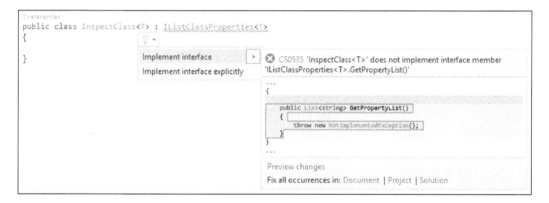

```
public class InspectClass<T> : IListClassProperties<T>
{

}
```
interface Chapter2.IListClassProperties<T>

'InspectClass<T>' does not implement interface member 'IListClassProperties<T>.GetPropertyList()'

Show potential fixes (Ctrl+.)

4. To show any potential fixes, type *Ctrl + .* (period) and implement the interface implicitly:

```
public class InspectClass<T> : IListClassProperties<T>
{

}
```
Implement interface

Implement interface explicitly

CS0535 'InspectClass<T>' does not implement interface member 'IListClassProperties<T>.GetPropertyList()'

```
...
{

    public List<string> GetPropertyList()
    {
        throw new NotImplementedException();
    }
}
...
```

Preview changes

Fix all occurrences in: Document | Project | Solution

5. This will create the `GetPropertyList()` method in your `InspectClass<T>` class without any implementation. You will add the implementation in a moment. If you try to run your code without adding any implementation to the `GetpropertyList()` method, the compiler will throw `NotImplementedException`:

```
public class InspectClass<T> : IListClassProperties<T>
{
    public List<string> GetPropertyList()
    {
        throw new NotImplementedException();
    }
}
```

6. Next, add a constructor to your `InspectClass<T>` class that takes a generic type parameter and sets it equal to the private variable `_classToInspect` that you also need to create. This is setting up the code that we will use to instantiate the `InspectClass<T>` object. We will pass to the object we need a list of properties from the constructor, and the constructor will set the private variable `_classToInspect` so that we can use it in our `GetPropertyList()` method implementation:

```
public class InspectClass<T> : IListClassProperties<T>
{
    T _classToInspect;
    public InspectClass(T classToInspect)
    {
        _classToInspect = classToInspect;
    }

    public List<string> GetPropertyList()
    {
        throw new NotImplementedException();
    }
}
```

7. To finish off our class, we need to add some implementation to the `GetPropertyList()` method. It is here that the LINQ query will be used to return a `List<string>` object of all the properties contained in the class supplied to the constructor:

```
public List<string> GetPropertyList()
{
    return _classToInspect.GetType().GetProperties().Select(p =>
p.Name).ToList();
}
```

8. Moving to our console application, go ahead and create a simple class called `Invoice`. This is one of several classes that can be used in the system, and the `Invoice` class is one of the smaller classes. It usually just holds invoice data specific to a record in the invoices records of the data store you connect to. We need to find a list of the properties in this class:

```
public class Invoice
{
    public int ID { get; set; }
    public decimal TotalValue { get; set; }
    public int LineNumber { get; set; }
    public string StockItem { get; set; }
    public decimal ItemPrice { get; set; }
    public int Qty { get; set; }
}
```

9. We can now make use of our `InspectClass<T>` generic class that implements the `IListClassProperties<T>` generic interface. To do this, we will create a new instance of the `Invoice` class. We will then instantiate the `InspectClass<T>` class, passing the type in the angle brackets and the `oInvoice` object to the constructor. We are now ready to call the `GetPropertyList()` method. The result is returned to a `List<string>` object called `lstProps`. We can then run `foreach` on the list, writing the value of each `property` variable to the console window:

```
Invoice oInvoice = new Invoice();
InspectClass<Invoice> oClassInspector = new
InspectClass<Invoice>(oInvoice);
List<string> lstProps = oClassInspector.GetPropertyList();

foreach(string property in lstProps)
{
    Console.WriteLine(property);
}
Console.ReadLine();
```

10. Go ahead and run the code to see the output generated by inspecting the properties of the `Invoice` class:

As you can see, the properties are listed as they exist in the `Invoice` class. The `IListClassProperties<T>` generic interface and the `InspectClass<T>` class don't care what type of class they need to inspect. They will take any class, run the code on it, and produce a result.

But the preceding implementation still poses a slight problem. Let's have a look at one of the variation of this problem:

1. Consider the following code in the console application:

```
InspectClass<int> oClassInspector = new InspectClass<int>(10);
List<string> lstProps = oClassInspector.GetPropertyList();
foreach (string property in lstProps)
{
    Console.WriteLine(property);
}
Console.ReadLine();
```

You can see that we have easily passed an integer value and type to the `InspectClass<T>` class, and the code does not show any warnings at all. In fact, if you ran this code, nothing would be returned and nothing outputs to the console window. What we need to do is implement the constraints on our generic class and interface.

2. At the end of the interface implementation after the class, add the `where T : class` clause. The code now needs to look like this:

```
public class InspectClass<T> : IListClassProperties<T> where T :
class
{
    T _classToInspect;
    public InspectClass(T classToInspect)
    {
        _classToInspect = classToInspect;
    }

    public List<string> GetPropertyList()
    {
        return _classToInspect.GetType().GetProperties().Select(p
=> p.Name).ToList();
    }
}
```

3. If we returned to our console application code, you will see that Visual Studio has underlined the `int` type passed to the `InspectClass<T>` class:

```
InspectClass<int> oClassInspector = new InspectClass<int>(10);
List<string> lstProps = oClassInspector.GetPropertyList();
foreach (string property in lstProps)
{
    Console.WriteLine(property);
}
Console.ReadLine();
```

The reason for this is because we have defined a constraint against our generic class and interface. We have told the compiler that we only accept reference types. Therefore, this applies to any class, interface array, type, or delegate. Our `Invoice` class will therefore be a valid type, and the constraint will not apply to it.

We can also be more specific in our type parameter constraints. The reason for this is that we perhaps do not want to constrain the parameters to reference types. If we, for example, wanted to button down the generic class and interface to only accept classes created inside our current system, we can implement a constraint that the argument for `T` needs to be derived from a specific object. Here, we can use abstract classes again:

1. Create an abstract class called `AcmeObject` and specify that all classes that inherit from `AcmeObject` implement a property called `ID`:

```
public abstract class AcmeObject
{
    public abstract int ID { get; set; }
}
```

2. We can now ensure that objects we create in our code for which we need to read the properties from are derived from `AcmeObject`. To apply the constraint, modify the generic class and place the `where T : AcmeObject` constraint after the interface implementation. Your code should now look like this:

```
public class InspectClass<T> : IListClassProperties<T> where T :
AcmeObject
{
    T _classToInspect;
    public InspectClass(T classToInspect)
    {
        _classToInspect = classToInspect;
    }

    public List<string> GetPropertyList()
    {
        return _classToInspect.GetType().GetProperties().Select(p
=>
p.Name).ToList();
    }
}
```

3. In the console application, modify the `Invoice` class to inherit from the `AcmeObject` abstract class. Implement the `ID` property as defined in the abstract class:

```
public class Invoice : AcmeObject
{
    public override int ID { get; set; }
```

```
        public decimal TotalValue { get; set; }
        public int LineNumber { get; set; }
        public string StockItem { get; set; }
        public decimal ItemPrice { get; set; }
        public int Qty { get; set; }
}
```

4. Create two more classes called `SalesOrder` and `CreditNote`. This time, however, only make the `SalesOrder` class inherit from `AcmeObject`. Leave the `CreditNote` object as is. This is so that we can clearly see how the constraint can be applied:

```
public class SalesOrder : AcmeObject
{
        public override int ID { get; set; }
        public decimal TotalValue { get; set; }
        public int LineNumber { get; set; }
        public string StockItem { get; set; }
        public decimal ItemPrice { get; set; }
        public int Qty { get; set; }
}

public class CreditNote
{
        public int ID { get; set; }
        public decimal TotalValue { get; set; }
        public int LineNumber { get; set; }
        public string StockItem { get; set; }
        public decimal ItemPrice { get; set; }
        public int Qty { get; set; }
}
```

5. Create the code needed to get the property list for the `Invoice` and `SalesOrder` classes. The code is straightforward, and we can see that Visual Studio does not complain about either of these two classes:

```
Invoice oInvoice = new Invoice();
InspectClass<Invoice> oInvClassInspector = new InspectClass<Invoic
e>(oInvoice);
List<string> invProps = oInvClassInspector.GetPropertyList();

foreach (string property in invProps)
{
        Console.WriteLine(property);
}
Console.ReadLine();
SalesOrder oSalesOrder = new SalesOrder();
```

```
InspectClass<SalesOrder> oSoClassInspector = new InspectClass<Sale
sOrder>(oSalesOrder);
List<string> soProps = oSoClassInspector.GetPropertyList();

foreach (string property in soProps)
{
    Console.WriteLine(property);
}
Console.ReadLine();
```

6. If, however, we had to try do the same for our `CreditNote` class, we will see that Visual Studio will warn us that we can't pass the `CreditNote` class to the `InspectClass<T>` class because the constraint we implemented only accepts objects that derive from our `AcmeObject` abstract class. By doing this, we have effectively taken control over exactly what we allow to be passed to our generic class and interface by means of constraints:

```
CreditNote oCreditNote = new CreditNote();
InspectClass<CreditNote> oCredClassInspector = new InspectClass<CreditNote>(oCreditNote);
List<string> credProps = oCredClassInspector.GetPropertyList();

foreach (string property in credProps)
{
    Console.WriteLine(property);
}
Console.ReadLine();
```

How it works...

Speaking of generic interfaces, we have seen that we can implement behavior on a generic class by implementing a generic interface. The power of using the generic class and generic interface is well illustrated earlier.

Having said that, we do believe that knowing when to use constraints is also important so that you can close down your generic classes to only accept the specific types that you want. This ensures that you don't get any surprises when someone accidently passes an integer to your generic class.

Finally, the constraints that you can use are as follows:

▶ where `T`: `struct`: The type argument must be any value types

▶ where `T`: `class`: The type argument must be any reference types

▶ where `T`: `new()`: The type argument needs to have a parameterless constructor

- ▶ `where T: <base class name>:` The type argument must derive from the given base class

- ▶ `where T: <T must derive from object>:` T The type argument must derive from the object after the colon

- ▶ `where T: <interface>:` The type argument must implement the interface specified

3

Object-Oriented
Programming in C#

This chapter will introduce you to the foundation of C# and **object-oriented programming** (**OOP**). In this chapter, you will cover the following recipes:

- ▸ Using inheritance in C#
- ▸ Using abstraction
- ▸ Leveraging encapsulation
- ▸ Implementing polymorphism
- ▸ Single responsibility principle
- ▸ Open/closed principle

Introduction

During your career as a creator of software, you will hear the term OOP many times. This design philosophy allows for objects to exist independently and can be reused by different sections of code. This is all made possible by what we refer to as the four pillars of OOP, namely inheritance, encapsulation, abstraction, and polymorphism.

In order to grasp this, you need to start thinking of objects (which are basically instantiated classes) that perform a specific task. Classes need to adhere to the SOLID design principle. This principle is explained here:

- **Single responsibility principle (SRP)**
- Open/closed principle
- **Liskov substitution principle (LSP)**
- Interface segregation principle
- Dependency inversion principle

Let's start off with an explanation of the four pillars of OOP, after which we will have a look at the SOLID principle in more detail.

Using inheritance in C#

In today's world, inheritance is usually associated with the end of things. In OOP, however, it is associated with the beginning of something new and better. When we create a new class, we can take an already existing class and have our new class inherit from it. This means that our new object will have all the features of the inherited class, as well as the additional features added to the new class. This is at the root of inheritance. We call a class that inherits from another a derived class.

Getting ready

To illustrate the concept of inheritance, we will create a few classes that inherit from another to form new, more feature-rich objects.

How to do it...

1. Create a new class library by right-clicking on your solution and selecting **Add** and then **New Project** from the context menu:

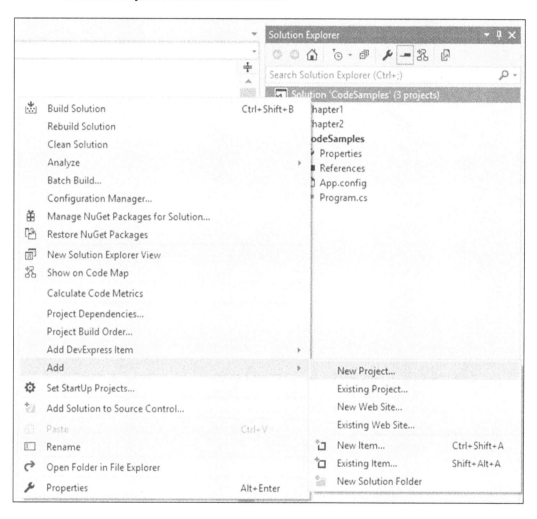

2. From the **Add New Project** dialog screen, select **Class Library** from the installed templates and call your class `Chapter3`:

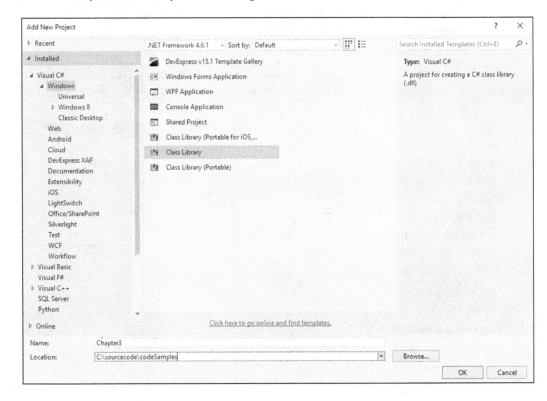

3. Your new class library will be added to your solution with a default name `Class1.cs`, which we renamed to `Recipes.cs` in order to distinguish the code properly. You can, however, rename your class to whatever you like if it makes more sense to you.

4. To rename your class, simply click on the class name in the **Solution Explorer** and select **Rename** from the context menu:

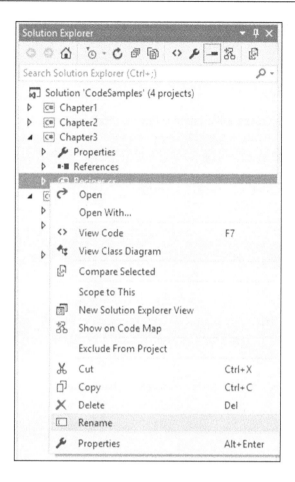

5. Visual Studio will ask you to confirm the renaming of all references to the code element **Class1** in the project. Just click on **Yes**:

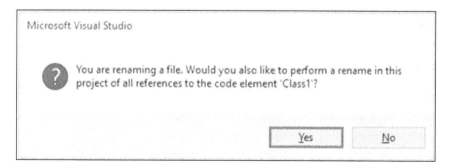

6. Now, let's create a new class called `SpaceShip`:

```
public class SpaceShip
{

}
```

7. Our `SpaceShip` class will contain a few methods that describe the basics of a spaceship. Go ahead and add these methods to your `SpaceShip` class:

```
public class SpaceShip
{
    public void ControlBridge()
    {

    }
    public void MedicalBay(int patientCapacity)
    {

    }
    public void EngineRoom(int warpDrives)
    {

    }
    public void CrewQuarters(int crewCapacity)
    {

    }
    public void TeleportationRoom()
    {

    }
}
```

Because the `SpaceShip` class forms part of all other intergalactic vessels, it becomes the blueprint for every other vessel.

8. Next, we want to create a `Destroyer` class. To accomplish this, we will create a `Destroyer` class and use a colon after the class name to indicate that we want to inherit from another class (the `SpaceShip` class). Therefore, the following needs to be added when creating the `Destroyer` class:

```
public class Destroyer : SpaceShip
{

}
```

We can also say that the `Destroyer` class is derived from the `SpaceShip` class. The `SpaceShip` class is therefore the base class of all other intergalactic vessels.

9. Next, add a few methods to the `Destroyer` class that are unique to a destroyer. These methods belong only to the `Destroyer` class and not to the `SpaceShip` class:

```
public class Destroyer : SpaceShip
{
    public void WarRoom()
    {

    }
    public void Armory(int payloadCapacity)
    {

    }

    public void WarSpecialists(int activeBattalions)
    {

    }
}
```

10. Finally, create a third class called `Annihilator`. This is the most powerful intergalactic vessel and is used to wage war on planets. Let the `Annihilator` class inherit from the `Destroyer` class by creating the class and marking it as derived from the `Destroyer` class as follows `Annihilator : Destroyer`:

```
public class Annihilator : Destroyer
{

}
```

11. Finally, add a few methods to the `Annihilator` class that only belong to this type of `SpaceShip` class:

```
public class Annihilator : Destroyer
{
    public void TractorBeam()
    {

    }

    public void PlanetDestructionCapability()
```

```
        {

        }
    }
```

12. Inside the console application, add a reference to the Chapter3 class library by right-clicking on **References** under the **CodeSamples** project and selecting **Add Reference** from the context menu:

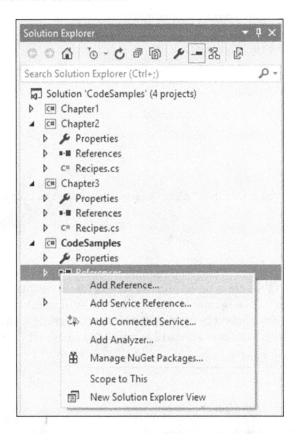

13. In the **Reference Manager** window, select the Chapter3 solution under **Projects | Solutions**. This will allow you to use the classes we just created in your console application:

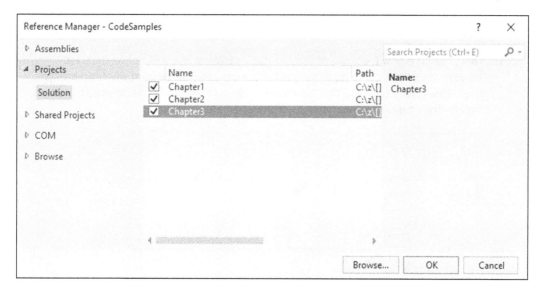

14. What we see now is that when we create a new instance of the `SpaceShip` class, only the methods defined in that class are available to us. This is because the `SpaceShip` class does not inherit from any other class:

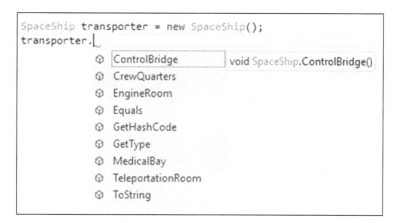

15. Go ahead and create the `SpaceShip` class with its methods in the console application:

```
SpaceShip transporter = new SpaceShip();
transporter.ControlBridge();
transporter.CrewQuarters(1500);
transporter.EngineRoom(2);
transporter.MedicalBay(350);
transporter.TeleportationRoom();
```

You will see that these are the only methods available to us when instantiating a new instance of this class.

16. Next, create a new instance of the `Destroyer` class. You will notice that the `Destroyer` class contains more methods than what we defined when we created the class. This is because the `Destroyer` class is inheriting the `SpaceShip` class and therefore inherits the methods of the `SpaceShip` class:

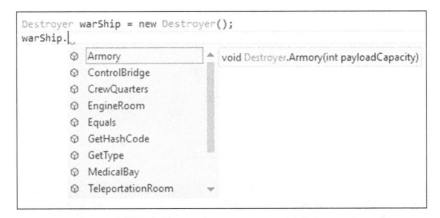

17. Go ahead and create the `Destroyer` class with all its methods in the console application:

```
Destroyer warShip = new Destroyer();
warShip.Armory(6);
warShip.ControlBridge();
warShip.CrewQuarters(2200);
warShip.EngineRoom(4);
warShip.MedicalBay(800);
warShip.TeleportationRoom();
warShip.WarRoom();
warShip.WarSpecialists(1);
```

18. Finally, create a new instance of the `Annihilator` class. This class contains all the methods of the `Destroyer` class as well as the methods from the `SpaceShip` class. This is because `Annihilator` inherits from `Destroyer`, which, in turn, inherits from `SpaceShip`:

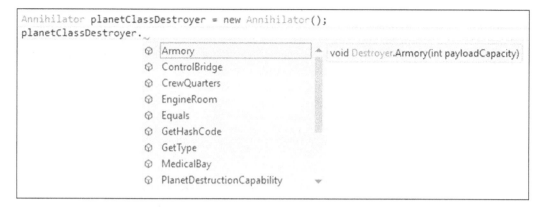

```
Annihilator planetClassDestroyer = new Annihilator();
planetClassDestroyer.
```

☉	Armory	void Destroyer.Armory(int payloadCapacity)
☉	ControlBridge	
☉	CrewQuarters	
☉	EngineRoom	
☉	Equals	
☉	GetHashCode	
☉	GetType	
☉	MedicalBay	
☉	PlanetDestructionCapability	

19. Go ahead and create the `Annihilator` class with all its methods in the console application:

```
Annihilator planetClassDestroyer = new Annihilator();
planetClassDestroyer.Armory(12);
planetClassDestroyer.ControlBridge();
planetClassDestroyer.CrewQuarters(4500);
planetClassDestroyer.EngineRoom(7);
planetClassDestroyer.MedicalBay(3500);
planetClassDestroyer.PlanetDestructionCapability();
planetClassDestroyer.TeleportationRoom();
planetClassDestroyer.TractorBeam();
planetClassDestroyer.WarRoom();
planetClassDestroyer.WarSpecialists(3);
```

How it works...

We can see that inheritance allowed us to easily extend our classes by reusing functionality that already exists within another class created earlier. You also need to be aware though that any changes to the `SpaceShip` class will be inherited up the stack to the top-most derived class.

Inheritance is a very powerful feature of C#, which allows developers to write less code and reuse working and tested methods.

Using abstraction

With abstraction, we take from the object we want to create the basic functionality that all objects derived from the abstracted object must have. To explain this in simple terms, we abstract the common functionality and put it in a single class that will be used to provide this shared functionality to all classes that inherit from it.

Getting ready

To explain abstraction, we will use abstract classes. Imagine that you are dealing with trainee space astronauts who need to progress through the ranks as they get trained. The truth is that once you as trainee learn a new skill, that skill is learned and will remain with you even though you learn more advanced ways to do things. You must also implement all the previous skills learned in the new object you create. Abstract classes demonstrate this concept very nicely.

How to do it...

1. Create an abstract class called `SpaceCadet`. This is the first type of astronaut you can be when starting with training. The abstract class and its members are defined using the `abstract` keyword. A thing to note is that abstract classes cannot be instantiated. The members represent the skills that `SpaceCadet` will have, such as negotiation and basic weapons training:

    ```
    public abstract class SpaceCadet
    {
        public abstract void ChartingStarMaps();
        public abstract void BasicCommunicationSkill();
        public abstract void BasicWeaponsTraining();
        public abstract void Negotiation();
    }
    ```

2. Next, create another abstract class called `SpacePrivate`. This abstract class inherits from the `SpaceCadet` abstract class. What we are basically saying is that when a space cadet is trained as a space private, they will still have all the skills learned as a space cadet:

    ```
    public abstract class SpacePrivate : SpaceCadet
    {
        public abstract void AdvancedCommunicationSkill();
        public abstract void AdvancedWeaponsTraining();
        public abstract void Persuader();
    }
    ```

3. To demonstrate this, create a class called `LabResearcher` and inherit the `SpaceCadet` abstract class. Inheriting from the abstract class is done by defining a colon and abstract class name after the newly created class name. This tells the compiler that the `LabResearcher` class inherits from the `SpaceCadet` class:

    ```
    public class LabResearcher : SpaceCadet
    {

    }
    ```

Because we are inheriting an abstract class, the compiler will underline the LabResearcher class name to warn us that the derived class does not implement any of the methods in the SpaceCadet abstract class.

4. If you hover your mouse over the squiggly line, you will see that the lightbulb tip provides us with the issues discovered:

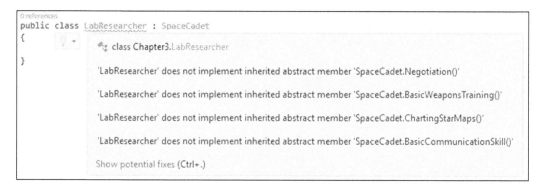

5. Visual Studio does a great job of providing a solution to the issues discovered. By typing *Ctrl + .* (Control key and dot), you can let Visual Studio show you some potential fixes (in this case, only one fix) for the issues identified:

```
0 references
public class LabResearcher : SpaceCadet
{
}

        Implement Abstract Class              ⊗ CS0534 'LabResearcher' does not implement inherited abstract member
                                                 'SpaceCadet.ChartingStarMaps()'
                                                 ...
                                                 {
                                                     public override void BasicCommunicationSkill()
                                                     {
                                                         throw new NotImplementedException();
                                                     }

                                                     public override void BasicWeaponsTraining()
                                                     {
                                                         throw new NotImplementedException();
                                                     }

                                                     public override void ChartingStarMaps()
                                                     {
                                                         throw new NotImplementedException();
                                                     }

                                                     public override void Negotiation()
                                                     {
                                                         throw new NotImplementedException();
                                                     }
                                                 }
                                                 ...
                                                 Preview changes
                                                 Fix all occurrences in: Document | Project | Solution
```

6. After Visual Studio has added the required methods, you will see that these are the same methods defined in the `SpaceCadet` abstract class. Abstract classes, therefore, require the classes inheriting from the abstract class to implement the methods defined in the abstract class. You will also notice that the methods added to the `LabResearcher` class contain no implementation and will throw an exception if used as is:

```
public class LabResearcher : SpaceCadet
{
    public override void BasicCommunicationSkill()
    {
        throw new NotImplementedException();
    }

    public override void BasicWeaponsTraining()
    {
        throw new NotImplementedException();
    }

    public override void ChartingStarMaps()
    {
        throw new NotImplementedException();
    }

    public override void Negotiation()
    {
        throw new NotImplementedException();
    }
}
```

7. Next, create a class called `PlanetExplorer` and make this class inherit from the `SpacePrivate` abstract class. You will remember that the `SpacePrivate` abstract class inherited from the `SpaceCadet` abstract class:

```
public class PlanetExplorer : SpacePrivate
{

}
```

8. Visual Studio will once again warn you that your new class does not implement the methods of the abstract class that you are inheriting from. Here, however, you will notice that the lightbulb tip informs you that you are not implementing any of the methods in the `SpacePrivate` and `SpaceCadet` abstract classes. This is because the `SpacePrivate` abstract class is inheriting from the `SpaceCadet` abstract class:

```
0 references
public class PlanetExplorer : SpacePrivate
{
          ♀ ▾          ⚙ class Chapter3.PlanetExplorer
}
                        'PlanetExplorer' does not implement inherited abstract member 'SpacePrivate.AdvancedCommunicationSkill()'

                        'PlanetExplorer' does not implement inherited abstract member 'SpaceCadette.BasicCommunicationSkill()'

                        'PlanetExplorer' does not implement inherited abstract member 'SpacePrivate.AdvancedWeaponsTraining()'

                        'PlanetExplorer' does not implement inherited abstract member 'SpaceCadette.BasicWeaponsTraining()'

                        'PlanetExplorer' does not implement inherited abstract member 'SpaceCadette.ChartingStarMaps()'

                        'PlanetExplorer' does not implement inherited abstract member 'SpaceCadette.Negotiation()'

                        'PlanetExplorer' does not implement inherited abstract member 'SpacePrivate.Persuader()'

                        Show potential fixes (Ctrl+.)
```

9. To fix the issues identified, type *Ctrl + .* (Control key and dot) and let Visual Studio show you some potential fixes (in this case, only one fix) for the issues identified:

```
class PlanetExplorer : SpacePrivate
   ♀ ▾
      Implement Abstract Class          ▸        ⊗ CS0534 'PlanetExplorer' does not implement inherited abstract member
                                                   'SpacePrivate.AdvancedCommunicationSkill()'
                                                 ...
                                                 {
                                                     public override void AdvancedCommunicationSkill()
                                                     {
                                                         throw new NotImplementedException();
                                                     }

                                                     public override void AdvancedWeaponsTraining()
                                                     {
                                                         throw new NotImplementedException();
                                                     }

                                                     public override void BasicCommunicationSkill()
                                                     {
                                                         throw new NotImplementedException();
                                                     }

                                                     public override void BasicWeaponsTraining()
                                                     {
                                                         throw new NotImplementedException();
                                                     }

                                                     public override void ChartingStarMaps()
                                                     {
                                                         throw new NotImplementedException();
                                                     }

                                                     public override void Negotiation()
                                                     {
                                                         throw new NotImplementedException();
                                                     }

                                                     public override void Persuader()
                                                     {
                                                         throw new NotImplementedException();
                                                     }
                                                 }
                                                 ...
                                                 Preview changes
                                                 Fix all occurrences in: Document | Project | Solution
```

10. After the fixes have been added to your code, you will see that the `PlanetExplorer` class contains all the methods in the `SpacePrivate` and `SpaceCadet` abstract classes:

```csharp
public class PlanetExplorer : SpacePrivate
{
    public override void AdvancedCommunicationSkill()
    {
        throw new NotImplementedException();
    }

    public override void AdvancedWeaponsTraining()
    {
        throw new NotImplementedException();
    }

    public override void BasicCommunicationSkill()
    {
        throw new NotImplementedException();
    }

    public override void BasicWeaponsTraining()
    {
        throw new NotImplementedException();
    }

    public override void ChartingStarMaps()
    {
        throw new NotImplementedException();
    }

    public override void Negotiation()
    {
        throw new NotImplementedException();
    }

    public override void Persuader()
    {
        throw new NotImplementedException();
    }
}
```

How it works...

Abstraction has allowed us to define a common set of functionality that is to be shared among all the classes that derive from the abstract classes. The difference between inheriting from the abstract class and a normal class is that with an abstract class, you have to implement all the methods defined in that abstract class.

This makes the class easy to version and change. If you need to add new functionality, you can do so by adding that functionality to the abstract class without breaking any of the existing code. Visual Studio will require that all inherited classes implement the new method defined in the abstract class.

You can, therefore, be assured that the change applied will be implemented in all your classes that derive from the abstract classes in your code.

Leveraging encapsulation

What is encapsulation? Simply put, it is hiding the inner workings of a class that aren't necessary for the implementation of that class. Think of encapsulation as follows: most people who own a car know that it runs on gas. They don't need to know the inner workings of an internal combustion engine to be able to use a car. They only need to know that they need to fill it up with gas when it is close to empty and that they need to check the oil and tyre pressure. Even then, it is usually not done by the car owner. This is true for classes and encapsulation.

The owner of the class is the one who uses it. The inner workings of that class need not be exposed to the developer using the class. The class is, therefore, like a black box. You know that the class will be consistent in its functionality, given the correct set of parameters. How exactly the class gets to the output is of no concern to the developer as long as the input is correct.

Getting ready

To illustrate the concept of encapsulation, we will create a class that is somewhat complex in its inner workings. We need to calculate the **thrust to weight ratio** (**TWR**) of a space shuttle to determine whether it will be able to take off vertically. It needs to exert more thrust than its weight to counteract gravity and get into a stable orbit. This also depends on which planet the shuttle takes off from, because different planets exert different gravitational forces on objects on their surface. In simple terms, the TWR must be greater than one.

How to do it...

1. Create a new class called `LaunchSuttle`. Then, add the following private variables to the class for engine thrust; the mass of the shuttle; the local gravitational acceleration; the constant values for the gravity of the Earth, Moon, and Mars (these are constants because they will never change); the universal gravitational constant; and an enumerator for the planet we are dealing with:

```
public class LaunchShuttle
{
    private double _EngineThrust;
    private double _TotalShuttleMass;
    private double _LocalGravitationalAcceleration;

    private const double EarthGravity = 9.81;
    private const double MoonGravity = 1.63;
    private const double MarsGravity = 3.75;
    private double UniversalGravitationalConstant;

    public enum Planet { Earth, Moon, Mars }
}
```

2. To our class, we will add three overloaded constructors that are essential to perform the calculation of the TWR based on the known facts at the time of instantiation (we assume that we will always know the engine thrust capability and mass of the shuttle). We will pass the gravitational acceleration for the first constructor. This is useful if we know beforehand what that value will be. For example, the gravitational acceleration of the Earth is 9.81 m/s^2.

   The second constructor will use the `Planet` enumerator to calculate the TWR that uses the constant variable values.

   The third constructor will use the radius and mass of the planet to calculate the gravitational acceleration when those values are knows to return the TWR:

```
public LaunchShuttle(double engineThrust, double
totalShuttleMass, double gravitationalAcceleration)
{
    _EngineThrust = engineThrust;
    _TotalShuttleMass = totalShuttleMass;
    _LocalGravitationalAcceleration =
    gravitationalAcceleration;

}

public LaunchShuttle(double engineThrust, double
totalShuttleMass, Planet planet)
```

```
{
    _EngineThrust = engineThrust;
    _TotalShuttleMass = totalShuttleMass;
    SetGraviationalAcceleration(planet);


}

public LaunchShuttle(double engineThrust, double
totalShuttleMass, double planetMass, double planetRadius)
{
    _EngineThrust = engineThrust;
    _TotalShuttleMass = totalShuttleMass;
    SetUniversalGravitationalConstant();
    _LocalGravitationalAcceleration =
    Math.Round(CalculateGravitationalAcceleration
    (planetRadius, planetMass), 2);
}
```

3. In order to use the second overloaded constructor that passes the `Planet` enumerator as a parameter to the class, we need to create another method that has been scoped as `private` to calculate the gravitational acceleration. We also need to set the `_LocalGravitationalAcceleration` variable to the specific constant that matches the enumerator value. This method is something that the user of the class does not need to see in order to use the class. It is, therefore, scoped as `private` in order to hide that functionality from the user:

```
private void SetGraviationalAcceleration(Planet planet)
{
    switch (planet)
    {
        case Planet.Earth:
            _LocalGravitationalAcceleration = EarthGravity;
            break;
        case Planet.Moon:
            _LocalGravitationalAcceleration = MoonGravity;
            break;
        case Planet.Mars:
            _LocalGravitationalAcceleration = MarsGravity;
            break;
        default:
            break;
    }
}
```

4. Of the following methods, only one is defined as public and will, therefore, be visible to the user of the class. Create the private methods to set the universal gravitational constant, to calculate the TWR, and to calculate the gravitational acceleration. These are all scoped as private, because the developer does not need to know what these methods do in order to use the class:

```csharp
private void SetUniversalGravitationalConstant()
{
    UniversalGravitationalConstant = 6.6726 * Math.Pow(10,
    -11);
}

private double CalculateThrustToWeightRatio()
{
    // TWR = Ft/m.g > 1
    return _EngineThrust / (_TotalShuttleMass *
    _LocalGravitationalAcceleration);
}

private double CalculateGravitationalAcceleration(double
radius, double mass)
{
    return (UniversalGravitationalConstant * mass) /
    Math.Pow(radius, 2);
}

public double TWR()
{
    return Math.Round(CalculateThrustToWeightRatio(), 2);
}
```

5. Finally, in your console application, create the following variables with their known vales:

```csharp
double thrust = 220; // kN
double shuttleMass = 16.12; // t
double graviatatonalAccelerationEarth = 9.81;
double earthMass = 5.9742 * Math.Pow(10, 24);
double earthRadius = 6378100;
double thrustToWeightRatio = 0;
```

6. Create a new instance of the `LaunchShuttle` class and pass it the values needed to calculate the TWR:

```
LaunchShuttle NasaShuttle1 = new LaunchShuttle(thrust,
shuttleMass, graviatatonalAccelerationEarth);
thrustToWeightRatio = NasaShuttle1.TWR();
Console.WriteLine(thrustToWeightRatio);
```

7. When you use the dot operator on the `NasaShuttle1` variable, you will notice that IntelliSense only shows the `TWR` method. The class exposes nothing of the inner workings of how it gets to the calculated TWR value. The only thing that the developer knows is that the `LaunchShuttle` class will consistently return the correct TWR value, given the same input parameters:

```
LaunchShuttle NasaShuttle1 = new LaunchShuttle(thrust, shuttleMass, graviatatonalAccelerationEarth);
thrustToWeightRatio = NasaShuttle1.

                          ⊘  Equals
                          ⊘  GetHashCode
                          ⊘  GetType
                          ⊘  ToString
                          ⊘  TWR                    double LaunchShuttle.TWR()
```

8. To test this, create two more instances of the `LaunchShuttle` class and call a different constructor each time:

```
LaunchShuttle NasaShuttle2 = new LaunchShuttle(thrust,
shuttleMass, LaunchShuttle.Planet.Earth);
thrustToWeightRatio = NasaShuttle2.TWR();
Console.WriteLine(thrustToWeightRatio);

LaunchShuttle NasaShuttle3 = new LaunchShuttle(thrust,
shuttleMass, earthMass, earthRadius);
thrustToWeightRatio = NasaShuttle3.TWR();
Console.WriteLine(thrustToWeightRatio);

Console.Read();
```

9. If you run your console application, you will see that the same value is returned for the TWR. The value indicates that a shuttle weighing 16.12 tons with a rocket that puts out 220 kilonewtons of thrust will be able to lift off the surface of the Earth (if only just):

How it works...

The class uses the scoping rules to hide certain functionality inside the class from the developer using the class. As mentioned earlier, the developer does not need to know how the calculations are done to return the value for the TWR. This all aids in making the class more useful and easy to implement. Here is a list of the various scopes available in C#, along with their uses:

▸ `Public`: This is used with variables, properties, types, and methods and is visible anywhere.

▸ `Private`: This is used with variables, properties, types, and methods and is visible only in the block where they are defined.

▸ `Protected`: This is used with variables, properties, and methods. Don't think of this in terms of public or private. The protected scope is only visible inside the class in which it is used, as well as in any inherited classes.

▸ `Friend`: This is used with variables, properties, and methods and can only be used by code in the same project or assembly.

▸ `Protected Friend`: This is used with variables, properties, and methods and is a combination (as the name suggests) of the protected and friend scopes.

Implementing polymorphism

Polymorphism is a concept that is quite easy to grasp once you have looked at and understood the other pillars of OOP. Polymorphism literally means that something can have many forms. This means that from a single interface, you can create multiple implementations.

There are two subsections to this, namely static and dynamic polymorphism. With static polymorphism, you are dealing with the overloading of methods and functions. You can use the same method, but perform many different tasks.

With dynamic polymorphism, you are dealing with the creation and implementation of abstract classes. These abstract classes act as a blueprint that tells you what a derived class should implement. The following section looks at both.

Getting ready

We will begin by illustrating the use of an abstract class, which is an example of dynamic polymorphism. We will then create overloaded constructors as an example of static polymorphism.

How to do it...

1. Create an abstract class called Shuttle and give it a member called TWR, which is the calculation of the TWR of the shuttle:

```
public abstract class Shuttle
{
    public abstract double TWR();
}
```

2. Next, create a class called NasaShuttle and have it inherit from the abstract class Shuttle, by putting the abstract class name after a colon at the end of the NasaShuttle class declaration:

```
public class NasaShuttle : Shuttle
{

}
```

3. Visual Studio will underline the `NasaShuttle` class because you have told the compiler that the class inherits from an abstract class, but you have not yet implemented the members of that abstract class:

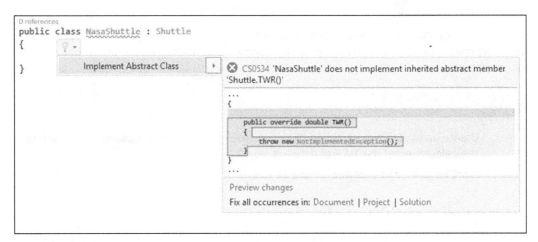

4. To fix the issues identified, type *Ctrl + .* (Control key and dot) and let Visual Studio show you some potential fixes (in this case, only one fix) for the issues identified:

5. Visual Studio then adds the missing implementation to your `NasaShuttle` class. By default, it will add it as not implemented, because you are required to provide implementation for the abstract member you overrode in the abstract class:

```csharp
public class NasaShuttle : Shuttle
{
    public override double TWR()
    {
        throw new NotImplementedException();
    }
}
```

6. Create another class called `RoscosmosShuttle` and inherit from the same `Shuttle` abstract class:

```
public class RoscosmosShuttle : Shuttle
{

}
```

7. Visual Studio will underline the `RoscosmosShuttle` class because you have told the compiler that the class inherits from an abstract class, but you have not yet implemented the members of that abstract class:

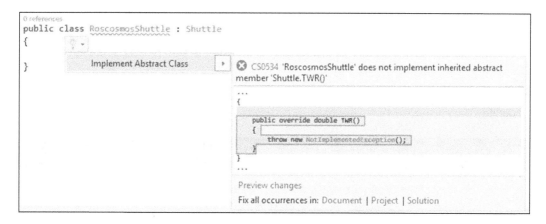

8. To fix the issues identified, type *Ctrl + .* (Control key and dot) and let Visual Studio show you some potential fixes (in this case, only one fix) for the issues identified:

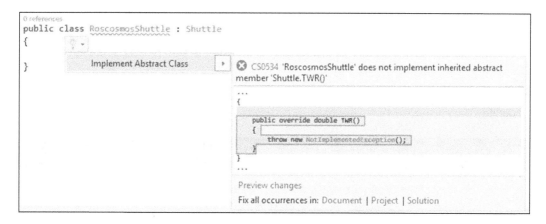

9. The overridden method is then added to the `RoscosmosShuttle` class as not implemented. You have just seen an example of dynamic polymorphism in action:

```
public class RoscosmosShuttle : Shuttle
{
    public override double TWR()
    {
```

```
            throw new NotImplementedException();
        }
    }
```

10. To see an example of static polymorphism, create the following overloaded constructor for `NasaShuttle`. The constructor name stays the same, but the signature of the constructor changes, which makes it overloaded:

```
public NasaShuttle(double engineThrust, double
totalShuttleMass, double gravitationalAcceleration)
{

}

public NasaShuttle(double engineThrust, double
totalShuttleMass, double planetMass, double planetRadius)
{

}
```

How it works...

Polymorphism is something you will easily be using already by simply applying good object oriented principles to the design of your classes. With the abstract `Shuttle` class, we saw that the class took on the shape of the `NasaShuttle` class and the `RoscosmosShuttle` class when it was used to derive those new classes from its abstraction. The constructor of the `NasaShuttle` class was then overridden to provide the same method name, but implemented using different signatures.

This is at the heart of polymorphism. Most likely, you have been using it without knowing about it.

Single responsibility principle

When talking about SOLID principles, we will start off with the SRP. Here, we are actually saying that a class has a specific task that it needs to fulfil and it should not do anything else.

Getting ready

You will create a new class and write code to log an error to the database when an exception is thrown on adding more troops to the star ship, causing it to be over capacity.

How to do it...

1. Create a new class called `StarShip`:

```
public class Starship
{

}
```

2. To your class, add a new method that will set the maximum troop capacity of the `StarShip` class:

```
public void SetMaximumTroopCapacity(int capacity)
{

}
```

3. Inside this method, add a `trycatch` clause that will attempt to set the maximum troop capacity, but for some reason, it will fail. Upon failure, it will write the error to the log table inside the database:

```
try
{
    // Read current capacity and try to add more
}
catch (Exception ex)
{
    string connectionString = "connection string goes
    here";
    string sql = $"INSERT INTO tblLog (error, date) VALUES
    ({ex.Message}, GetDate())";
    using (SqlConnection con = new
    SqlConnection(connectionString))
    {
        SqlCommand cmd = new SqlCommand(sql);
        cmd.CommandType = CommandType.Text;
        cmd.Connection = con;
        con.Open();
        cmd.ExecuteNonQuery();
    }
    throw ex;
}
```

How it works...

If you have code that looks like the preceding one, you are in contravention of the SRP. The `StarShip` class is no longer responsible for just itself and things that have to do with star ships. It now has to fulfill the role of logging errors to the database too. You see the problem here is that the database-logging code does not belong in the `catch` clause of the `SetMaximumTroopCapacity` method. A better approach would be to create a separate `DatabaseLogging` class with methods to create connections and write exceptions to the appropriate log table. You will also find that you are going to have to write that logging code in multiple places (in every `catch` clause). If you are finding that you are repeating code (by copying and pasting from other areas), you probably need to put that code into a common class, and you have likely broken the SRP rule.

Open/closed principle

When creating classes, we need to ensure that the class prohibits any breaking modifications by needing to change internal code. We say that such a class is closed. If we need to change it somehow, we can do so by extending the class. This extensibility is where we say that the class is open for extensions.

Getting ready

You will create a class that determines the skills of a trooper by looking at the class of trooper. We will show you the way many developers create such a class and the way it can be created using the open/closed principle.

How to do it...

1. Create a class called `StarTrooper`:

    ```
    public class StarTrooper
    {

    }
    ```

2. To this class, add an enumerator called `TrooperClass` to identify the type of trooper we want to return the skills of. Also, create a `List<string>` variable to contain the skills of the specific trooper class. Finally, create a method called `GetSkills` that returns the specific set of skills for the given trooper class.

The class is quite straightforward, but the implementation of the code is something we see a lot. Sometimes, instead of a `switch` statement, you will see a whole lot of `if else` statements. While the functionality of the code is clear, it is not easy to add another class of trooper to the `StarTrooper` class without changing code. Assume that you now have to add an additional `Engineer` class to the `StarTrooper` class. You would have to modify the `TrooperClass` enumeration and the code in the `switch` statement.

This changing of code can cause you to introduce bugs into code that was previously working fine. We now see that the `StarTrooper` class is not closed and can't be extended easily to accommodate additional `TrooperClass` objects:

```
public enum TrooperClass { Soldier, Medic, Scientist }
List<string> TroopSkill;

public List<string> GetSkills(TrooperClass troopClass)
{
    switch (troopClass)
    {
        case TrooperClass.Soldier:
        return TroopSkill = new List<string>(new
        string[] { "Weaponry", "TacticalCombat",
        "HandToHandCombat" });

        case TrooperClass.Medic:
        return TroopSkill = new List<string>(new
        string[] { "CPR", "AdvancedLifeSupport" });

        case TrooperClass.Scientist:
        return TroopSkill = new List<string>(new
        string[] { "Chemistry",
        "MollecularDeconstruction", "QuarkTheory" });

        default:
            return TroopSkill = new
            List<string>(new string[]
            { "none" });
    }
}
```

3. The solution to this problem is inheritance. Instead of having to change code, we extend it. Start off by rewriting the above `StarTrooper` class and create a `Trooper` class. The `GetSkills` method is declared as `virtual`:

```
public class Trooper
{
    public virtual List<string> GetSkills()
    {
        return new List<string>(new string[] { "none" });
    }
}
```

4. Now, we can easily create derived classes for the `Soldier`, `Medic`, and `Scientist` trooper classes available. Create the following derived classes that inherit from the `Trooper` class. You can see that the `override` keyword is used when creating the `GetSkills` method:

```
public class Soldier : Trooper
{
    public override List<string> GetSkills()
    {
        return new List<string>(new string[] { "Weaponry",
        "TacticalCombat", "HandToHandCombat" });
    }
}


public class Medic : Trooper
{
    public override List<string> GetSkills()
    {
        return new List<string>(new string[] { "CPR",
        "AdvancedLifeSupport" });
    }
}


public class Scientist : Trooper
{
    public override List<string> GetSkills()
    {
        return new List<string>(new string[] { "Chemistry",
        "MollecularDeconstruction", "QuarkTheory" });
    }
}
```

5. The code becomes extremely easy to implement when extending the class to add an additional class of `Trooper`. If we now want to add the `Engineer` class, we would simply override the `GetSkills` method after inheriting from the `Trooper` class created earlier:

```
public class Engineer : Trooper
{
public override List<string> GetSkills()
    {
        return new List<string>(new string[] {
        "Construction", "Demolition" });
    }
}
```

How it works...

The classes derived from the `Trooper` class are extensions of the `Trooper` class. We can say that each class is closed, because modifying it does not necessitate changing the original code. The `Trooper` class is also extensible because we have been able to easily extend the class by creating derived classes from it.

Another by-product of this design is smaller, more manageable code that is easier to read and understand.

4

Composing Event-Based Programs Using Reactive Extensions

This chapter deals with **Reactive Extensions** (**Rx**). To understand Rx, we will cover the following recipes:

- ▸ Installing Rx
- ▸ Events versus observables
- ▸ Using LINQ to perform queries
- ▸ Using schedulers in Rx
- ▸ Debugging lambda expressions

Introduction

Often, during your day-to-day dealings with developing applications in C#, you will have to use asynchronous programming. You might also have to deal with many data sources. Think of a web service that returns the current exchange rates, a Twitter search returning a stream of related data, or even different events generated by multiple computers. Rx provides an elegant solution in the form of the `IObserver<T>` interface.

You use the `IObserver<T>` interface to subscribe to the events. Then, the `IObservable<T>` interface, which maintains a list of `IObserver<T>` interfaces, will notify them on the change of state. In essence, Rx will stick together multiple data sources (social media, RSS feeds, UI events, and so on) that generate data. Rx, therefore, brings these data sources together in one interface. In fact, Rx can be thought of as consisting of three sections:

- **Observables**: The interface that brings together and represents all these data streams
- **Language-Integrated Query** (**LINQ**): The ability to use LINQ to query these multiple data streams
- **Schedulers**: Parametrizing concurrency using schedulers

The question on many minds might be why developers should use (or find use for) Rx. Here are a few examples where Rx are really useful:

- Creating a search that has an autocomplete function. You don't want the code to perform a search for each value you type into the search area. Rx allows you to throttle the search.
- Making the UI of your application more responsive.
- Being notified when data changes instead of having to poll the data for changes. Think of real-time stock prices.

To keep up to date with Rx, you can have a look at the GitHub page: `https://github.com/Reactive-Extensions/Rx.NET`.

Installing Rx

Before we can begin exploring Rx, we need to install it. The easiest way to do this is using NuGet.

Getting ready

For this chapter on Rx, we will not create a separate class. All the code will be written in a console application.

How to do it...

1. Right-click on your solution and select **Manage NuGet Packages for Solution...** from the context menu:

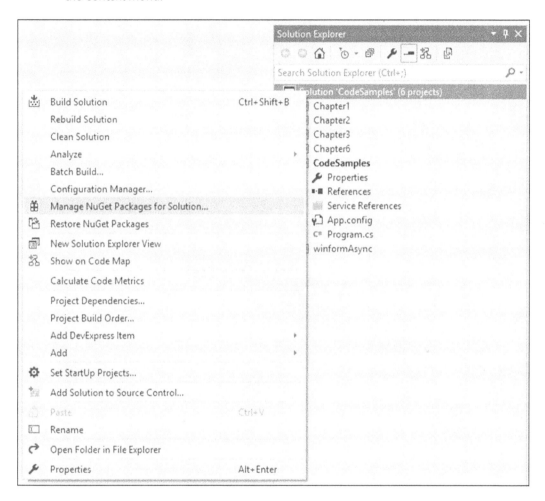

2. In the window that is displayed afterwards, type `System.Reactive` in the search text box and search for the NuGet installer:

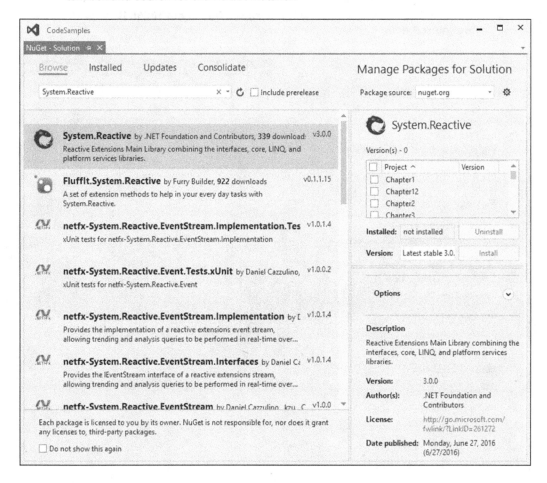

3. At the time of writing this book, the last stable release was version 3.0.0. Next, select the projects that you want to install Rx on. For simplicity sake, we just selected it to be installed project wide:

4. The next screenshot that is displayed is a confirmation dialog box, asking you to confirm the changes to the project. It will show a preview of the changes it will be making to each project. If you are happy with the changes, click on the **OK** button:

5. A license agreement might be presented to you in the last dialog screen, which you will need to accept. To continue, click on the **I Accept** button.

6. After the installation is complete, you will see the references added to Rx under the **References** node in your project. These are as follows:

    ❑   `System.Reactive.Core`

    ❑   `System.Reactive.Interfaces`

    ❑   `System.Reactive.Linq`

    ❑   `System.Reactive.PlatformServices`

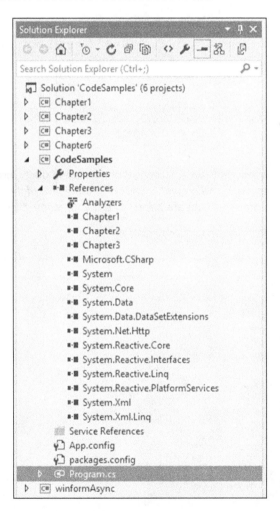

How it works...

NuGet is by far the easiest way to add additional components to your projects. As you can see from the added references, `System.Reactive` is the main assembly. To gain a better understanding of `System.Reactive`, view the assemblies in **Object Browser**. To do this, double-click on any of the assemblies in the **References** option of your project:

`System.Reactive.Linq` contains all the querying functionality in Rx. You will also notice that `System.Reactive.Concurrency` contains all the schedulers.

Events versus observables

Being developers, we should all be quite familiar with events. Most developers have been creating events since we started writing code. In fact, if you have even dropped a button control on a form and double-clicked the button to create the method that handles the click of the button, you have created an event. In .NET, we can declare events using the `event` keyword, publish to the event by invoking it, and subscribe to that event by adding a handler to the event. We therefore have the following operations:

- Declare
- Publish
- Subscribe

With Rx, we have a similar structure where we declare a data stream, publish data to that stream, and subscribe to it.

Getting ready

First, we will see how an event works in C#. We will then see the working of an event using Rx and, in doing so, highlight the differences.

How to do it...

1. In your console application, add a new class called `DotNet`. To this class, add a property called `AvailableDatatype`:

```
public class DotNet
{
    public string  AvailableDatatype { get; set; }
}
```

2. In the main program class, add a new static action event called `types`. Basically, this is just a delegate and will receive some value, in our case, the available .NET data types:

```
class Program
{
    // Static action event
    static event Action<string> types;

    static void Main(string[] args)
    {

    }
}
```

3. Inside `void Main`, create a `List<DotNet>` class called `lstTypes`. Inside this list, add several values of type `DotNet` class. Here, we will just add hardcoded data of some of the data types in .NET:

```
List<DotNet> lstTypes = new List<DotNet>();
DotNet blnTypes = new DotNet();
blnTypes.AvailableDatatype = "bool";
lstTypes.Add(blnTypes);

DotNet strTypes = new DotNet();
strTypes.AvailableDatatype = "string";
lstTypes.Add(strTypes);

DotNet intTypes = new DotNet();
intTypes.AvailableDatatype = "int";
lstTypes.Add(intTypes);

DotNet decTypes = new DotNet();
decTypes.AvailableDatatype = "decimal";
lstTypes.Add(decTypes);
```

4. Our next task is to subscribe to this event with an event handler that is simply outputting the value of *x* to the console window. We will then raise the event each time we loop through our `lstTypes` list by adding the line `types(lstTypes[i].AvailableDatatype);`:

```
types += x =>
{
    Console.WriteLine(x);
};


for (int i = 0; i <= lstTypes.Count - 1; i++)
{
    types(lstTypes[i].AvailableDatatype);
}

Console.ReadLine();
```

 In reality, before raising an event, we should always check that the event isn't null. Only after this check should we raise the event. For brevity, we have not added this check before raising the event.

5. When you have added all the code from step 1 to step 4, your console application should look like this:

```
class Program
{
    // Static action event
    static event Action<string> types;

    static void Main(string[] args)
    {
        List<DotNet> lstTypes = new List<DotNet>();
        DotNet blnTypes = new DotNet();
        blnTypes.AvailableDatatype = "bool";
        lstTypes.Add(blnTypes);

        DotNet strTypes = new DotNet();
        strTypes.AvailableDatatype = "string";
        lstTypes.Add(strTypes);

        DotNet intTypes = new DotNet();
        intTypes.AvailableDatatype = "int";
        lstTypes.Add(intTypes);

        DotNet decTypes = new DotNet();
        decTypes.AvailableDatatype = "decimal";
        lstTypes.Add(decTypes);


        types += x =>
        {
            Console.WriteLine(x);
        };


        for (int i = 0; i <= lstTypes.Count - 1; i++)
        {
            types(lstTypes[i].AvailableDatatype);
        }

        Console.ReadLine();
    }
}
```

6. Running your application will set our list with values and then raise the event created to output the values of the list to the console window:

7. Let's see the working of events using Rx. Add a static `Subject` of `string`. You might also need to add the `System.Reactive.Subjects` namespace to your project as `Subjects` live in this separate namespace:

```
class Program
{

    static Subject<string> obsTypes = new Subject<string>();

    static void Main(string[] args)
    {

    }
}
```

8. After the code that created the list of `DotNet`, we used `+=` to wire up an event handler. This time round, we will use `Subscribe`. This is the `IObservable` portion of the code. After you have added this, raise the event using the `OnNext` keyword. This is the `IObserver` portion of the code. Therefore, as we loop through our list, we will call `OnNext` to pump out the values to the subscribed `IObservable` interface:

```
// IObservable
obsTypes.Subscribe(x =>
{
    Console.WriteLine(x);
});
```

```
        // IObserver
        for (int i = 0; i <= lstTypes.Count - 1; i++)
        {
            obsTypes.OnNext(lstTypes[i].AvailableDatatype);
        }

        Console.ReadLine();
```

9. When you have completed adding all the code, your application should look like this:

```
class Program
{

    static Subject<string> obsTypes = new Subject<string>();

    static void Main(string[] args)
    {
        List<DotNet> lstTypes = new List<DotNet>();
        DotNet blnTypes = new DotNet();
        blnTypes.AvailableDatatype = "bool";
        lstTypes.Add(blnTypes);

        DotNet strTypes = new DotNet();
        strTypes.AvailableDatatype = "string";
        lstTypes.Add(strTypes);

        DotNet intTypes = new DotNet();
        intTypes.AvailableDatatype = "int";
        lstTypes.Add(intTypes);

        DotNet decTypes = new DotNet();
        decTypes.AvailableDatatype = "decimal";
        lstTypes.Add(decTypes);


        // IObservable
        obsTypes.Subscribe(x =>
        {
            Console.WriteLine(x);
        });

        // IObserver
        for (int i = 0; i <= lstTypes.Count - 1; i++)
        {
            obsTypes.OnNext(lstTypes[i].AvailableDatatype);
```

```
        }

        Console.ReadLine();
    }
}
```

10. When you run your application, you will see the same items output to the console window as earlier:

How it works...

In Rx, we can declare an event stream with the `Subject` keyword. So, we have a source of events that we can publish to using `OnNext`. To see those values in the console window, we subscribed to the event stream using `Subscribe`.

Rx allows you to have objects that are just publishers or just subscribers. This is because the `IObservable` and `IObserver` interfaces are in fact separate. Also, note that in Rx, the observables can be passed as parameters, returned as results, and stored in variables, which makes them first class:

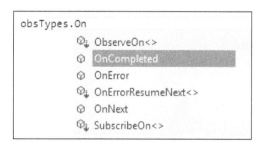

Rx also allows you to specify that the event stream is completed or that an error occurred. This really sets Rx apart from events in .NET. Also, it is important to note that including the `System.Reactive.Linq` namespace in your project allows developers to write queries over the `Subject` type because a `Subject` is an `IObservable` interface:

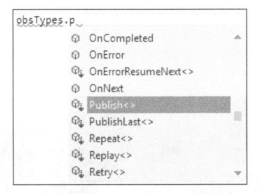

This is another feature that sets Rx apart from the events in .NET.

Using LINQ to perform queries

Rx allow developers to use the `IObservable` interface that represents synchronous data streams to write queries using LINQ. To recap, Rx can be thought of as consisting of three sections:

- ▶ **Observables**: The interface that brings together and represents all these data streams
- ▶ **Language-Integrated Query** (**LINQ**): The ability to use LINQ to query these multiple data streams
- ▶ **Schedulers**: Parametrizing concurrency using schedulers

In this recipe, we will be looking at the LINQ functionality of Rx in more detail.

Getting ready

As observables are just data streams, we can use LINQ to query them. In the following recipe, we will output text to the screen based on a LINQ query.

How to do it...

1. Start by adding a new Windows Forms project to your solution:

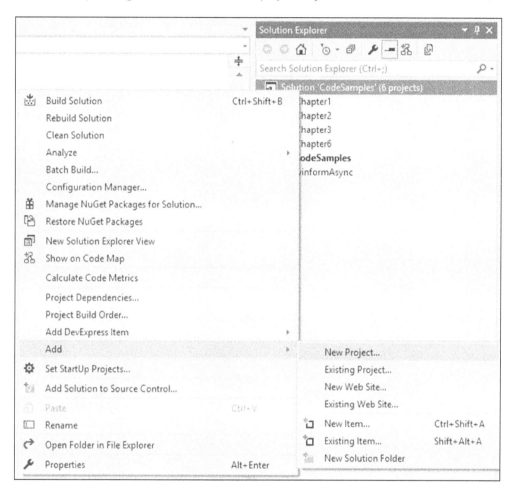

2. Call the project `winformRx` and click on the **OK** button:

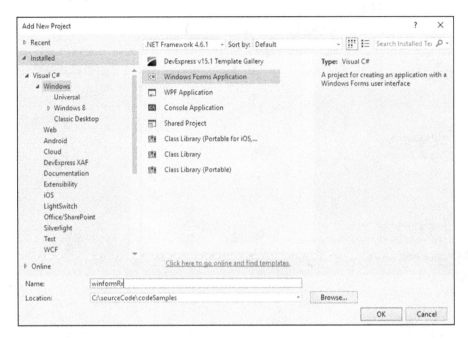

3. In **Toolbox**, search for the **TextBox** control and add it to your form:

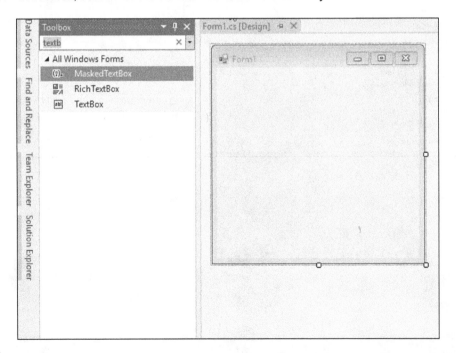

4. Finally, add a label control to your form:

5. Right-click on your `winformRx` project and select **Manage NuGet Packages...** from the context menu:

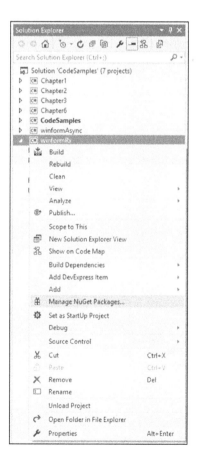

6. In the search text box, enter `System.Reactive` to search for the NuGet package and click on the **Install** button:

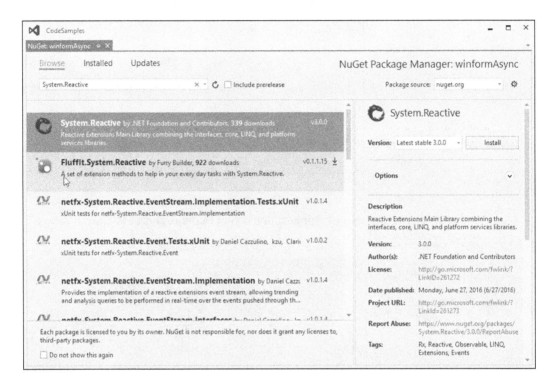

7. Visual Studio will ask you to review the changes it's about to make to your project. Click on the **OK** button:

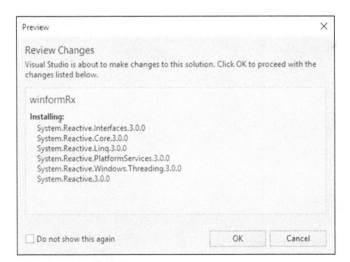

8. Before the installation starts, you might need to accept the license agreement by clicking on the **I Accept** button:

9. After the installation completes, you should see the newly added references to your winformRx project if you expand the **References** for the project:

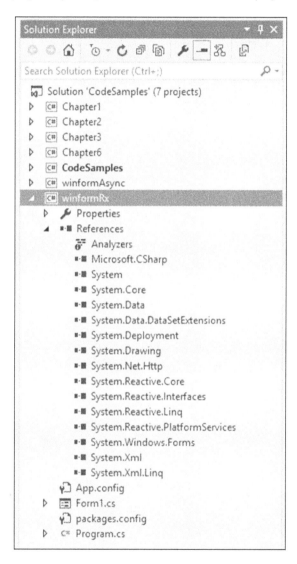

10. Finally, right-click on the project and set `winformRx` as your startup project by clicking on **Set as StartUp Project** from the context menu:

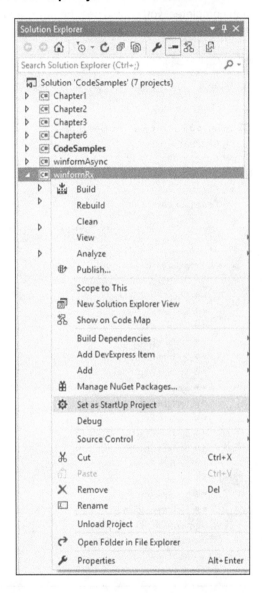

11. Create the form load event handler for the form by double-clicking anywhere on the Windows Form. To this form, add the `Observable` keyword. You will notice that the keyword is immediately underlined. This is because you are missing the reference to the LINQ assembly of `System.Reactive`:

```
1 reference
private void Form1_Load(object sender, EventArgs e)
{
    Observable
    The name 'Observable' does not exist in the current context

    Show potential fixes (Ctrl+.)

}
```

12. To add this, press *Ctrl + .* (period) to bring up the possible suggestions to fix the issue. Select to add the `using System.Reactive.Linq` namespace to your project:

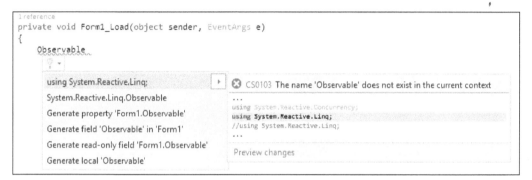

13. Continue adding the following code to your form load event. Basically, you are using LINQ and telling the compiler that you want to select the text from the event pattern that matches the text changed event of the text box on the form called `textBox1`. After you have done that, add a subscription to the variable and tell it to output whatever it finds in the text to the label on the form called `label1`:

```
private void Form1_Load(object sender, EventArgs e)
{
    var searchTerm =
    Observable.FromEventPattern<EventArgs>(textBox1,
    "TextChanged")
    .Select(x => ((TextBox)x.Sender).Text);

    searchTerm.Subscribe(trm => label1.Text = trm);
}
```

When we added the text box and label to our form, we left the control names as default. If, however, you changed the default names, you would need to specify those names instead of `textBox1` and `label1` for the controls on the form.

14. Click on the run button to run your application. The Windows Form will be displayed with the text box and label on it:

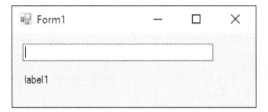

15. Notice that the text is output to the label on the form as you type:

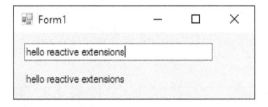

16. Let's jazz things up a bit by adding a `Where` condition to the LINQ statement. We will specify that the `text` string must only select the text when it ends with a period. This means that the text will only be displayed in the label after each full sentence. As you can see, we aren't doing anything special here. We are merely using standard LINQ to query our data stream and return the results to our `searchTerm` variable:

```
private void Form1_Load(object sender, EventArgs e)
{
    var searchTerm =
    Observable.FromEventPattern<EventArgs>(textBox1,
    "TextChanged")
    .Select(x => ((TextBox)x.Sender).Text)
    .Where(text => text.EndsWith("."));

    searchTerm.Subscribe(trm => label1.Text = trm);
}
```

17. Run your application and start typing in a line of text. You will see that nothing is output to the label control as you type, as was evident in the previous example before we added in our `Where` condition:

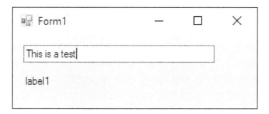

18. Add a period and start adding a second line of text:

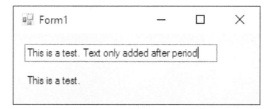

19. You will see that only after each period, the text entered is added to the label. Our `Where` condition is, therefore, working perfectly:

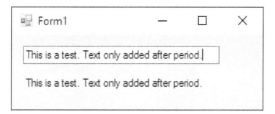

How it works...

The LINQ aspect of Rx allows developers to construct observables. Here are some examples:

- ▶ `Observable.Empty<>`: Returns an empty observable sequence
- ▶ `Observable.Return<>`: Returns an observable sequence containing a single element
- ▶ `Observable.Throw<>`: Returns an observable sequence terminating with an exception
- ▶ `Observable.Never<>`: Returns a non-terminating observable sequence infinite in duration

The use of LINQ in Rx allows the developer to manipulate and filter the data stream to return exactly what they need.

Using schedulers in Rx

Sometimes, we need to have an `IObservable` subscription run at a specific time. Imagine having to synchronize events across servers in geographically different areas and time zones. You might also need to read data from a queue while preserving the order in which the events occur. Another example would be to perform some kind of I/O task that could take some time to complete. Schedulers come in very handy in these situations.

Getting ready

Additionally, you can consider reading up more on using schedulers on MSDN. Have a look at `https://msdn.microsoft.com/en-us/library/hh242963(v=vs.103).aspx`.

How to do it...

1. If you haven't already done so, create a new Windows Form application and call it `winformRx`. Open the form designer and in **Toolbox**, search for the **TextBox** control and add it to your form:

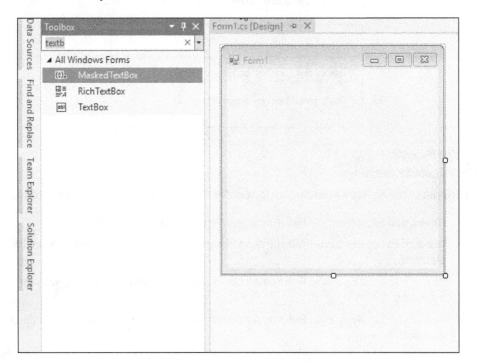

2. Next, add a label control to your form:

3. Double-click on your Windows Form designer to create the onload event handler. Inside this handler, add some code to read the text entered into the text box and only display that text 5 seconds after the user has stopped typing. This is achieved using the `Throttle` keyword. Add a subscription to the `searchTerm` variable, writing the result of the text input to the label control's text property:

```
private void Form1_Load(object sender, EventArgs e)
{
    var searchTerm =
    Observable.FromEventPattern<EventArgs>(textBox1,
    "TextChanged")
    .Select(x => ((TextBox)x.Sender).Text)
    .Throttle(TimeSpan.FromMilliseconds(5000));

    searchTerm.Subscribe(trm => label1.Text = trm);
}
```

Note that you might need to add `System.Reactive.Linq` in your `using` statements.

4. Run your application and start typing in some text into the text box. Immediately, we will receive an exception. It is a cross-thread violation. This occurs when there is an attempt to update the UI from a background thread. The `Observable` interface is running a timer from `System.Threading`, which isn't on the same thread as the UI. Luckily, there is an easy way to overcome this. Well, it turns out that the UI-threading capabilities lie in a different assembly, which we found easiest to get via the **Package Manager Console**:

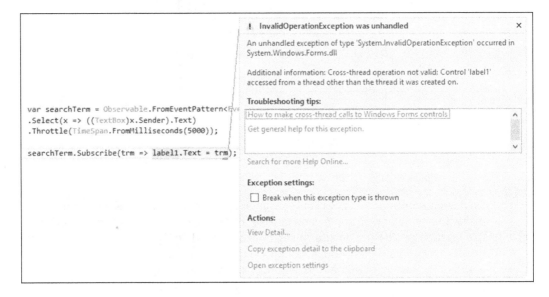

```
var searchTerm = Observable.FromEventPattern<Eve
.Select(x => ((TextBox)x.Sender).Text)
.Throttle(TimeSpan.FromMilliseconds(5000));

searchTerm.Subscribe(trm => label1.Text = trm);
```

> **! InvalidOperationException was unhandled**   ×
>
> An unhandled exception of type 'System.InvalidOperationException' occurred in System.Windows.Forms.dll
>
> Additional information: Cross-thread operation not valid: Control 'label1' accessed from a thread other than the thread it was created on.
>
> **Troubleshooting tips:**
>
> How to make cross-thread calls to Windows Forms controls
>
> Get general help for this exception.
>
> Search for more Help Online...
>
> **Exception settings:**
>
> ☐ Break when this exception type is thrown
>
> **Actions:**
>
> View Detail...
>
> Copy exception detail to the clipboard
>
> Open exception settings

5. Click on **View | Other Windows | Package Manager Console** to access the **Package Manager Console**:

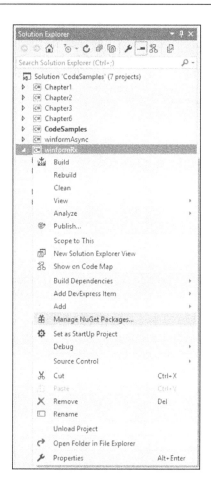

6. Enter the following command: PM> Install-Package System.Reactive.
Windows.Forms

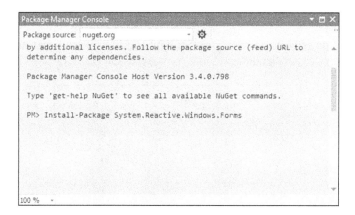

Please note that you need to ensure that the **Default project** selection is set to `winformRx` in the **Package Manager Console**. If you don't see this option, resize the **Package Manager Console** screen width until the option is displayed. This way you can be certain that the package is added to the correct project.

7. After the installation completes, modify your code in the onload event handler and change `searchTerm.Subscribe(trm => label1.Text = trm);`, which does the subscription, to look like this:

```
searchTerm.ObserveOn(new ControlScheduler(this)).Subscribe(trm =>
label1.Text = trm);
```

You will notice that we are using the `ObserveOn` method here. What this basically tells the compiler is that the `this` keyword in `new ControlScheduler(this)` is actually a reference to our Windows Form. Therefore, `ControlScheduler` will use the Windows Forms timers to create the interval to update our UI. The message happens on the correct thread, and we no longer have our cross-thread violation.

8. If you have not added the `System.Reactive.Concurrency` namespace to your project, Visual Studio will underline the `ControlScheduler` line of code with a squiggly line. Pressing *Ctrl + .* (the Control key and dot) will allow you to add the missing namespace:

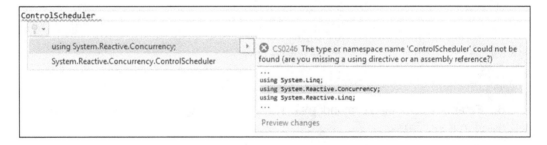

9. This means that `System.Reactive.Concurrency` contains a scheduler that can talk to Windows Forms controls so that it can do the scheduling. Run your application again and start typing some text into your text box:

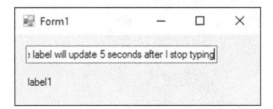

10. Five seconds after we stop typing, the throttle condition is fulfilled, and the text is output to our label:

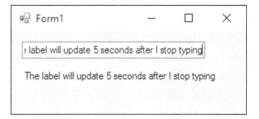

How it works...

What we need to keep in mind here from the code we created is that there are `ObserveOn` and `Subscribe`. You should not confuse the two. In most cases, when dealing with schedulers, you will use `ObserveOn`. The `ObserveOn` method allows you to parametrize where the `OnNext`, `OnCompleted`, and `OnError` messages run. With `Subscribe`, we parameterize where the actual subscribe and unsubscribe code runs.

We also need to remember that Rx use the threading timers (`System.Threading.Timer`) as a default, which is why we encountered the cross-thread violation earlier. As you saw though, we used schedulers to parameterize what timer to use. The way schedulers do this is by exposing three components. These are:

▸ The scheduler's ability to perform some action

▸ The order in which the action or work to be performed is executed

▸ A clock that allows the scheduler to have a notion of time

The use of a clock is important because it allows the developer to use timers on remote machines, for example (where there might be a time difference between you and them), to tell them to perform an action at a particular time.

Debugging lambda expressions

Visual Studio 2015 has added the ability for developers to debug lambda expressions. This is a fantastic addition to the features of our favorite IDE. It allows us to check the results of a lambda expression on the fly and modify the expression to test different scenarios.

Getting ready

We will create a very basic lambda expression and change it in the **Watch** window to produce a different value.

How to do it...

1. Add a class called `CSharpSix`. Add a property to this class called `FavoriteFeature`:

```
public class CSharpSix
{
    public string FavoriteFeature { get; set; }
}
```

2. Next, create a `List<CSharpSix>` object and add a few of your favorite C# 6 features to this list:

```
List<CSharpSix> FavCSharpFeatures = new List<CSharpSix>();
CSharpSix feature1 = new CSharpSix();
feature1.FavoriteFeature = "String Interpolation";
FavCSharpFeatures.Add(feature1);

CSharpSix feature2 = new CSharpSix();
feature2.FavoriteFeature = "Exception Filters";
FavCSharpFeatures.Add(feature2);

CSharpSix feature3 = new CSharpSix();
feature3.FavoriteFeature = "Nameof Expressions";
FavCSharpFeatures.Add(feature3);
```

3. Then, create an expression to return only the features starting with the `"Ex"` string. Here, we would obviously expect to see exception filters as a result:

```
var filteredFeature = FavCSharpFeatures.Where(feature =>
feature.FavoriteFeature.StartsWith("Ex"));
```

4. Place a breakpoint on the expression and run your application. When the code stops at the breakpoint, you can copy the lambda expression:

```
45
46   List<CSharpSix> FavCSharpFeatures = new List<CSharpSix>();
47   CSharpSix feature1 = new CSharpSix();
48   feature1.FavoriteFeature = "String Interpolation";
49   FavCSharpFeatures.Add(feature1);
50
51   CSharpSix feature2 = new CSharpSix();
52   feature2.FavoriteFeature = "Exception Filters";
53   FavCSharpFeatures.Add(feature2);
54
55   CSharpSix feature3 = new CSharpSix();
56   feature3.FavoriteFeature = "Nameof Expressions";
57   FavCSharpFeatures.Add(feature3);
58
59   var filteredFeature = FavCSharpFeatures.Where(feature =>   < 1ms elapsed
60   feature.FavoriteFeature.StartsWith("Ex"));
61
```

5. Paste the lambda expression into your **Watch** windows and change the string in the `StartsWith` method. You will see that the result has changed to the `"Nameof Expressions"` string:

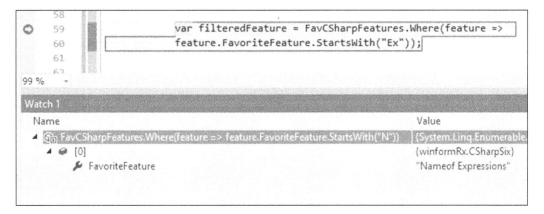

How it works...

Being able to debug lambda expressions allows us to change and debug a lambda expression easily. This is something that was not possible in previous versions of Visual Studio. It is obviously of great importance to know this tip when working with these expressions.

Another point to note is that you can do the same thing from the **Immediate** window in Visual Studio 2015, as well as pinned variables from the lambda expression.

5

Create Microservices on Azure Service Fabric

This chapter deals with the exciting world of microservices and **Azure Service Fabric**. In this chapter, we will cover the following recipes:

- Downloading and installing Service Fabric
- Creating a Service Fabric application with a stateless actor service
- Using Service Fabric Explorer

Introduction

Traditionally, developers wrote applications in a monolithic manner. This means one single executable that is broken up into components via classes and so on. Monolithic applications require a great deal of testing, and deployment is tedious due to the bulkiness of the monolithic application. Even though you might have multiple developer teams, they all need to have a solid understanding of the application as a whole.

Microservices is a technology that aims to address the issues surrounding monolithic applications and the traditional way of developing applications. With microservices, you can break the application into smaller bits (services) that can function on their own without being dependent on any of the other services. These smaller services can be stateless or stateful and are also smaller in scale in terms of functionality, making them easier to develop, test, and deploy. You can also version each microservice independently from the others. If one microservice is receiving more load than the others, you can scale only that service up to meet the demands placed on it. With monolithic applications, you would have to try and scale the whole application up in order to meet the demands for a single component within the application.

Take, for example, the workings of a popular online web store. It could consist of a shopping cart, shopper profile, order management, backend login, inventory management, billing, returns, and much more. Traditionally, a single web application is created to provide all these services. With microservices, you can isolate each service as a standalone, self-contained bit of functionality and code base. You can also dedicate a team of developers to work on a single portion of the web store. If this team is responsible for the inventory-management microservice, they would handle every aspect of it. This, for example, means everything from writing code and enhancing functionality, to testing and deployment.

Another excellent side effect of microservices is that it allows you to easily isolate any faults you might come across. Finally, you can also create microservices in any technology you want (C#, Java, VB.NET), as they are language independent.

Azure Service Fabric allows you to scale your microservices easily and increases application availability because it implements failover. When microservices are used with Fabric, microservices become a very powerful technology. Think of Azure Service Fabric as a **Platform as a Service (PaaS)** solution, on top of which your microservices sit. We call the collection that the microservices live on a Service Fabric cluster. Each microservice lives on a virtual machine, which is referred to as a node in the Service Fabric cluster. This Service Fabric cluster can live in the cloud or on a local machine. If a node becomes unavailable for any reason, the Service Fabric cluster will automatically redistribute the microservices to the other nodes so that the application remains available.

Finally, here is a word on the differences between stateful and stateless microservices. You are able to create a microservice as stateless or stateful. When a microservice relies on an external data store to persist data, it is stateless in nature. This simply means that the microservice does not maintain its state internally. A stateful microservice, on the other hand, maintains its own state by storing it locally on the server it resides on.

Downloading and installing Service Fabric

You will have to install and set up a local Service Fabric cluster on your PC before you can create and test Service Fabric applications.

Getting ready

We will download and install the **software development kit (SDK)** from the Azure site. This will allow us to create a local Service Fabric cluster on your local development machine.

How to do it...

1. From the Microsoft Azure site, download the SDK and access other resources, such as documentation, via the Service Fabric learning path, from `https://azure.microsoft.com/en-us/documentation/learning-paths/service-fabric/`:

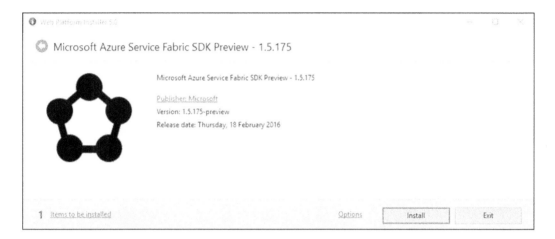

2. You will need to accept the license terms before the installation begins:

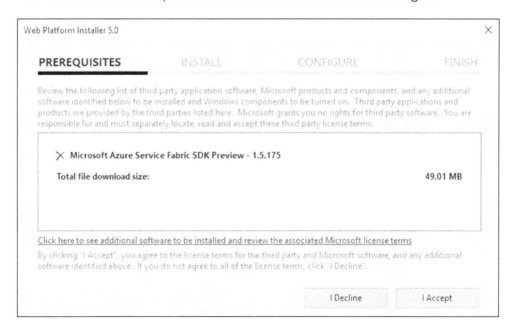

3. The web platform installer then starts downloading the Microsoft Azure Service Fabric runtime. Allow this process to complete:

4. After the download has completed, the install process will begin:

5. When the installation has completed, the following products would have been installed, which is also evident in the following screenshot:

- ❑ Microsoft Azure Service Fabric Runtime
- ❑ Microsoft Azure Service Fabric Core SDK Preview
- ❑ Microsoft Azure Service Fabric Visual Studio 2015 Tools Preview
- ❑ Microsoft Azure Service Fabric SDK Preview

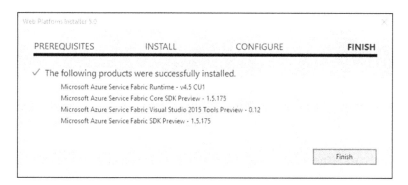

6. The next task is to open PowerShell as the administrator. In the Windows 10 Start menu, type the word `PowerShell`, and the search will immediately return the desktop application as a result. Right-click on the desktop application and select **Run as administrator** from the context menu:

7. Once Windows PowerShell has opened up, run the `Set-ExecutionPolicy` `-ExecutionPolicy Unrestricted -Force -Scope CurrentUser` command. The reason for this is that Service Fabric uses PowerShell scripts for the creation of the local development cluster. It is also used for the deployment of Visual Studio developed apps. Running this command prevents Windows from blocking those scripts:

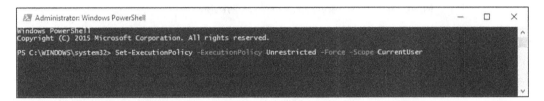

8. Next, create the local Service Fabric cluster. Enter the `& "$ENV:ProgramFiles\` `Microsoft SDKs\Service Fabric\ClusterSetup\DevClusterSetup.ps1"` command.

   This will create the local cluster needed to host Service Fabric applications:

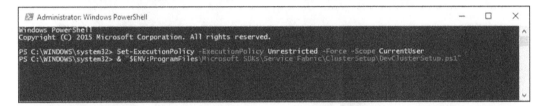

9. After the cluster is created, PowerShell will start the service:

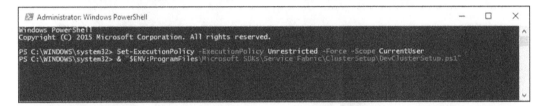

10. The process might take several minutes. Be sure to let it complete:

11. Once the naming service is ready, you can close PowerShell:

12. To view the created cluster, you can navigate to `http://localhost:19080/`
    `Explorer` on your local machine.

    This will give you a snapshot of the cluster's health and state. It will also show any
    applications running in the cluster:

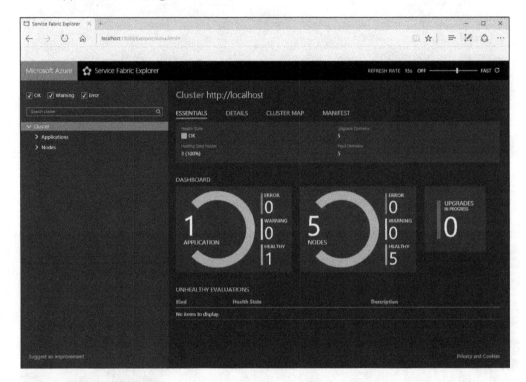

How it works...

As you can see, the Service Fabric cluster is essential for creating and running applications
created in Visual Studio. This will allow us to test applications directly on your local machine
before publishing them to the cloud.

Creating a Service Fabric application with a stateless actor service

As part of the introduction to this chapter, we looked at the difference between stateful and
stateless microservices. The Service Fabric application templates available are then further
divided into **Reliable Services** (stateful/stateless) and **Reliable Actors** (stateful/stateless).
When to use which one is something that will depend on the specific business requirement
of your application.

To put it simply though, if you wanted to create a service that should be exposed to many users of your application at any one time, a Reliable Service would probably be a good fit. Think of a service exposing the latest exchange rates that can be consumed by many users or applications at once.

Again, looking back to the introduction of this chapter, we used the example of an online web store with a shopping cart. A Reliable Actor could be a good fit for every customer buying items, so you could have a shopping cart actor. The Reliable Actor as part of the Service Fabric framework is based on the Virtual Actor pattern. Have a look at the article on the Virtual Actor pattern at `http://research.microsoft.com/en-us/projects/orleans/`.

To show you how easy it is to create a microservice using a stateless actor service as an example, we will use Visual Studio to publish a service to the Service Fabric cluster and call that service from a console (client) application.

Getting ready

To complete this recipe, you must ensure that you have installed your local Service Fabric cluster on your local machine.

How to do it...

1. In Visual Studio, create a new project by going to **File** | **New** | **Project**:

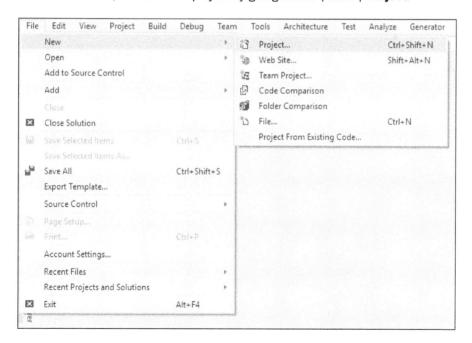

2. From the **Visual C#** node, expand the nodes until you see the **Cloud** node. When you click on it, you will see that Visual Studio now lists a new **Service Fabric Application** template. Select the **Service Fabric Application** template, call it sfApp, and click on **OK**:

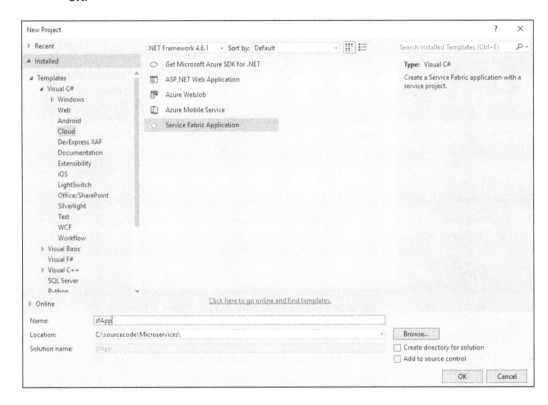

3. Next, select **Stateless Reliable Actor** from the **Create a Service** window that pops up. We just called ours `UtilitiesActor`:

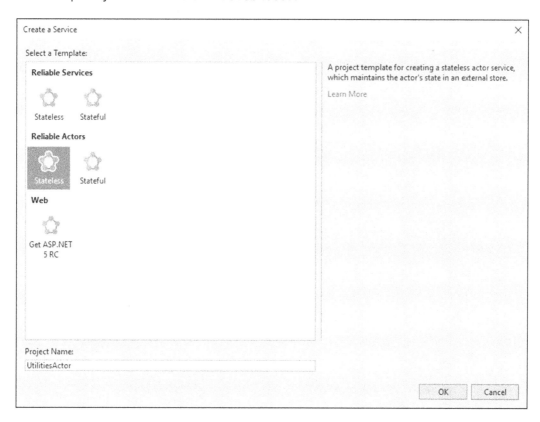

4. Once your solution is created, you will notice that it consists of three projects. These are:

    ❑ sfApp

    ❑ UtilitiesActor

    ❑ UtilitiesActor.Interfaces

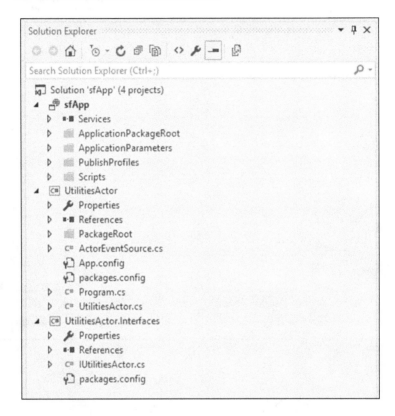

5. We will start off by modifying the IUtilitiesActor interface. This interface will simply require that UtilitiesActor implements a method called ValidateEmailAsync that takes an e-mail address as a parameter and returns a Boolean value indicating whether it is a valid email address or not:

```
namespace UtilitiesActor.Interfaces
{
    public interface IUtilitiesActor : IActor
    {
        Task<bool> ValidateEmailAsync(string
        emailToValidate);
    }
}
```

6. Next, open up your `UtilitiesActor` project and view the class. It will be underlined with a red squiggly line because it does not implement the interface member `ValidateEmailAsync()`:

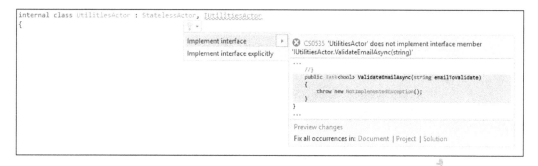

7. Using *Ctrl + .* (period), implement the interface. Remove all the other unnecessary default code (if any):

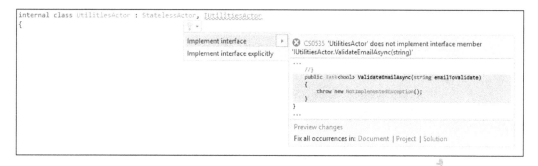

8. The implemented interface code inserted for you should look like this. At the moment, it only contains `NotImplementedException`. It is here that we will implement the code to validate the e-mail address:

```
namespace UtilitiesActor
{
    internal class UtilitiesActor : StatelessActor,
    IUtilitiesActor
    {
        public Task<bool> ValidateEmailAsync(string
        emailToValidate)
        {
            throw new NotImplementedException();
        }
    }
}
```

9. We will use a regular expression to validate the e-mail address passed to this method via the parameter. Regular expressions are very powerful. I have, however, in all my years of programming, never written my own expression. These are readily available on the Internet, and you can create a utilities class (or extension methods class) for your own projects to reuse. You can make use of regular expressions and other code that is often used.

   Finally, you will notice the `ActorEventSource` code. This is simply just to create **Event Tracing for Windows** (**ETW**) events that will help you see what is happening in your application from the diagnostic events window in Visual Studio. To open the diagnostic events window, go to **View, Other Windows** and click on **Diagnostic Events Viewer**:

```
internal class UtilitiesActor : StatelessActor,
IUtilitiesActor
{
    public async Task<bool> ValidateEmailAsync(string
    emailToValidate)
    {
        ActorEventSource.Current.ActorMessage(this, "Email
        Validation");

        return await
        Task.FromResult(Regex.IsMatch(emailToValidate,
        @"\A(?:[a-z0-9!#$%&'*+/=?^_`{|}~-]+(?:\.[a-z0-
        9!#$%&'*+/=?^_`{|}~-]+)*@(?:[a-z0-9](?:[a-z0-9-
        ]*[a-z0-9])?\.)+[a-z0-9](?:[a-z0-9-]*[a-z0-
        9])?)\Z", RegexOptions.IgnoreCase));
    }
}
```

10. Be sure to add a reference to the `System.Text.RegularExpressions` namespace. Without it, you will not be able to use the regular expressions. If you added the regular expression in your code without adding the reference, Visual Studio will display a red squiggly line under the `Regex` method:

```
return await Task.FromResult(Regex.IsMatch(emailToValidate, @"\A(?:[a-z0-9!#$%&'*
+/=?^_`{|}~-]+(?:\.[a    }!                                          -]*[a-
z0-9])?\.)+[a-z0-9](?:[a-z0        The name 'Regex' does not exist in the current context    ));

                                 Show potential fixes (Ctrl+.)
```

11. Using *Ctrl + .* (period), add the `using` statement to your project. This will bring the regular expression namespace into scope:

12. Now that we have created the interface and also added the implementation of that interface, it is time to add a client application that we will use for testing. Right-click on your solution and add a new project:

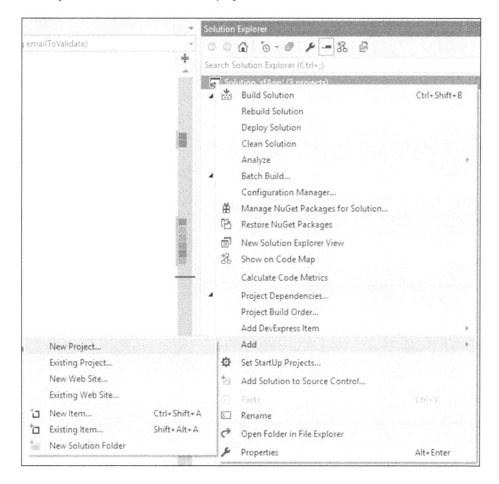

13. The easiest way is to add a simple console application. Call your client application `sfApp.Client` and click on the **OK** button:

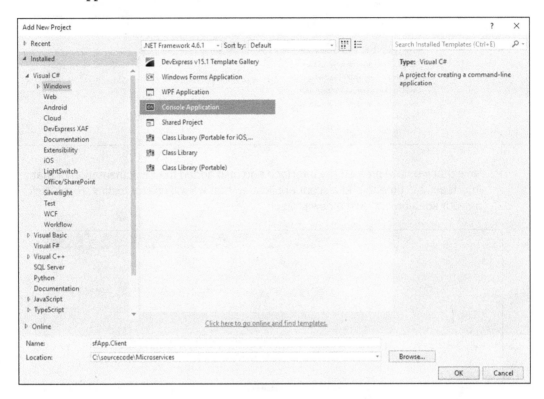

14. After you have added your console application to your solution, your solution should look like this:

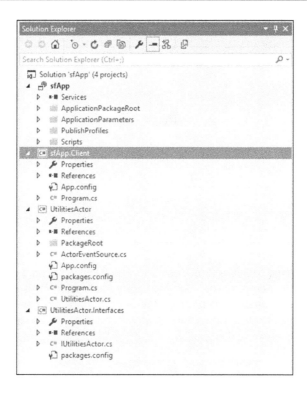

15. You will now need to add references to your client application. Right-click the **References** node in your `sfApp.Client` project and select **Add Reference** from the context menu:

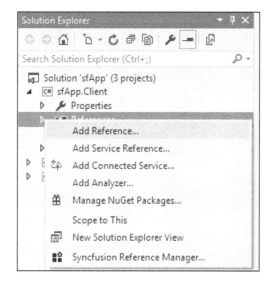

16. Start off by adding a reference to the `UtilitiesActor.Interfaces` project:

17. You will also need to add references to several Service Fabric **dynamic link libraries** (**DLLs**). When you created your Service Fabric application, it should have added a folder called `packages` to your project folder structure. Browse to this folder and add your Service Fabric DLLs from there. After you have added the required DLLs, your project should look like this:

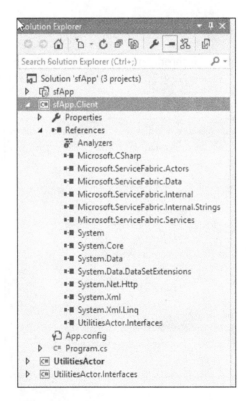

18. In the `Program.cs` file of your console application, you need to add the following code to the `Main` method:

```
namespace sfApp.Client
{
    class Program
    {
        static void Main(string[] args)
        {
            var actProxy =
            ActorProxy.Create<IUtilitiesActor>
            (ActorId.NewId(), "fabric:/sfApp");

            WriteLine("Utilities Actor {0} - Valid Email?:
            {1}", actProxy.GetActorId(),
            actProxy.ValidateEmailAsync
            ("validemail@gmail.com").Result);
            WriteLine("Utilities Actor {0} - Valid Email?:
            {1}", actProxy.GetActorId(),
            actProxy.ValidateEmailAsync
            ("invalid@email@gmail.com").Result);
            ReadLine();
        }
    }
}
```

All we are doing is creating a proxy for our actor and writing the output of the e-mail validation to the console window. Your client application is now ready.

19. Before we can run the client application, however, we need to publish our service first. In **Solution Explorer**, right-click on the `sfApp` service and click on **Publish** from the context menu:

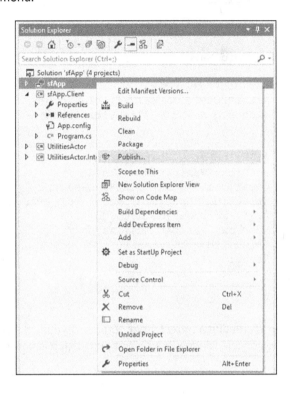

20. The **Publish Service Fabric Application** window will now be displayed. Click on the **Select...** button next to the **Connection endpoint** text box:

21. Select **Local Cluster** as your **Connection endpoint** and click on **OK**:

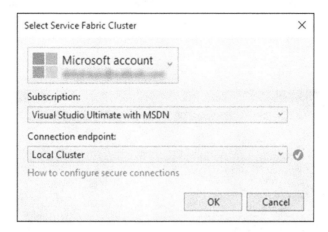

22. Change **Target profile** and **Application Parameters File** to `Local.xml`. When you are done, click on the **Publish** button:

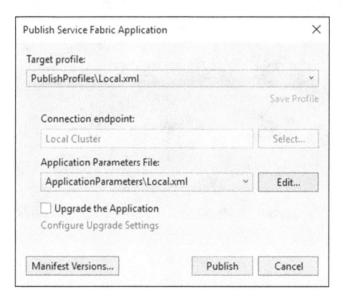

23. If you navigate to `http://localhost:19080/Explorer`, you will notice that the service you created has been published to your local Service Fabric cluster:

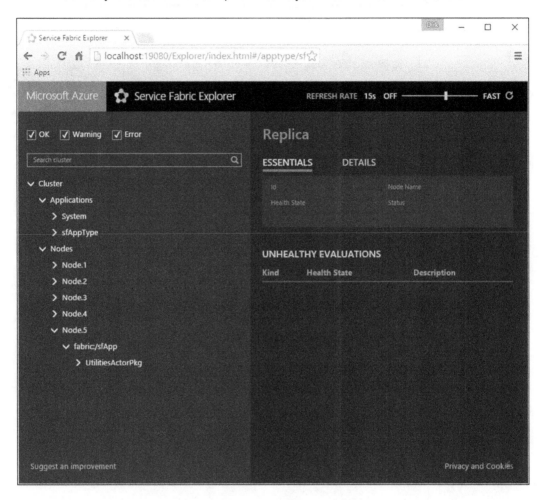

24. You are now ready to run your client application. Right-click on the `sfApp.Client` project, and select **Debug** and **Start new instance** from the context menu:

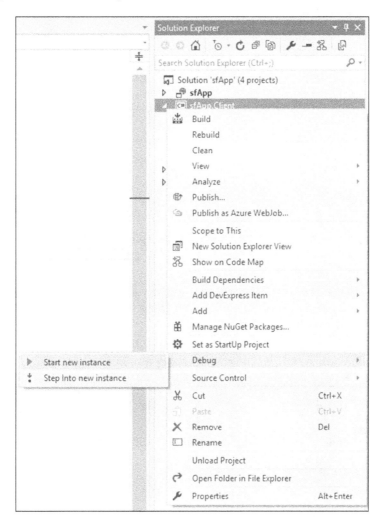

25. The console application calls the validate method to check the e-mail addresses, and displays the results to the console window. The results are as expected:

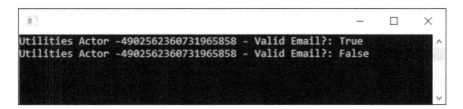

26. We can, however, be more specific when creating the actor ID. We can give it a specific name. Modify your proxy code and create a new `ActorId` method, and give it any string value:

```
var actProxy = ActorProxy.Create<IUtilitiesActor>(new
ActorId("Utilities"), "fabric:/sfApp");

WriteLine("Utilities Actor {0} - Valid Email?: {1}",
actProxy.GetActorId(),
actProxy.ValidateEmailAsync("validemail@gmail.com").Result)
;
WriteLine("Utilities Actor {0} - Valid Email?: {1}",
actProxy.GetActorId(),
actProxy.ValidateEmailAsync("invalid@email@gmail.com").Resu
lt);
ReadLine();
```

 The `ActorId` method can take a parameter of type `Guid`, `long` or `string`.

27. When you debug your client application again, you will notice that `Utilities Actor` now has a logical name (the same name you passed as a string value when creating a new `ActorId` method):

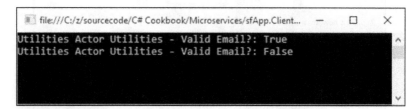

How it works...

Creating your Service Fabric application and publishing it locally is a perfect solution for testing your application before publishing it to the cloud. Creating small independent microservices allows developers many benefits related to testing, debugging, and deploying efficient and robust code that your applications can leverage to ensure maximum availability.

Using Service Fabric Explorer

There is another tool that you can use to visualize the Service Fabric cluster. It is a standalone tool that you can find by navigating to the local installation path at `%Program Files%\Microsoft SDKs\Service Fabric\Tools\ServiceFabricExplorer` and clicking on `ServiceFabricExplorer.exe`. When you run the application, it will automatically connect to your local Service Fabric cluster. It can display rich information regarding the applications on the cluster, the cluster nodes, the heath status of the applications and nodes, and any load on the applications in the cluster.

Getting ready

You must have already completed the installation of Service Fabric on your local machine for the Service Fabric Explorer to work. If you have not done so yet, follow the *Downloading and installing Service Fabric* recipe in this chapter.

How to do it...

1. When you start the Service Fabric Explorer, the following window will appear:

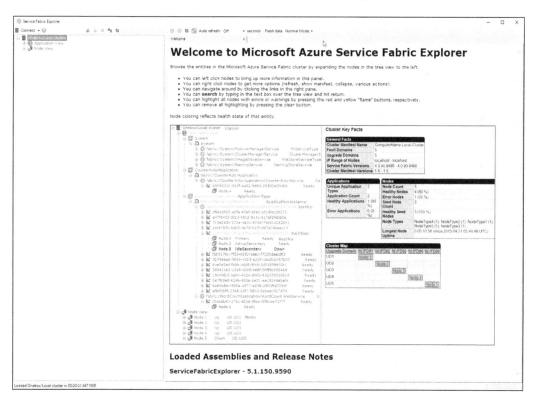

2. Note that the tree view to the left displays **Application View** and **Node View**:

3. The pane on the right-hand side will display information regarding the local cluster. This makes it easy for you to see the overall health of the local Service cluster:

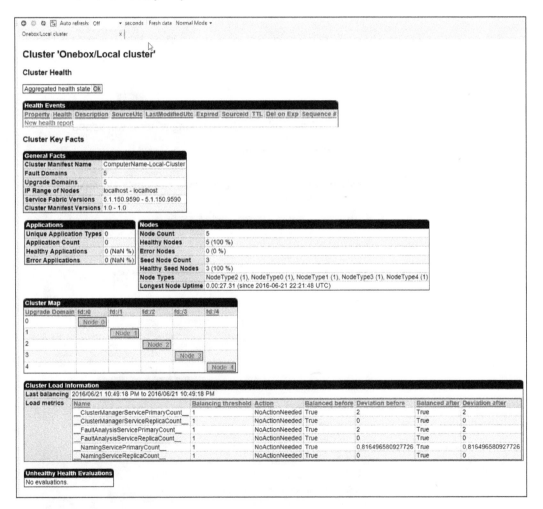

4. When you expand **Application View**, you will notice that our `sfApp` service has been published. Expanding it even further, you will see that the `sfApp` service has been published on **Node.2**. Expand **Node View** and **Node.2** to see the service active on that node:

5. To illustrate the scalability of microservices, right-click on **Node.2**, and from the context menu, stop the node. Then, click on the Refresh button at the top of the window to refresh the nodes and applications.

6. If you now had to go ahead and expand **Application View**, and looked at the service again, you will notice that the Service Fabric cluster noticed that **Node.2** was down. It then automatically pushed the service on to a new, healthy node (in this case, **Node.5**):

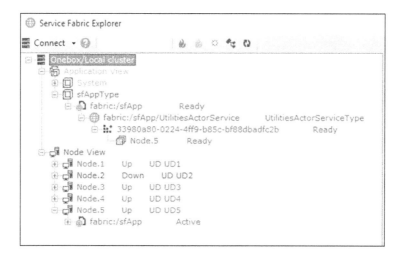

7. The local cluster nodes view in the right panel of the Service Fabric Explorer also reports that **Node.2** is down:

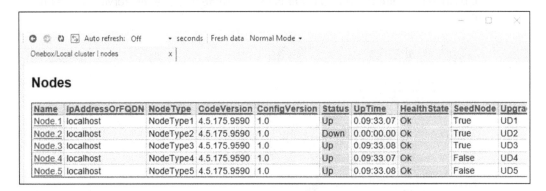

Name	IpAddressOrFQDN	NodeType	CodeVersion	ConfigVersion	Status	UpTime	HealthState	SeedNode	Upgra
Node.1	localhost	NodeType1	4.5.175.9590	1.0	Up	0.09:33.07	Ok	True	UD1
Node.2	localhost	NodeType2	4.5.175.9590	1.0	Down	0.00:00.00	Ok	True	UD2
Node.3	localhost	NodeType3	4.5.175.9590	1.0	Up	0.09:33.08	Ok	True	UD3
Node.4	localhost	NodeType4	4.5.175.9590	1.0	Up	0.09:33.07	Ok	False	UD4
Node.5	localhost	NodeType5	4.5.175.9590	1.0	Up	0.09:33.08	Ok	False	UD5

How it works...

The Service Fabric Explorer will allow you to see information on the selected node, and you will be able to drill down and see a rich amount of information regarding the Service Fabric cluster applications.

6
Making Apps Responsive with Asynchronous Programming

This chapter will introduce you to asynchronous programming. This chapter will cover the following recipes:

- ▸ Return types of asynchronous functions
- ▸ Handling tasks in asynchronous programming
- ▸ Exception handling in asynchronous programming

Introduction

Asynchronous programming is an exciting feature in C#. It allows you to continue program execution on the main thread while a long-running task runs in its own thread separately from the main thread. When this long-running task is complete, it will let the main thread know that it has completed (or failed). The benefit of asynchronous programming is that it improves the responsiveness of your application. The best way to learn and understand asynchronous programming is to experience it. The following recipes will illustrate some of the basics to you.

Return types of asynchronous functions

In asynchronous programming, the `async` methods can have three possible return types. These are:

- `void`
- `Task`
- `Task<TResult>`

We will have a look at each return type in the following recipe.

Getting ready

What could be the use of a `void` return type in asynchronous methods? Generally, `void` is used with event handlers. Just bear in mind that `void` returns nothing, so you can't wait for it. Therefore, if you call a `void` return type asynchronous method, your calling code should be able to continue executing code without having to wait for the asynchronous method to complete.

With asynchronous methods that have a return type of `Task`, you can utilize the `await` operator to pause the execution of the current thread until the called asynchronous method has completed. Keep in mind that an asynchronous method that returns a type of `Task` basically does not return an operand. Therefore, if it was written as a synchronous method, it would be a `void` return type method. This statement might be confusing, but it will become clear in the following recipes.

Finally, asynchronous methods that have a `return` statement have a return type of `TResult`. In other words, if the asynchronous method returns a Boolean, you would create an asynchronous method with a return type of `Task<bool>`.

Let's start with the `void` return type asynchronous method.

How to do it...

1. Create a new class library by right-clicking on your solution and selecting **Add** and then **New Project** from the context menu:

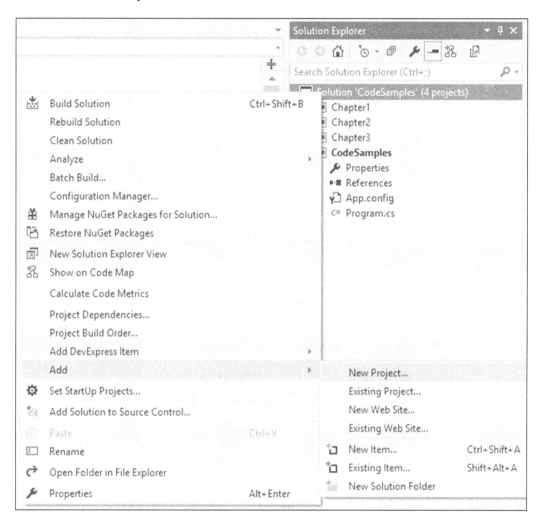

2. From the **Add New Project** dialog screen, select **Class Library** from the installed templates and call your class `Chapter6`:

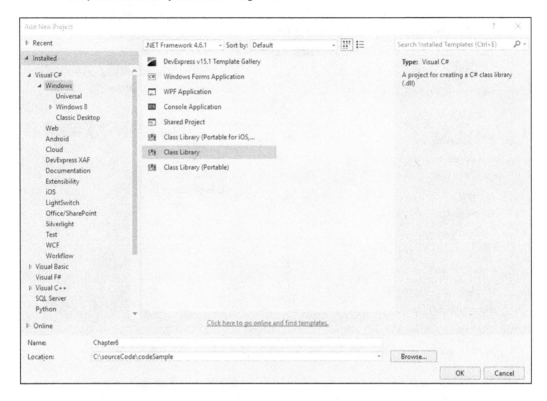

3. Your new class library will be added to your solution with a default name of `Class1.cs`, which we renamed to `Recipes.cs` in order to distinguish the code properly. You can, however, rename your class to whatever you like, if it makes more sense to you.

4. To rename your class, simply click on the class name in **Solution Explorer** and select **Rename** from the context menu:

5. Visual Studio will ask you to confirm the new names of all references to the code element **Class1** in the project. Just click on **Yes**:

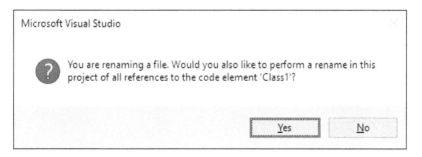

6. The next step is to add another new project. Right-click on the solution and select **Add** and then **New Project** from the context menu:

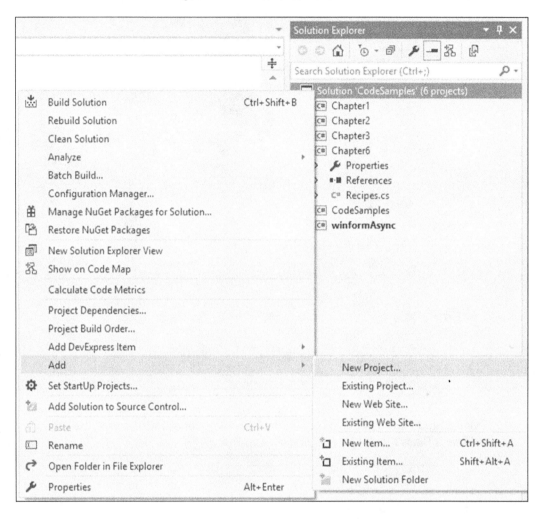

7. This time, you will be creating a new Windows Forms application for your solution. We need to do this so that we can create a button click event. We called our project `winformAsync`:

8. Your **Solution Explorer** will now look similar to the following screenshot, with the Winforms application added:

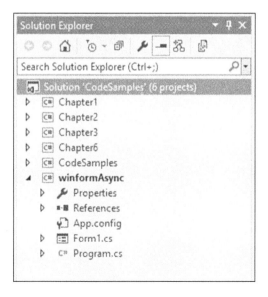

9. After you have added your Winforms application, add a reference to the Chapter6 class you created earlier. To do this, right-click on **References** under the **winformAsync** project and click on the **Add Reference** menu item from the context menu:

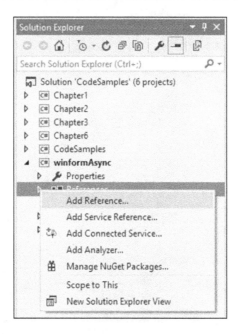

10. From the **Reference Manager** screen, select the Chapter6 class, which is found under the **Projects | Solution** node in the tree view to the left. Then, click on the **OK** button:

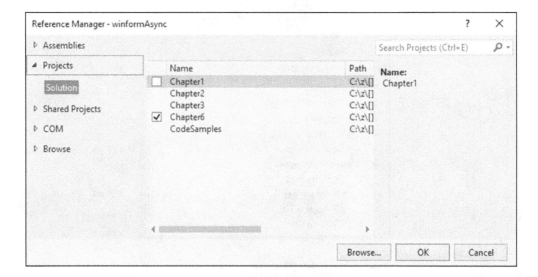

11. Another important step is to set the **winformAsync** project as the startup project in the solution. To do this, right-click the **winformAsync** project and select the **Set as StartUp Project** menu item from the context menu:

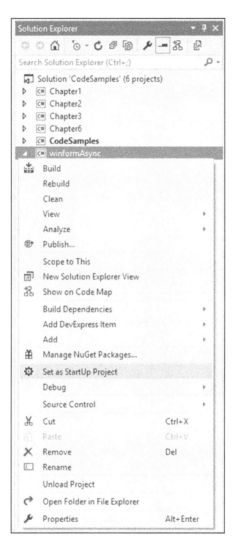

12. On the **winformAsync** form designer, open **Toolbox** and select the **Button** control, which is found under the **All Windows Forms** node:

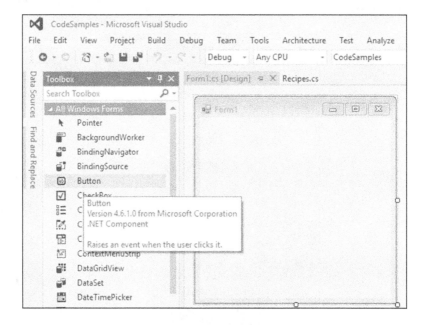

13. Drag the button control onto the **Form1** designer:

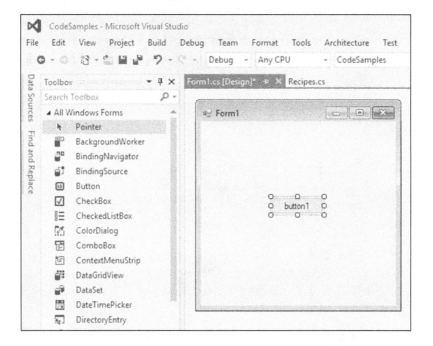

14. With the button control selected, double-click on the control to create the click event in the code behind. Visual Studio will insert the event code for you:

```
namespace winformAsync
{
    public partial class Form1 : Form
    {
        public Form1()
        {
            InitializeComponent();
        }

        private void button1_Click(object sender, EventArgs e)
        {

        }
    }
}
```

15. Change the `button1_Click` event and add the `async` keyword to the click event. This is an example of a `void` returning an asynchronous method:

```
private async void button1_Click(object sender, EventArgs e)
{

}
```

16. In the `Chapter6` class library, add a new class called `AsyncDemo`:

```
public class AsyncDemo
{
}
```

17. The next method to add to the `AsyncDemo` class is the asynchronous method that returns `TResult` (in this case, a Boolean). This method simply checks whether the current year is a leap year. It then returns a Boolean to the calling code:

```
async Task<bool> TaskOfTResultReturning_AsyncMethod()
{
    return await
    Task.FromResult<bool>
    (DateTime.IsLeapYear(DateTime.Now.Year));
}
```

18. The next method to add is the `void` returning method that returns a `Task` type so that it allows you to await the method. The method itself does not return any result, making it a `void` returning method. However, in order to use the `await` keyword, you return the `Task` type from this asynchronous method:

```
async Task TaskReturning_AsyncMethod()
{
    await Task.Delay(5000);
    Console.WriteLine("5 second delay");
}
```

19. Finally, add a method that will call the previous asynchronous methods and display the result of the leap year check. You will notice that we are using the `await` keyword with both method calls:

```
public async Task LongTask()
{
    bool isLeapYear = await
    TaskOfTResultReturning_AsyncMethod();
    Console.WriteLine($"{DateTime.Now.Year} {(isLeapYear ?
    " is " : " is not ")} a leap year");
    await TaskReturning_AsyncMethod();
}
```

20. In the button click, add the following code that calls the long-running task asynchronously:

```
private async void button1_Click(object sender, EventArgs e)
{
    Console.WriteLine("Button Clicked");
    Chapter6.AsyncDemo oAsync = new Chapter6.AsyncDemo();
    await oAsync.LongTask();
    Console.WriteLine("Button Click Ended");
}
```

21. Running your application will display the Windows Forms application:

22. Before clicking on the **button1** button, ensure that the **Output** window is visible:

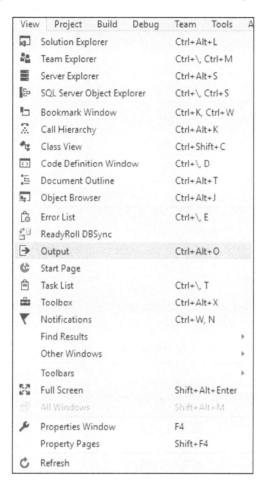

View	Project	Build	Debug	Team	Tools	A
Solution Explorer				Ctrl+Alt+L		
Team Explorer				Ctrl+\, Ctrl+M		
Server Explorer				Ctrl+Alt+S		
SQL Server Object Explorer				Ctrl+\, Ctrl+S		
Bookmark Window				Ctrl+K, Ctrl+W		
Call Hierarchy				Ctrl+Alt+K		
Class View				Ctrl+Shift+C		
Code Definition Window				Ctrl+\, D		
Document Outline				Ctrl+Alt+T		
Object Browser				Ctrl+Alt+J		
Error List				Ctrl+\, E		
ReadyRoll DBSync						
Output				Ctrl+Alt+O		
Start Page						
Task List				Ctrl+\, T		
Toolbox				Ctrl+Alt+X		
Notifications				Ctrl+W, N		
Find Results				▸		
Other Windows				▸		
Toolbars				▸		
Full Screen				Shift+Alt+Enter		
All Windows				Shift+Alt+M		
Properties Window				F4		
Property Pages				Shift+F4		
Refresh						

23. From the **View** menu, click on the **Output** menu item or type *Ctrl + Alt + O* to display the **Output** window. This will allow us to see the `Console.Writeline()` outputs as we have added them to the code in the `Chapter6` class and in the Windows application.

24. Clicking on the **button1** button will display the outputs to our **Output** window. Throughout this code execution, the form remains responsive:

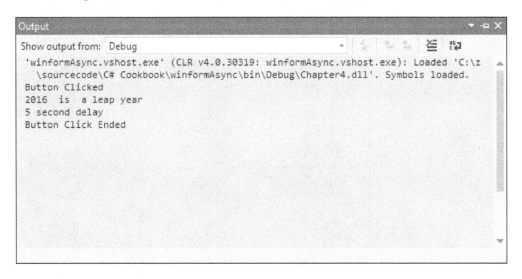

25. Finally, you can also use the `await` operator in separate calls. Modify the code in the `LongTask()` method as follows:

```
public async Task LongTask()
{
    Task<bool> blnIsLeapYear =
    TaskOfTResultReturning_AsyncMethod();

    for (int i = 0; i <= 10000; i++)
    {
        // Do other work that does not rely on
        blnIsLeapYear before awaiting
    }

    bool isLeapYear = await
    TaskOfTResultReturning_AsyncMethod();

    Console.WriteLine($"{DateTime.Now.Year} {(isLeapYear ?
    " is " : " is not ")} a leap year");
```

```
Task taskReturnMethhod = TaskReturning_AsyncMethod();

for (int i = 0; i <= 10000; i++)
{
    // Do other work that does not rely on
    taskReturnMethhod before awaiting
}

await taskReturnMethhod;
}
```

How it works...

In the preceding code, we have seen the `void` returning type asynchronous method that was used in the `button1_Click` event. We also created a `Task` returning method that returns nothing (that would be a `void` if used in synchronous programming), but returning `Task` type allows us to await the method. Finally, we created a `Task<TResult>` returning method that performs some task and returns the result to the calling code.

Handling tasks in asynchronous programming

Task-Based Asynchronous Pattern (**TAP**) is now the recommended method to create asynchronous code. It executes asynchronously on a thread from the thread pool and does not execute synchronously on the main thread of your application. It allows us to check the task's state by calling the `Status` property.

Getting ready

We will create a task to read a very large text file. This will be accomplished using an asynchronous `Task`.

How to do it...

1. Create a large text file (we called ours `taskFile.txt`) and place it in your `C:\temp` folder:

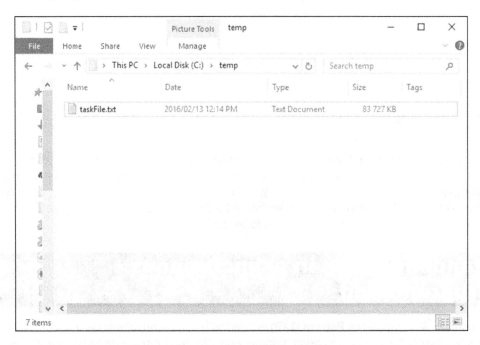

2. In the `AsyncDemo` class, create a method called `ReadBigFile()` that returns a `Task<TResult>` type, which will be used to return an integer of bytes read from our big text file:

```
public Task<int> ReadBigFile()
{

}
```

3. Add the following code to open and read the file bytes. You will see that we are using the `ReadAsync()` method that asynchronously reads a sequence of bytes from the stream and advances the position in that stream by the number of bytes read from that stream. You will also notice that we are using a buffer to read those bytes:

```
public Task<int> ReadBigFile()
{
    var bigFile = File.OpenRead(@"C:\temp\taskFile.txt");
    var bigFileBuffer = new byte[bigFile.Length];
    var readBytes = bigFile.ReadAsync(bigFileBuffer, 0,
    (int)bigFile.Length);
```

```
        return readBytes;
    }
```

Exceptions you can expect to handle from the `ReadAsync()` method are
`ArgumentNullException`, `ArgumentOutOfRangeException`,
`ArgumentException`, `NotSupportedException`,
`ObjectDisposedException` and `InvalidOperatorException`.

4. Finally, add the final section of code just after the `var readBytes = bigFile.`
`ReadAsync(bigFileBuffer, 0, (int)bigFile.Length);` line that uses a
lambda expression to specify the work that the task needs to perform. In this case,
it is to read the bytes in the file:

```
public Task<int> ReadBigFile()
{
    var bigFile = File.OpenRead(@"C:\temp\taskFile.txt");
    var bigFileBuffer = new byte[bigFile.Length];
    var readBytes = bigFile.ReadAsync(bigFileBuffer, 0, (int)
bigFile.Length);
    readBytes.ContinueWith(task =>
    {
        if (task.Status == TaskStatus.Running)
            Console.WriteLine("Running");
        else if (task.Status == TaskStatus.RanToCompletion)
            Console.WriteLine("RanToCompletion");
        else if (task.Status == TaskStatus.Faulted)
            Console.WriteLine("Faulted");

        bigFile.Dispose();
    });
    return readBytes;
}
```

5. If not done so in the previous recipe, add a button to your Windows Forms application's Forms Designer. On the **winformAsync** form designer, open **Toolbox** and select the **Button** control, which is found under the **All Windows Forms** node:

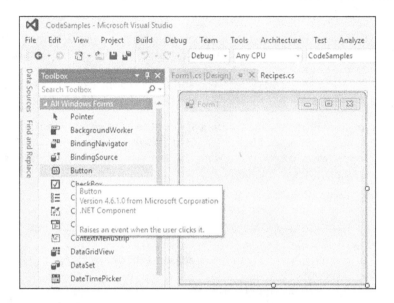

6. Drag the button control onto the **Form1** designer:

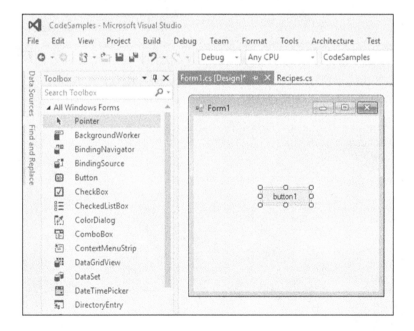

7. With the button control selected, double-click the control to create the click event in the code behind. Visual Studio will insert the event code for you:

```
namespace winformAsync
{
    public partial class Form1 : Form
    {
        public Form1()
        {
            InitializeComponent();
        }

        private void button1_Click(object sender, EventArgs e)
        {

        }
    }
}
```

8. Change the `button1_Click` event and add the `async` keyword to the click event. This is an example of a `void` returning an asynchronous method:

```
private async void button1_Click(object sender, EventArgs e)
{

}
```

9. Now, make sure that you add code to call the `AsyncDemo` class's `ReadBigFile()` method asynchronously. Remember to read the result from the method (which are the bytes read) into an integer variable:

```
private async void button1_Click(object sender, EventArgs e)
{
    Console.WriteLine("Start file read");
    Chapter6.AsyncDemo oAsync = new Chapter6.AsyncDemo();
    int readResult = await oAsync.ReadBigFile();
    Console.WriteLine("Bytes read = " + readResult);
}
```

10. Running your application will display the Windows Forms application:

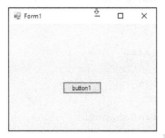

11. Before clicking on the **button1** button, ensure that the **Output** window is visible:

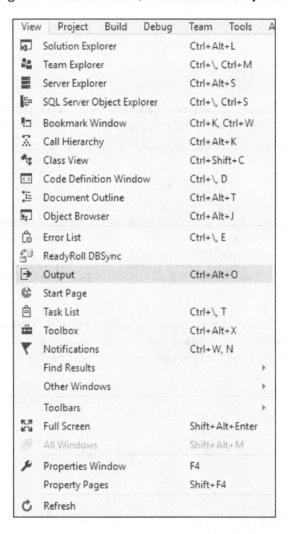

12. From the **View** menu, click on the **Output** menu item or type *Ctrl + Alt + O* to display
    the **Output** window. This will allow us to see the `Console.Writeline()` outputs
    as we have added them to the code in the `Chapter6` class and in the Windows
    application.

13. Clicking on the **button1** button will display the outputs in our **Output** window.
    Throughout this code execution, the form remains responsive:

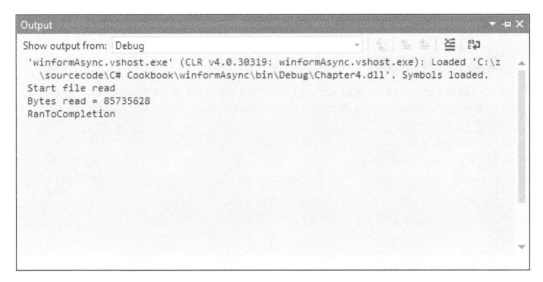

 Take note though that the information displayed in your **Output** window
will differ from the screenshot. This is because the file you used is
different from mine.

How it works...

The task is executed on a separate thread from the thread pool. This allows the application to
remain responsive while the large file is being processed. Tasks can be used in multiple ways
to improve your code. This recipe is but one example.

Exception handling in asynchronous programming

Exception handling in asynchronous programming has always been a challenge. This was
especially true in the catch blocks. As of C# 6, you are now allowed to write asynchronous
code inside the `catch` and `finally` block of your exception handlers.

Getting ready

The application will simulate the action of reading a logfile. Assume that a third-party system always makes a backup of the logfile before processing it in another application. While this processing is happening, the logfile is deleted and recreated. Our application, however, needs to read this logfile on a periodic basis. We, therefore, need to be prepared for the case where the file does not exist in the location we expect it in. Therefore, we will purposely omit the main logfile, so that we can force an error.

How to do it...

1. Create a text file and two folders to contain the logfiles. We will, however, only create a single logfile in the `BackupLog` folder. The `MainLog` folder will remain empty:

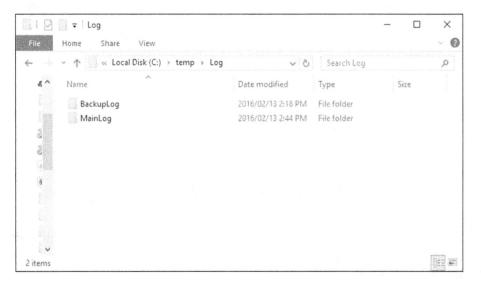

2. In our `AsyncDemo` class, write a method to read the main logfile in the `MainLog` folder:

```
private async Task<int> ReadMainLog()
{
    var bigFile =
    File.OpenRead(@"C:\temp\Log\MainLog\taskFile.txt");
    var bigFileBuffer = new byte[bigFile.Length];
    var readBytes = bigFile.ReadAsync(bigFileBuffer, 0,
    (int)bigFile.Length);
    await readBytes.ContinueWith(task =>
    {
        if (task.Status == TaskStatus.RanToCompletion)
```

```
            Console.WriteLine("Main Log RanToCompletion");
        else if (task.Status == TaskStatus.Faulted)
            Console.WriteLine("Main Log Faulted");

        bigFile.Dispose();
    });
    return await readBytes;
}
```

3. Create a second method to read the backup file in the `BackupLog` folder:

```
private async Task<int> ReadBackupLog()
{
    var bigFile =
    File.OpenRead(@"C:\temp\Log\BackupLog\taskFile.txt");
    var bigFileBuffer = new byte[bigFile.Length];
    var readBytes = bigFile.ReadAsync(bigFileBuffer, 0,
    (int)bigFile.Length);
    await readBytes.ContinueWith(task =>
    {
        if (task.Status == TaskStatus.RanToCompletion)
            Console.WriteLine("Backup Log
            RanToCompletion");
        else if (task.Status == TaskStatus.Faulted)
            Console.WriteLine("Backup Log Faulted");

        bigFile.Dispose();
    });
    return await readBytes;
}
```

 In actual fact, we would probably only create a single method to read the logfiles, passing only the path as a parameter. In a production application, creating a class and overriding a method to read the different logfile locations would be a better approach. For the purposes of this recipe, however, we specifically wanted to create two separate methods so that the different calls to the asynchronous methods are clearly visible in the code.

4. We will then create a main `ReadLogFile()` method that tries to read the main logfile. As we have not created the logfile in the `MainLog` folder, the code will throw a `FileNotFoundException`. It will then run the asynchronous method and await that in the `catch` block of the `ReadLogFile()` method (something that was impossible in the previous versions of C#), returning the bytes read to the calling code:

```
public async Task<int> ReadLogFile()
{
    int returnBytes = -1;
    try
```

```
{
    Task<int> intBytesRead = ReadMainLog();
    returnBytes = await ReadMainLog();
}
catch (Exception ex)
{
    try
    {
        returnBytes = await ReadBackupLog();
    }
    catch (Exception)
    {
        throw;
    }
}
return returnBytes;
}
```

5. If not done so in the previous recipe, add a button to your Windows Forms application's Forms Designer. On the **winformAsync** Forms Designer, open **Toolbox** and select the **Button** control, which is found under the **All Windows Forms** node:

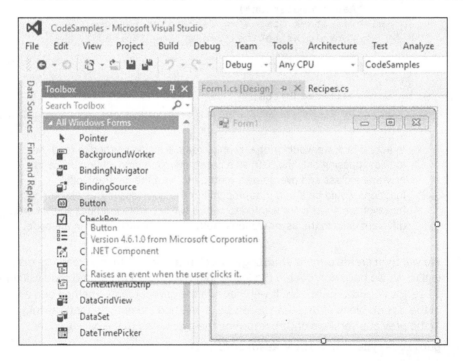

6. Drag the button control onto the **Form1** designer:

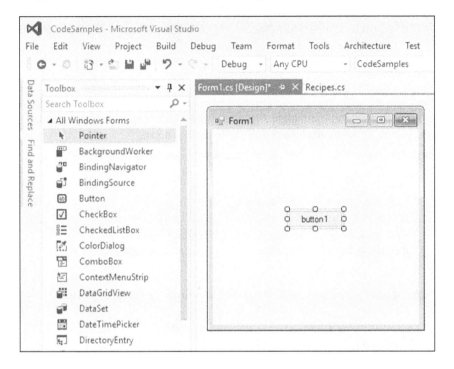

7. With the button control selected, double-click on the control to create the click event in the code behind. Visual Studio will insert the event code for you:

```
namespace winformAsync
{
    public partial class Form1 : Form
    {
        public Form1()
        {
            InitializeComponent();
        }

        private void button1_Click(object sender, EventArgs e)
        {

        }
    }
}
```

8. Change the `button1_Click` event and add the `async` keyword to the click event. This is an example of a `void` returning an asynchronous method:

```
private async void button1_Click(object sender, EventArgs e)
{

}
```

9. Next, we will write the code to create a new instance of the `AsyncDemo` class and attempt to read the main logfile. In a real-world example, it is at this point that the code does not know that the main logfile does not exist:

```
private async void button1_Click(object sender, EventArgs
e)
{
    Console.WriteLine("Read backup file");
    Chapter6.AsyncDemo oAsync = new Chapter6.AsyncDemo();
    int readResult = await oAsync.ReadLogFile();
    Console.WriteLine("Bytes read = " + readResult);
}
```

10. Running your application will display the Windows Forms application:

11. Before clicking on the **button1** button, ensure that the **Output** window is visible:

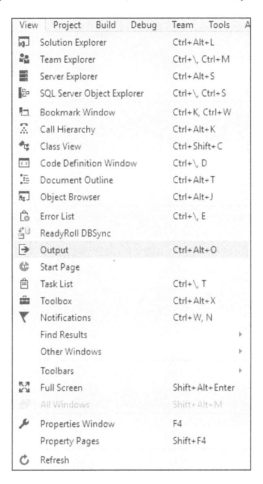

12. From the **View** menu, click on the **Output** menu item or type *Ctrl + Alt + O* to display the **Output** window. This will allow us to see the `Console.Writeline()` outputs as we have added them to the code in the `Chapter6` class and in the Windows application.

13. To simulate a file not found exception, we deleted the file from the `MainLog` folder. You will see that the exception is thrown, and the `catch` block runs the code to read the backup logfile instead:

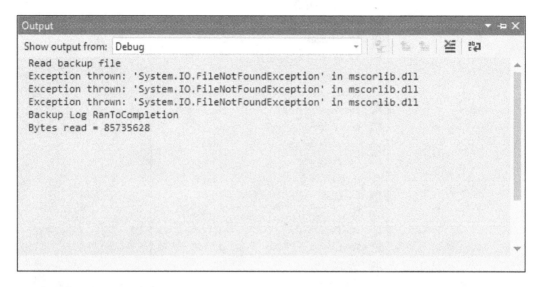

```
Output                                                                    ▼ ⊏ X
Show output from:  Debug                                    ▼   ≱   ⬩ ⬩   ⤨  ᵇᵅ₂
Read backup file
Exception thrown: 'System.IO.FileNotFoundException' in mscorlib.dll
Exception thrown: 'System.IO.FileNotFoundException' in mscorlib.dll
Exception thrown: 'System.IO.FileNotFoundException' in mscorlib.dll
Backup Log RanToCompletion
Bytes read = 85735628
```

How it works...

The fact that we can await in `catch` and `finally` blocks allows developers much more flexibility, because asynchronous results can consistently be awaited throughout the application. As you can see from the code we wrote, as soon as the exception was thrown, we asynchronously read the file read method for the backup file.

7

High Performance Programming Using Parallel and Multithreading in C#

This chapter takes a look at improving your code's performance using multithreading and parallel programming. In this chapter, we will cover the following recipes:

- ▸ Creating and aborting a low-priority background thread
- ▸ Increasing maximum thread pool size
- ▸ Creating multiple threads
- ▸ Locking one thread until the contended resources are available
- ▸ Invoking parallel calls to methods using `Parallel.Invoke`
- ▸ Using a parallel `foreach` loop to run multiple threads
- ▸ Cancelling a parallel `foreach` loop
- ▸ Catching errors in parallel `foreach` loops
- ▸ Debugging multiple threads

Introduction

If you can find a single-core CPU in a computer today, it will probably mean that you are standing in a museum. Every new computer today utilizes the advantages of multiple cores. Programmers can take advantage of this extra processing power in their own applications. As applications have grown in size and complexity, in many cases they actually need to utilize multithreading.

While not every situation is always suited for the implementation of multithreaded code logic, it is good to know how to use multithreading to improve the performance of your applications. This chapter will take you through the fundamentals of this exciting technology in C# programming.

Creating and aborting a low-priority background thread

The reason we want to have a look at a background thread specifically is because by default, all threads created by the main app thread or `Thread` class constructor are foreground threads. So, what exactly separates a foreground thread from a background thread? Well, background threads are identical to foreground threads with the exception that if all foreground threads are terminated, the background threads are stopped too. This is useful if you have a process in your application that must not stop the application from terminating. In other words, while your application is running, the background thread must continue to run.

Getting ready

We will create a simple application that defines the thread created as a background thread. It will then suspend, resume, and abort the thread.

How to do it...

1. Create a new class library by right-clicking on your solution and selecting **Add** and then **New Project** from the context menu:

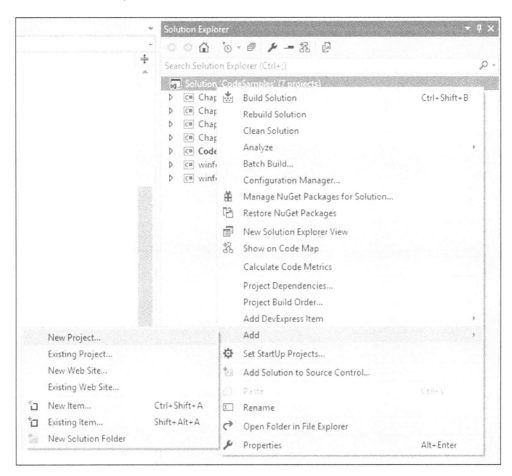

2. From the **Add New Project** dialog screen, select **Class Library** from the installed templates and call your class `Chapter7`:

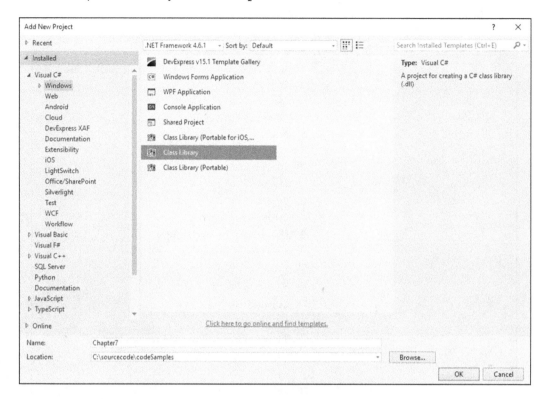

3. Your new class library will be added to your solution with a default name `Class1.cs`, which we renamed to `Recipes.cs` in order to distinguish the code properly. You can, however, rename your class to whatever you like if that makes more sense to you.

4. To rename your class, simply click on the class name in **Solution Explorer** and select **Rename** from the context menu:

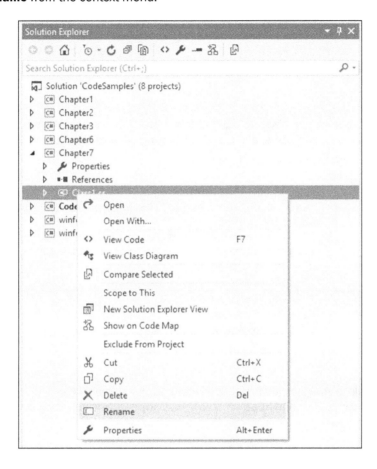

5. Visual Studio will ask you to confirm a rename of all references to the code element **Class1** in the project. Just click on **Yes**:

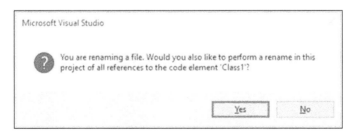

6. The following class is added to your `Chapter7` library project:

```
namespace Chapter7
{
    public class Recipes
    {

    }
}
```

7. Inside the `Recipes` class, add a method called `DoBackgroundTask()` with the `public void` modifiers, and add the following console output to it:

```
public void DoBackgroundTask()
    {
        WriteLine($"Thread
        {Thread.CurrentThread.ManagedThreadId} has a
        threadstate of
        {Thread.CurrentThread.ThreadState} with
        {Thread.CurrentThread.Priority} priority");
        WriteLine($"Start thread sleep at
        {DateTime.Now.Second} seconds");
        Thread.Sleep(3000);
        WriteLine($"End thread sleep at
        {DateTime.Now.Second} seconds");
    }
```

 Make sure that you have added the `using` statements for `System.Threading` and `static System.Console` to your `using` statements.

8. Inside the console application called `CodeSamples`, added previously, add a reference to the `Chapter7` class library by right-clicking on **References** under the `CodeSamples` project and selecting **Add Reference** from the context menu:

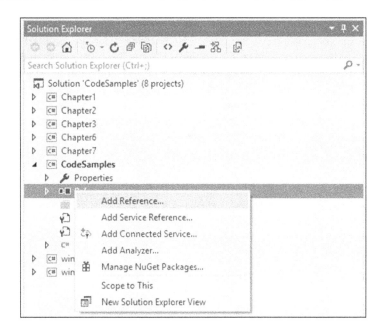

9. In the **Reference Manager** window, select the `Chapter7` solution by going to **Projects | Solutions**. This will allow you to use the classes we just created in your console application:

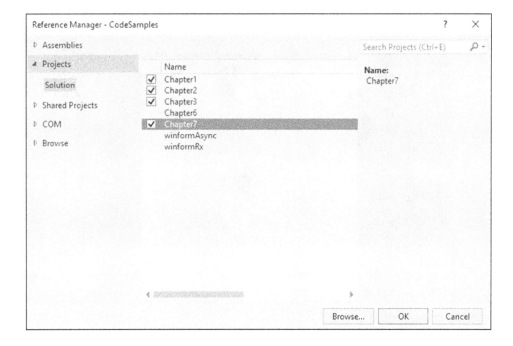

10. In the `void Main` method, create a new instance of your `Recipes` class and add it to a new thread called `backgroundThread`. Define this newly created thread to be a background thread and then start it. Finally, set the thread to sleep for five seconds. We need to do this because we have created a background thread that is set to sleep for three seconds. Background threads do not prohibit foreground threads from terminating. Therefore, if the main application thread (which is by default a foreground thread) terminates before the background thread completes, the application will terminate and also terminate the background thread:

```
static void Main(string[] args)
{
    Chapter7.Recipes oRecipe = new Chapter7.Recipes();
    var backgroundThread = new
    Thread(oRecipe.DoBackgroundTask);
    backgroundThread.IsBackground = true;
    backgroundThread.Start();
    Thread.Sleep(5000);
}
```

 Please note that you might need to add the `using System.Threading;` directive.

11. Run your console application by pressing *F5*. You will see that we have created a background thread with a normal priority:

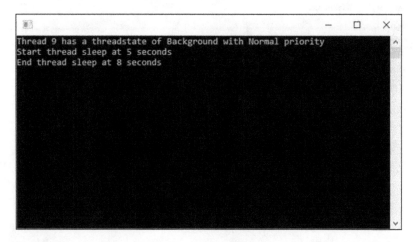

12. Let's modify our thread and set its priority down to low. Add this line of code to your console application: `backgroundThread.Priority = ThreadPriority.Lowest;`. This line will downgrade the thread priority:

```
Chapter7.Recipes oRecipe = new Chapter7.Recipes();
var backgroundThread = new Thread(oRecipe.DoBackgroundTask);
```

```
backgroundThread.IsBackground = true;
backgroundThread.Priority = ThreadPriority.Lowest;
backgroundThread.Start();
Thread.Sleep(5000);
```

13. Run your console application again. This time, you will see that the thread priority has been set to the lowest priority:

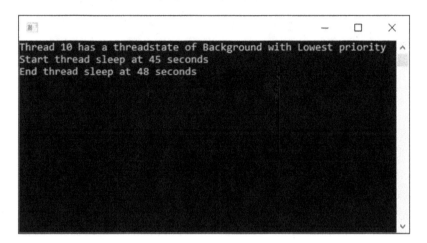

14. Go back to your `DoBackgroundTask()` method and add `Thread.CurrentThread.Abort();` right before `Thread.Sleep(3000);` is called. This line will prematurely kill the background thread. Your code should look like this:

```
public void DoBackgroundTask()
{
    WriteLine($"Thread
    {Thread.CurrentThread.ManagedThreadId}
    has a threadstate of {Thread.CurrentThread.ThreadState}
    with {Thread.CurrentThread.Priority} priority");
    WriteLine($"Start thread sleep at {DateTime.Now.Second}
    seconds");
    Thread.CurrentThread.Abort();
    Thread.Sleep(3000);
    WriteLine($"End thread sleep at {DateTime.Now.Second}
    seconds");
}
```

15. When you run your console application, you will see that the thread is aborted before the `Thread.Sleep` method is called. Aborting a thread in this way, however, is generally not recommended:

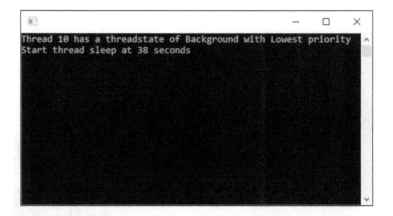

```
Thread 10 has a threadstate of Background with Lowest priority
Start thread sleep at 38 seconds
```

How it works...

Being able to create a background thread is a great way to work on a different thread from the main thread while not interfering with the process of the main application thread. Another added benefit is that the background thread is terminated as soon as the main application thread is completed. This process ensures that your application will terminate gracefully.

Increasing maximum thread pool size

The thread pool in .NET resides in the `System.Threading.ThreadPool` class. Generally, there is a lot of discussion around creating your own threads as opposed to using the thread pool. Popular thinking dictates that the thread pool should be used for brief jobs. This is because the thread pool is limited in size. There are many other processes in the system that will use the thread pool. You therefore do not want your application to hog all the threads in the thread pool.

The rule is that you can't set the number of maximum worker or completion threads to be less than the number of processors on your computer. You are also not allowed to set the maximum worker or completion threads to less than the minimum thread pool size.

Getting ready

We will read the number of processors on the current computer. Then, we will get the minimum and maximum allowable thread pool size, generate a random number between the minimum and maximum thread pool size, and set the maximum number of threads on the thread pool.

How to do it...

1. Create a new method called `IncreaseThreadPoolSize()` in the `Recipes` class:

```
public class Recipes
{
    public void IncreaseThreadPoolSize()
    {

    }
}
```

2. Start by adding the code to read the number of processors on the current machine using `Environment.ProcessorCount`:

```
public class Recipes
{
    public void IncreaseThreadPoolSize()
    {
        int numberOfProcessors =
        Environment.ProcessorCount;
        WriteLine($"Processor Count =
        {numberOfProcessors}");
    }
}
```

3. Next, we will retrieve the maximum and minimum threads available in the thread pool:

```
int maxworkerThreads;
int maxconcurrentActiveRequests;
int minworkerThreads;
int minconcurrentActiveRequests;
ThreadPool.GetMinThreads(out minworkerThreads, out
minconcurrentActiveRequests);
WriteLine($"ThreadPool minimum Worker = {minworkerThreads}
and minimum Requests = {minconcurrentActiveRequests}");

ThreadPool.GetMaxThreads(out maxworkerThreads, out
maxconcurrentActiveRequests);
WriteLine($"ThreadPool maximum Worker = {maxworkerThreads}
and maximum Requests = {maxconcurrentActiveRequests}");
```

4. Then, we will generate a random number between the maximum and minimum number of threads in the thread pool:

```
Random rndWorkers = new Random();
int newMaxWorker = rndWorkers.Next(minworkerThreads,
maxworkerThreads);
WriteLine($"New Max Worker Thread generated =
{newMaxWorker}");

Random rndConRequests = new Random();
int newMaxRequests =
rndConRequests.Next(minconcurrentActiveRequests,
maxconcurrentActiveRequests);
WriteLine($"New Max Active Requests generated =
{newMaxRequests}");
```

5. We now need to attempt to set the maximum number of threads in the thread pool by calling the SetMaxThreads method and setting it to our new random maximum value for the worker threads and the completion port threads. Any requests above this maximum number will be queued until the thread pool threads become active again. If the SetMaxThreads method is successful, the method will return true; otherwise, it will return false. It is a good idea to ensure that the SetMaxThreads method is successful:

```
bool changeSucceeded =
ThreadPool.SetMaxThreads(newMaxWorker, newMaxRequests);
if (changeSucceeded)
{
    WriteLine("SetMaxThreads completed");
    int maxworkerThreadCount;
    int maxconcurrentActiveRequestCount;
    ThreadPool.GetMaxThreads(out maxworkerThreadCount, out
    maxconcurrentActiveRequestCount);
    WriteLine($"ThreadPool Max Worker =
    {maxworkerThreadCount} and Max Requests =
    {maxconcurrentActiveRequestCount}");
}
else
    WriteLine("SetMaxThreads failed");
```

 Worker threads is the maximum number of worker threads in the thread pool, while the completion port threads is the maximum number of asynchronous I/O threads in the thread pool.

6. When you have added all the code in the steps listed, your `IncreaseThreadPoolSize()` method should look like this:

```
public class Recipes
{
    public void IncreaseThreadPoolSize()
    {
        int numberOfProcessors =
        Environment.ProcessorCount;
        WriteLine($"Processor Count =
        {numberOfProcessors}");

        int maxworkerThreads;
        int maxconcurrentActiveRequests;
        int minworkerThreads;
        int minconcurrentActiveRequests;
        ThreadPool.GetMinThreads(out minworkerThreads, out
        minconcurrentActiveRequests);
        WriteLine($"ThreadPool minimum Worker =
        {minworkerThreads} and minimum Requests =
        {minconcurrentActiveRequests}");

        ThreadPool.GetMaxThreads(out maxworkerThreads, out
        maxconcurrentActiveRequests);
        WriteLine($"ThreadPool maximum Worker =
        {maxworkerThreads} and maximum Requests =
        {maxconcurrentActiveRequests}");

        Random rndWorkers = new Random();
        int newMaxWorker =
        rndWorkers.Next(minworkerThreads,
        maxworkerThreads);
        WriteLine($"New Max Worker Thread generated =
        {newMaxWorker}");

        Random rndConRequests = new Random();
        int newMaxRequests =
        rndConRequests.Next(minconcurrentActiveRequests,
        maxconcurrentActiveRequests);
        WriteLine($"New Max Active Requests generated =
        {newMaxRequests}");

        bool changeSucceeded =
        ThreadPool.SetMaxThreads(newMaxWorker,
        newMaxRequests);
        if (changeSucceeded)
        {
```

```
            WriteLine("SetMaxThreads completed");
            int maxworkerThreadCount;
            int maxconcurrentActiveRequestCount;
            ThreadPool.GetMaxThreads(out
            maxworkerThreadCount, out
            maxconcurrentActiveRequestCount);
            WriteLine($"ThreadPool Max Worker =
            {maxworkerThreadCount} and Max Requests =
            {maxconcurrentActiveRequestCount}");
        }
        else
            WriteLine("SetMaxThreads failed");

    }
}
```

7. Head on over to your console application and create a new instance of your `Recipe` class, and call the `IncreaseThreadPoolSize()` method:

```
Chapter7.Recipes oRecipe = new Chapter7.Recipes();
oRecipe.IncreaseThreadPoolSize();
Console.ReadLine();
```

8. Finally, run your console application and take note of the output:

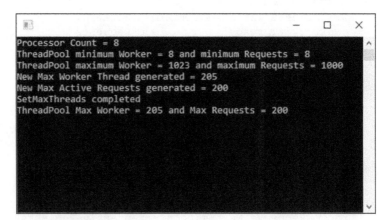

How it works...

From the console application, we can see that the processor count is 8. The minimum number of thread pool threads, therefore, also equals 8. We then read the maximum thread pool size and generate a random number between the minimum and maximum numbers. Lastly, we set the maximum thread pool size to our randomly generated minimum and maximum.

While this is only a proof of concept and not something one would do in a production application (setting the thread pool to a random number), it clearly illustrates the ability to set the thread pool to a value specified by the developer.

 The code in this recipe was compiled for 32 bit. Try changing your application to a 64-bit application and run the code again. See the difference 64 bit makes.

Creating multiple threads

Sometimes, we need to create multiple threads. Before we can continue, however, we need to wait for these threads to complete doing whatever they need to do. For this, the use of tasks is best suited.

Getting ready

Make sure that you have added the `using System.Threading.Tasks;` statement to the top of your `Recipes` class.

How to do it...

1. Create a new method called `MultipleThreadWait()` in your `Recipes` class. Then, create a second method called `RunThread()` with the `private` modifier, which takes an integer of seconds to make the thread sleep. This will simulate the process of doing some work for a variable amount of time:

```
public class Recipes
{
    public void MultipleThreadWait()
    {

    }

    private void RunThread(int sleepSeconds)
    {

    }
}
```

 In reality, you would probably not call the same method. You could, for all intents and purposes, call three separate methods. Here, however, for the sake of simplicity, we will call the same method with different sleep durations.

2. Add the following code to your `MultipleThreadWait()` method. You will notice that we are creating three tasks that then create three threads. We will then fire off these three threads and make them sleep for 3, 5, and 2 seconds. Finally, we will call the `Task.WaitAll` method to wait before continuing the execution of the application:

```
Task thread1 = Task.Factory.StartNew(() => RunThread(3));
Task thread2 = Task.Factory.StartNew(() => RunThread(5));
Task thread3 = Task.Factory.StartNew(() => RunThread(2));

Task.WaitAll(thread1, thread2, thread3);
WriteLine("All tasks completed");
```

3. Then, in the `RunThread()` method, we will read the current thread ID and then make the thread sleep for the amount of milliseconds supplied. This is just the integer value for the seconds multiplied by 1000:

```
int threadID = Thread.CurrentThread.ManagedThreadId;

WriteLine($"Sleep thread {threadID} for {sleepSeconds}
seconds at {DateTime.Now.Second} seconds");
Thread.Sleep(sleepSeconds * 1000);
WriteLine($"Wake thread {threadID} at {DateTime.Now.Second}
seconds");
```

4. When you have completed the code, your `Recipes` class should look like this:

```
public class Recipes
{
    public void MultipleThreadWait()
    {
        Task thread1 = Task.Factory.StartNew(() =>
        RunThread(3));
        Task thread2 = Task.Factory.StartNew(() =>
        RunThread(5));
        Task thread3 = Task.Factory.StartNew(() =>
        RunThread(2));

        Task.WaitAll(thread1, thread2, thread3);
        WriteLine("All tasks completed");
    }

    private void RunThread(int sleepSeconds)
    {
        int threadID =
        Thread.CurrentThread.ManagedThreadId;
```

```
            WriteLine($"Sleep thread {threadID} for
            {sleepSeconds} seconds at {DateTime.Now.Second}
            seconds");
            Thread.Sleep(sleepSeconds * 1000);
            WriteLine($"Wake thread {threadID} at
            {DateTime.Now.Second} seconds");
        }
    }
```

5. Finally, add a new instance of the `Recipe` class to your console application and call the `MultipleThreadWait()` method:

    ```
    Chapter7.Recipes oRecipe = new Chapter7.Recipes();
    oRecipe.MultipleThreadWait();
    Console.ReadLine();
    ```

6. Run your console application and view the output produced:

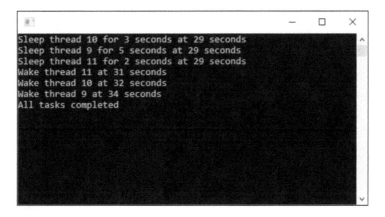

How it works...

You will notice that three threads (`thread 9`, `thread 10`, and `thread 11`) are created. These are then paused by making them sleep for various amounts of time. After each thread wakes, the code waits for all three threads to complete before continuing the execution of the application code.

Locking one thread until the contended resources are available

There are instances where we want to give sole access to a process to a specific thread. We can do this using the `lock` keyword. This will execute this process in a thread-safe manner. Therefore, when a thread runs the process, it will gain exclusive access to the process for the duration of the lock scope. If another thread tries to gain access to the process inside the locked code, it will be blocked and have to wait its turn until the lock is released.

Getting ready

For this example, we will use tasks. Make sure that you have added the `using System.Threading.Tasks;` statement to the top of your `Recipes` class.

How to do it...

1. In the `Recipes` class, add an object called `threadLock` with the `private` modifier. Then, add two methods called `LockThreadExample()` and `ContendedResource()` that take an integer of seconds to sleep as a parameter:

```
public class Recipes
{
    private object threadLock = new object();
    public void LockThreadExample()
    {

    }

    private void ContendedResource(int sleepSeconds)
    {

    }
}
```

 It is considered a best practice to define the object to lock on as private.

2. Add three tasks to the `LockThreadExample()` method. They will create threads that try to access the same section of code simultaneously. This code will wait until all the threads have completed before terminating the application:

```
Task thread1 = Task.Factory.StartNew(() =>
ContendedResource(3));
Task thread2 = Task.Factory.StartNew(() =>
ContendedResource(5));
Task thread3 = Task.Factory.StartNew(() =>
ContendedResource(2));

Task.WaitAll(thread1, thread2, thread3);
WriteLine("All tasks completed");
```

3. In the `ContendedResource()` method, create a lock using the `private` `threadLock` object and then make the thread sleep for the amount of seconds passed to the method as a parameter:

```
int threadID = Thread.CurrentThread.ManagedThreadId;
lock (threadLock)
{
    WriteLine($"Locked for thread {threadID}");
    Thread.Sleep(sleepSeconds * 1000);
}
WriteLine($"Lock released for thread {threadID}");
```

4. Back in the console application, add the following code to instantiate a new `Recipes` class and call the `LockThreadExample()` method:

```
Chapter7.Recipes oRecipe = new Chapter7.Recipes();
oRecipe.LockThreadExample();
Console.ReadLine();
```

5. Run the console application and see the information output to the console window:

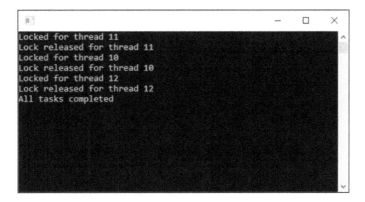

How it works...

We can see that `thread 11` gained exclusive access to the contended resource. At the same time, `thread 11` and `thread 12` tried to access the contended resource locked by `thread 11`. This then caused the other two threads to wait until `thread 11` had completed and released the lock. The result of this is that the code is executed in an orderly manner, as can be seen in the console window output. Each thread waits its turn until it can access the resource and lock its thread.

Invoking parallel calls to methods using Parallel.Invoke

`Parallel.Invoke` allows us to execute tasks in (you guessed it) parallel. Sometimes, you need to perform operations simultaneously and, in so doing, speed up processing. You can therefore expect that the total time taken to process the tasks is equal to the longest running process. Using `Parallel.Invoke` is quite easy.

Getting ready

Make sure that you have added the `using System.Threading.Tasks;` statement to the top of your `Recipes` class.

How to do it...

1. Start off by creating two methods in the `Recipes` class called `ParallelInvoke()` and `PerformSomeTask()`, which take an integer of seconds to sleep as the parameter:

```
public class Recipes
{
    public void ParallelInvoke()
    {

    }

    private void PerformSomeTask(int sleepSeconds)
    {

    }
}
```

2. Add the following code to the `ParallelInvoke()` method. This code will call `Paralell.Invoke` to run the `PerformSomeTask()` method:

```
WriteLine($"Parallel.Invoke started at
{DateTime.Now.Second} seconds");
Parallel.Invoke(
    () => PerformSomeTask(3),
    () => PerformSomeTask(5),
    () => PerformSomeTask(2)
    );

WriteLine($"Parallel.Invoke completed at
{DateTime.Now.Second} seconds");
```

3. In the `PerformSomeTask()` method, make the thread sleep for the amount of seconds passed to the method as the parameter (converting the seconds to milliseconds by multiplying it by `1000`):

```
int threadID = Thread.CurrentThread.ManagedThreadId;
WriteLine($"Sleep thread {threadID} for {sleepSeconds}
seconds");
Thread.Sleep(sleepSeconds * 1000);
WriteLine($"Thread {threadID} resumed");
```

4. When you have added all the code, your `Recipes` class should look like this:

```
public class Recipes
{
    public void ParallelInvoke()
    {
        WriteLine($"Parallel.Invoke started at
        {DateTime.Now.Second} seconds");
        Parallel.Invoke(
            () => PerformSomeTask(3),
            () => PerformSomeTask(5),
            () => PerformSomeTask(2)
            );

        WriteLine($"Parallel.Invoke completed at
        {DateTime.Now.Second} seconds");
    }

    private void PerformSomeTask(int sleepSeconds)
    {
        int threadID =
        Thread.CurrentThread.ManagedThreadId;
        WriteLine($"Sleep thread {threadID} for
        {sleepSeconds} seconds");
```

```
            Thread.Sleep(sleepSeconds * 1000);
            WriteLine($"Thread {threadID} resumed");
        }
    }
```

5. In the console application, instantiate a new instance of the `Recipes` class and call the `ParallelInvoke()` method:

```
Chapter7.Recipes oRecipe = new Chapter7.Recipes();
oRecipe.ParallelInvoke();
Console.ReadLine();
```

6. Run the console application and look at the output produced in the console window:

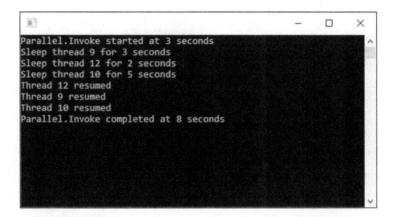

How it works...

Because we are running all these threads in parallel, we can assume that the longest process will denote the total duration of the all the tasks. This means that the total duration of the process will be 5 seconds because the longest task will take 5 seconds to complete (we set `thread 10` to sleep for a maximum of 5 seconds).

As we can see, the time difference between the start and the end of `Parallel.Invoke` is exactly 5 seconds.

Using a parallel foreach loop to run multiple threads

A while ago, during a work retreat (yes, the company I work for is really that cool), Graham Rook, who is one of my colleagues, showed me a parallel `foreach` loop. It certainly speeds up processing a great deal. But here's the rub. It makes no sense using a parallel `foreach` loop if you're dealing with small amounts of data or little tasks. The parallel `foreach` loop excels when there is bulk processing to do or huge amounts of data to process.

Getting ready section...

Getting ready

We will start off by looking at where the parallel `foreach` loop does not perform better than the standard `foreach` loop. For this, we will create a small list of 500 items and just iterate over the list, writing the items to the console window.

For the second example that illustrates the power of the parallel `foreach` loop, we will use the same list and create a file for each item in the list. The power and benefit of the parallel `foreach` loop will be evident in the second example.

How to do it...

1. Start off by creating two methods in the `Recipes` class. Call one method `ReadCollectionForEach()` and pass it a parameter of `List<string>`. Create a second method called `ReadCollectionParallelForEach()` that also accepts a parameter of `List<string>`:

```
public class Recipes
{
    public double ReadCollectionForEach(List<string>
    intCollection)
    {

    }

    private double
    ReadCollectionParallelForEach(List<string> intCollection)
    {

    }
}
```

2. In the `ReadCollectionForEach()` method, add a standard `foreach` loop that will iterate over the collection of strings passed to it and write the value it finds to the console window. Then, clear the console window. Use a timer to keep track of the total seconds elapsed during the `foreach` loop:

```
var timer = Stopwatch.StartNew();
foreach (string integer in intCollection)
{
    WriteLine(integer);
    Clear();
}
return timer.Elapsed.TotalSeconds;
```

3. In the second method, called `ReadCollectionParallelForEach()`, do the same. However, instead of using a standard `foreach` loop, add a `Parallel.ForEach` loop. You will notice that the `Parallel.ForEach` loop looks slightly different. The signature of `Parallel.ForEach` requires that you pass it an enumerable data source (`List<string> intCollection`) and define an action, which is the delegate that is invoked for every iteration (`integer`):

```
var timer = Stopwatch.StartNew();
Parallel.ForEach(intCollection, integer =>
{
    WriteLine(integer);
    Clear();
});
return timer.Elapsed.TotalSeconds;
```

4. When you have added all the required code, your `Recipes` class should look like this:

```
public class Recipes
{
    public double ReadCollectionForEach(List<string>
    intCollection)
    {
        var timer = Stopwatch.StartNew();
        foreach (string integer in intCollection)
        {
            WriteLine(integer);
            Clear();
        }
        return timer.Elapsed.TotalSeconds;
    }


    public double
    ReadCollectionParallelForEach(List<string>
    intCollection)
    {
        var timer = Stopwatch.StartNew();
        Parallel.ForEach(intCollection, integer =>
        {
            WriteLine(integer);
            Clear();
        });
        return timer.Elapsed.TotalSeconds;
    }
}
```

5. In the console application, create the `List<string>` collection and pass it to the two methods created in the `Recipes` class. You will notice that we are only creating a collection of 500 items. After the code is completed, return the time elapsed in seconds and output it to the console window:

```
List<string> integerList = new List<string>();
for (int i = 0; i <= 500; i++)
{
    integerList.Add(i.ToString());
}
Chapter7.Recipes oRecipe = new Chapter7.Recipes();
double timeElapsed1 =
oRecipe.ReadCollectionForEach(integerList);
double timeElapsed2 =
oRecipe.ReadCollectionParallelForEach(integerList);
WriteLine($"foreach executed in {timeElapsed1}");
WriteLine($"Parallel.ForEach executed in {timeElapsed2}");
```

6. Run your application. From the output displayed, you will see that the performance gain using the `Parallel.ForEach` loop is negligible. In fact, in this case, the `Parallel.ForEach` loop only improved performance by 0.4516 percent:

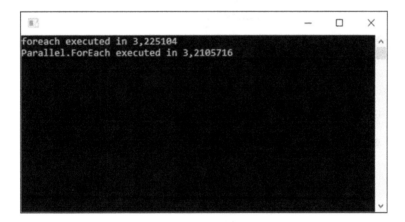

7. Let's use a different example now. We will create a process-intensive task and measure the performance gain that the `Parallel.ForEach` loop will give us. Create two methods called `CreateWriteFilesForEach()` and `CreateWriteFilesParallelForEach()`, which both take the `List<string>` collection as the parameter:

```
public class Recipes
{
    public void CreateWriteFilesForEach(List<string>
    intCollection)
    {
```

```
    }

    private void
    CreateWriteFilesParallelForEach(List<string>
    intCollection)
    {

    }
}
```

8. Add the following code to the `CreateWriteFilesForEach()` method. This code starts the timer and executes the standard `foreach` loop on the `List<string>` object. It then writes the elapsed time out to the console window:

```
WriteLine($"Start foreach File method");
var timer = Stopwatch.StartNew();
foreach (string integer in intCollection)
{

}
WriteLine($"foreach File method executed in
{timer.Elapsed.TotalSeconds} seconds");
```

9. Inside the `foreach` loop, add the code to check whether a file exists with the specific name created by appending the `integer` value to the filename portion of the `filePath` variable. Create the file (ensuring that you use `Dispose` method in order not to lock the file when trying to write to it) and write some text to the newly created file:

```
string filePath =
$"C:\\temp\\output\\ForEach_Log{integer}.txt";
if (!File.Exists(filePath))
{
    File.Create(filePath).Dispose();
    using (StreamWriter sw = new StreamWriter(filePath,
    false))
    {
        sw.WriteLine($"{integer}. Log file start:
        {DateTime.Now.ToUniversalTime().ToString()}");
    }
}
```

10. Next, add this code to the `CreateWriteFilesParallelForEach()` method, which basically performs the same function as the `CreateWriteFilesForEach()` method, but uses a `Parallel.ForEach` loop to create and write files:

```
WriteLine($"Start Parallel.ForEach File method");
var timer = Stopwatch.StartNew();
```

```
Parallel.ForEach(intCollection, integer =>
{

});
WriteLine($"Parallel.ForEach File method executed in
{timer.Elapsed.TotalSeconds} seconds");
```

11. Add the slightly modified file-creation code inside the `Parallel.ForEach` loop:

```
string filePath =
$"C:\\temp\\output\\ParallelForEach_Log{integer}.txt";
if (!File.Exists(filePath))
{
    File.Create(filePath).Dispose();
    using (StreamWriter sw = new StreamWriter(filePath,
    false))
    {
        sw.WriteLine($"{integer}. Log file start:
        {DateTime.Now.ToUniversalTime().ToString()}");
    }
}
```

12. When you are done, your code needs to look like this:

```
public class Recipes
{
    public void CreateWriteFilesForEach(List<string>
    intCollection)
    {
        WriteLine($"Start foreach File method");
        var timer = Stopwatch.StartNew();
        foreach (string integer in intCollection)
        {
            string filePath =
            $"C:\\temp\\output\\ForEach_Log{integer}.txt";
            if (!File.Exists(filePath))
            {
                File.Create(filePath).Dispose();
                using (StreamWriter sw = new
                StreamWriter(filePath, false))
                {
                    sw.WriteLine($"{integer}. Log file
                    start: {DateTime.Now.ToUniversalTime()
                    .ToString()}");
                }
            }
        }
    }
```

```
            WriteLine($"foreach File method executed in
            {timer.Elapsed.TotalSeconds} seconds");
        }

        public void
        CreateWriteFilesParallelForEach(List<string>
        intCollection)
        {
            WriteLine($"Start Parallel.ForEach File method");
            var timer = Stopwatch.StartNew();
            Parallel.ForEach(intCollection, integer =>
            {
                string filePath =
                $"C:\\temp\\output\\ParallelForEach_Log
                {integer}.txt";
                if (!File.Exists(filePath))
                {
                    File.Create(filePath).Dispose();
                    using (StreamWriter sw = new
                    StreamWriter(filePath, false))
                    {
                        sw.WriteLine($"{integer}. Log file
                        start: {DateTime.Now.ToUniversalTime()
                        .ToString()}");
                    }
                }
            });
            WriteLine($"Parallel.ForEach File method executed
            in {timer.Elapsed.TotalSeconds} seconds");
        }
    }
```

13. Heading over to the console application, modify the `List<string>` object slightly and increase the count from `500` to `1000`. Then, call the file methods created in the `Recipes` class:

```
List<string> integerList = new List<string>();
for (int i = 0; i <= 1000; i++)
{
    integerList.Add(i.ToString());
}

Chapter7.Recipes oRecipe = new Chapter7.Recipes();
oRecipe.CreateWriteFilesForEach(integerList);
oRecipe.CreateWriteFilesParallelForEach(integerList);
ReadLine();
```

14. Finally, when you are ready, make sure that you have the `C:\temp\output` directory and that there aren't any other files in that directory. Run your application and review the output to the console window. This time round, we can see that the `Parallel.ForEach` loop has made a huge difference. The performance gain is massive and heralds a 60.7074 percent performance increase over the standard `foreach` loop:

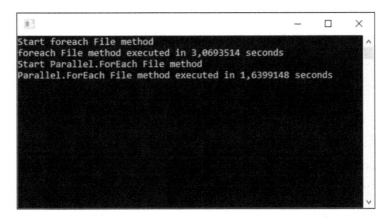

```
Start foreach File method
foreach File method executed in 3,0693514 seconds
Start Parallel.ForEach File method
Parallel.ForEach File method executed in 1,6399148 seconds
```

How it works...

From the examples used in this recipe, it is clear that the use of the parallel `foreach` loop should be considered carefully. If you are dealing with relatively low volumes of data or non-process intensive transactions, the parallel `foreach` loop will not benefit your application's performance much. In some instances, the standard `foreach` loop could be much faster than the parallel `foreach` loop. If, however, you find your application running into performance issues when processing large amounts of data or running processor-intensive tasks, give the parallel `foreach` loop a try. It just might surprise you.

Cancelling a parallel foreach loop

When dealing with parallel `foreach` loops, the obvious question is how one would terminate the loop prematurely based on a certain condition, such as a timeout. As it turns out, the parallel `foreach` loop is quite easy to terminate prematurely.

Getting ready

We will create a method that takes a collection of items and loops through this collection in a parallel `foreach` loop. It will also be aware of a timeout value that, if exceeded, will terminate the loop and exit the method.

How to do it...

1. Start off by creating a new method called `CancelParallelForEach()` in the `Recipes` class, which takes two parameters. One is a collection of `List<string>`, while the other is an integer specifying a timeout value. When the timeout value is exceeded, the `Parallel.ForEach` loop must terminate:

```csharp
public class Recipes
{
    public void CancelParallelForEach(List<string>
    intCollection, int timeOut)
    {

    }
}
```

2. Inside the `CancelParallelForEach()` method, add a timer to keep track of the elapsed time. This will signal the loop that the timeout threshold has been exceeded and that the loop needs to exit. Create the `Parallel.ForEach` method, defining a state. In each iteration, check the elapsed time against the timeout, and if the time is exceeded, break out of the loop:

```csharp
var timer = Stopwatch.StartNew();
Parallel.ForEach(intCollection, (integer, state) =>
{
    Thread.Sleep(1000);
    if (timer.Elapsed.Seconds > timeOut)
    {
        WriteLine($"Terminate thread
        {Thread.CurrentThread.ManagedThreadId}.
        Elapsed time {timer.Elapsed.Seconds} seconds");
        state.Break();
    }
    WriteLine($"Processing item {integer} on thread
    {Thread.CurrentThread.ManagedThreadId}");
});
```

3. In the console application, create the `List<string>` object and add `1000` items to it. Call the `CancelParallelForEach()` method with a timeout of only 5 seconds:

```csharp
List<string> integerList = new List<string>();
for (int i = 0; i <= 1000; i++)
{
    integerList.Add(i.ToString());
}

Chapter7.Recipes oRecipe = new Chapter7.Recipes();
```

```
oRecipe.CancelParallelForEach(integerList, 5);
WriteLine($"Parallel.ForEach loop terminated");
ReadLine();
```

4. Run your console application and review the output results:

```
Processing item 9 on thread 8
Processing item 16 on thread 17
Processing item 379 on thread 13
Processing item 754 on thread 11
Processing item 629 on thread 16
Processing item 255 on thread 10
Processing item 132 on thread 9
Processing item 13 on thread 15
Processing item 879 on thread 14
Processing item 504 on thread 12
Terminate thread 21. Elapsed time 6 seconds
Processing item 507 on thread 21
Terminate thread 19. Elapsed time 6 seconds
Processing item 259 on thread 19
Terminate thread 18. Elapsed time 6 seconds
Processing item 135 on thread 18
Terminate thread 8. Elapsed time 6 seconds
Processing item 10 on thread 8
Terminate thread 17. Elapsed time 6 seconds
Processing item 17 on thread 17
Terminate thread 16. Elapsed time 6 seconds
Terminate thread 20. Elapsed time 6 seconds
Processing item 383 on thread 20
Terminate thread 11. Elapsed time 6 seconds
Processing item 755 on thread 11
Terminate thread 9. Elapsed time 6 seconds
Processing item 133 on thread 9
Terminate thread 10. Elapsed time 6 seconds
Processing item 256 on thread 10
Terminate thread 14. Elapsed time 6 seconds
Processing item 880 on thread 14
Processing item 630 on thread 16
Terminate thread 13. Elapsed time 6 seconds
Processing item 380 on thread 13
Terminate thread 15. Elapsed time 6 seconds
Terminate thread 12. Elapsed time 6 seconds
Processing item 505 on thread 12
Processing item 14 on thread 15
Terminate thread 22. Elapsed time 7 seconds
Processing item 632 on thread 22
Parallel.ForEach loop terminated
```

How it works...

You can see from the console window output that as soon as the elapsed time exceeded the timeout value, the parallel loop was notified to cease the execution of iterations beyond the current iteration at the system's earliest convenience. Having this kind of control over the Parallel.ForEach loop allows developers to avoid runaway loops and give the user control to cancel a loop operation by clicking on a button, or automatically having the application terminate when the timeout value has been reached.

Catching errors in parallel foreach loops

With parallel `foreach` loops, developers can wrap the loop in a `try catch` statement. Care needs to be taken, however, because the `Parallel.ForEach` will throw `AggregatedException`, which has the exceptions it encounters over several threads rolled into one.

Getting ready

We will create a `List<string>` object that contains a collection of machine IP addresses. The `Parallel.ForEach` loop will check the IP addresses to see whether the machines on the other end of the given IP are alive. It does this by pinging the IP address. The method that performs the `Parallel.ForEach` loop will also be given the minimum required alive machines as an integer value. If the minimum number of machines alive is not met, an exception is thrown.

How to do it...

1. In the `Recipes` class, add a method called `CheckClientMachinesOnline()` that takes as parameters a `List<string>` collection of IP addresses and an integer that specifies the minimum number of machines required to be online. Add a second method called `MachineReturnedPing()` that will receive an IP address to ping. For our purpose, we will just return `false` to mimic a dead machine (the ping to the IP address timed out):

```
public class Recipes
{
    public void CheckClientMachinesOnline(List<string>
    ipAddresses, int minimumLive)
    {

    }

    private bool MachineReturnedPing(string ip)
    {
        return false;
    }
}
```

2. Inside the `CheckClientMachinesOnline()` method, add the `Parallel.ForEach` loop and create the `ParallelOptions` variable, which will specify the degree of parallelism. Wrap all this code inside a `try catch` statement and catch `AggregateException`:

```
try
{
    int machineCount = ipAddresses.Count();
```

```
var options = new ParallelOptions();
options.MaxDegreeOfParallelism = machineCount;
int deadMachines = 0;

Parallel.ForEach(ipAddresses, options, ip =>
{

});
}
catch (AggregateException aex)
{
    WriteLine("An AggregateException has occurred");
    throw;
}
```

3. Inside the `Parallel.ForEach` loop, write the code to check whether the machine is online by calling the `MachineReturnedPing()` method. In our example, this method will always return `false`. You will notice that we are keeping track of the offline machine count via the `Interlocked.Increment` method. This is just a way of incrementing a variable across the threads of the `Parallel.ForEach` loop:

```
if (MachineReturnedPing(ip))
{

}
else
{
    if (machineCount - Interlocked.Increment(ref
    deadMachines) < minimumLive)
    {
        WriteLine($"Machines to check = {machineCount}");
        WriteLine($"Dead machines = {deadMachines}");
        WriteLine($"Minimum machines required =
        {minimumLive}");
        WriteLine($"Live Machines = {machineCount -
        deadMachines}");

        throw new Exception($"Minimum machines requirement
        of {minimumLive} not met");
    }
}
```

4. If you have added all the code correctly, your `Recipes` class will look like this:

```csharp
public class Recipes
{
    public void CheckClientMachinesOnline(List<string>
    ipAddresses, int minimumLive)
    {
        try
        {
            int machineCount = ipAddresses.Count();
            var options = new ParallelOptions();
            options.MaxDegreeOfParallelism = machineCount;
            int deadMachines = 0;

            Parallel.ForEach(ipAddresses, options, ip =>
            {
                if (MachineReturnedPing(ip))
                {

                }
                else
                {
                    if (machineCount -
                    Interlocked.Increment(ref deadMachines)
                    < minimumLive)
                    {
                        WriteLine($"Machines to check =
                        {machineCount}");
                        WriteLine($"Dead machines =
                        {deadMachines}");
                        WriteLine($"Minimum machines
                        required = {minimumLive}");
                        WriteLine($"Live Machines =
                        {machineCount - deadMachines}");

                        throw new Exception($"Minimum
                        machines requirement of
                        {minimumLive} not met");
                    }
                }
            });
        }
        catch (AggregateException aex)
        {
            WriteLine("An AggregateException has
            occurred");
            throw;
        }
    }
}
```

```
private bool MachineReturnedPing(string ip)
{
    return false;
}
}
```

5. In the console application, create the `List<string>` object to store a
   collection of dummy IP addresses. Instantiate your `Recipes` class and call the
   `CheckClientMachinesOnline()` method, passing the collection of IP addresses
   and a minimum number of machines required to be online to it:

```
List<string> ipList = new List<string>();
for (int i = 0; i <= 10; i++)
{
    ipList.Add($"10.0.0.{i.ToString()}");
}

try
{
    Chapter7.Recipes oRecipe = new Chapter7.Recipes();
    oRecipe.CheckClientMachinesOnline(ipList, 2);
}
catch (Exception ex)
{
    WriteLine(ex.InnerException.Message);
}
ReadLine();
```

6. Run your application and review the output in the console window:

```
Machines to check = 11
Dead machines = 11
Minimum machines required = 2
Live Machines = 0
Machines to check = 11
Dead machines = 11
Minimum machines required = 2
Live Machines = 0
An AggregateException has occurred
Minimum machines requirement of 2 not met
```

How it works...

From the console window output, you can see that the minimum number of machines required to be online was not achieved. The application then threw an exception and caught it from the `Parallel.ForEach` loop. Being able to handle exceptions in parallel loops such as this one is essential to maintain the stability of your application by being able to handle exceptions as they occur.

We encourage you to play around a little with the `Parallel.ForEach` loop and drill into some of the inner methods of the `AggregareException` class to really understand it better.

Debugging multiple threads

Debugging multiple threads in Visual Studio is tricky, especially since these threads are all running at the same time. Luckily, we have a few tools available to us as developers to use to get a better understanding of what is happening in our multithreaded applications.

Getting ready

While debugging multithreaded applications, you can access various windows by going to **Debug | Windows** in Visual Studio.

How to do it...

1. Start debugging your multithreaded application after adding a breakpoint somewhere in the code. You can access various debugging windows by going to **Debug | Windows** in Visual Studio:

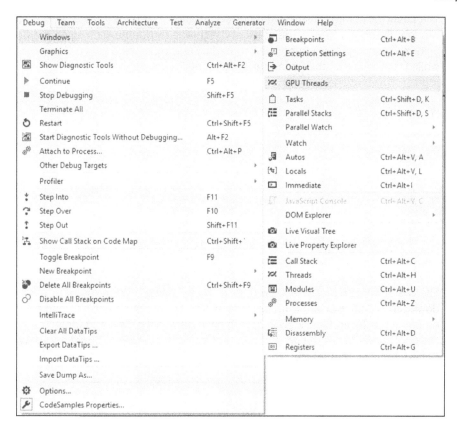

2. The first window available to you is the **Threads** window. Access it by going to **Debug | Windows** in Visual Studio or type *Ctrl + Alt + H*. In here, you can right-click on a thread to watch and flag it. If you have given your threads names, you will see that name appear in the **Name** column. To give your thread a name, you could add the following code to your application, which runs the method on a separate thread:

```
int threadID = Thread.CurrentThread.ManagedThreadId;
Thread.CurrentThread.Name = $"New Thread{threadID}";
```

You will also be able to see the currently active thread in the debugger. It will be marked with a yellow arrow. Then, there is the managed ID, which is the same ID you would have used to create the unique thread name earlier on.

The **Location** column displays the current method that the thread is in. The **Threads** window allows you to view the stack of the thread by double-clicking on the **Location** field. You can also freeze and thaw threads. Freezing stops a thread from executing, while thawing allows the frozen thread to continue as normal:

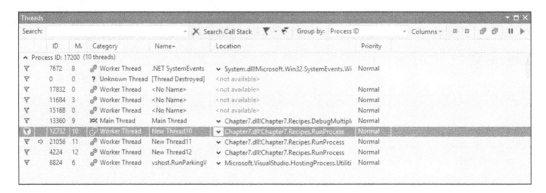

3. The **Tasks** window can be accessed by going to **Debug | Windows** or by holding down *Ctrl + Shift + D* and then pressing *K*. You will notice that the thread you flagged earlier in the **Threads** window is also flagged here in the **Tasks** window. The status of the task shows the status at that moment and can be **Active**, **Deadlocked**, **Waiting**, **Scheduled**, or **Completed**:

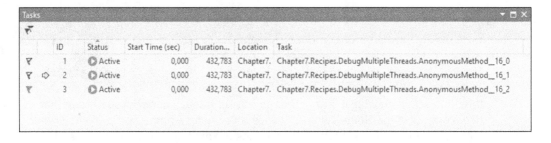

4. The **Parallel Stacks** window can be accessed by going to **Debug | Windows** in Visual Studio or by holding down *Ctrl + Shift + D*, and then pressing the S key. Here, you can see a graphical view of the tasks and threads. You can switch between the **Threads** and **Tasks** view by making a selection in the dropdown list in the upper-left corner of the **Parallel Stacks** window:

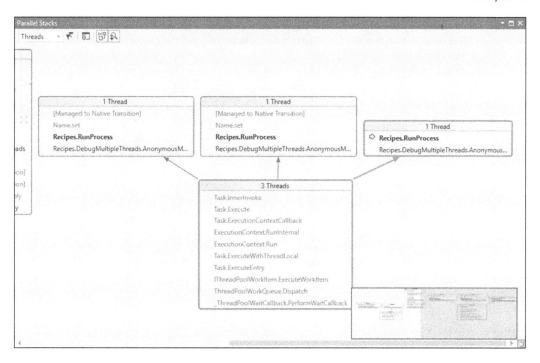

5. Changing the selection to **Tasks** will show you the current tasks in the debug session:

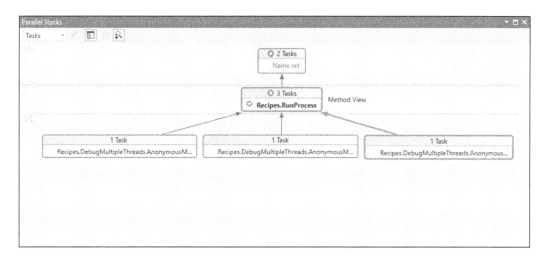

6. The next window, and undoubtedly my favorite is the **Parallel Watch** window. It is in fact identical to the standard **Watch** window in Visual Studio, but this watches values across all threads in your application. You can type in any valid C# expression into **Parallel Watch** and see the values as they are at that moment in the debug session. As you can see, we have added the `sleepSeconds` variable and the name of the thread to the watch:

How it works...

Being able to use the debugging tools for multithreaded applications effectively in Visual Studio makes it much easier to understand the structure of your application and helps you identify possible bugs, bottlenecks, and areas of concern.

We encourage you to learn more about the various debugging windows available to you.

8
Code Contracts

This chapter will introduce you to code contracts. This is a very powerful technology and one that will enable you to secure your code from unnecessary errors. This is especially true when you are writing a class that is shared between several developers. Code contracts allow you to inspect and handle data passed to your method under contract. If the contract fails its validation, you can take decisive action within your method to handle this eventuality. This chapter will cover the following recipes:

- ▸ Downloading, installing, and integrating code contracts into Visual Studio
- ▸ Creating code contract preconditions
- ▸ Creating code contract postconditions
- ▸ Creating code contract invariant
- ▸ Creating code contract `Assert` and `Assume` methods
- ▸ Creating code contract `ForAll` method
- ▸ Creating code contract `ValueAtReturn` method
- ▸ Creating code contract `Result` method
- ▸ Using code contracts on abstract classes
- ▸ Using contract abbreviator methods
- ▸ Creating tests using IntelliTest
- ▸ Using code contracts in extension methods

Introduction

You might be wondering what code contracts are exactly. To explain it in layman's terms, a code contract is a definition that you add to your methods. It tells the compilers that the method under contract will always adhere to specific conditions. An example of this is that the method will never return a null value to the calling code or that the method will always expect a parameter greater than a specific value. If any of these conditions are not met, your code can emit an exception, and the developer integrating with your class will be prompted to refine their calling code. On the flip side, when a developer calls your class, they can be sure that the method under contract will always behave in a specific way and never deviate from it.

Code contracts really stand out when working within a team of developers, but implementing this technology in a single-developer solution will only improve your code.

Downloading, installing, and integrating code contracts into Visual Studio

Before you can use code contracts in your applications, you need to download and install them. The easiest way of doing this is via extensions and updates. After the installation is complete, you will need to define a few settings for the code contracts to start functioning against the code they are implemented in. Let's have a look at the following recipe.

Getting ready

First, we will create a new class and add it to our Visual Studio project. We will then get the Code Contracts installer and install it for our project.

How to do it...

1. Create a new class by right-clicking on your solution and selecting **Add** and then **New Project** from the context menu:

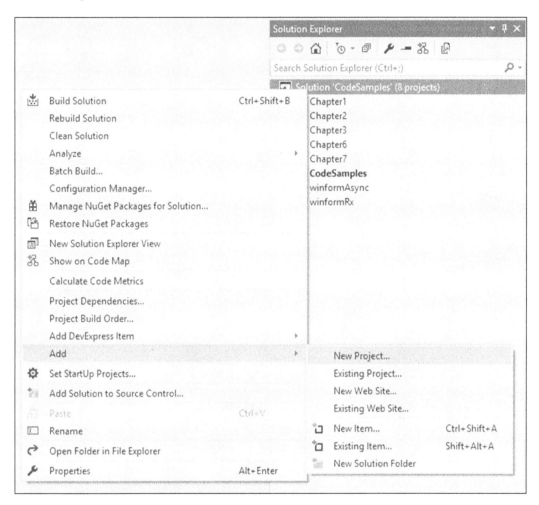

2. From the **Add New Project** dialog screen, select **Class Library** from the installed templates and call your class Chapter8:

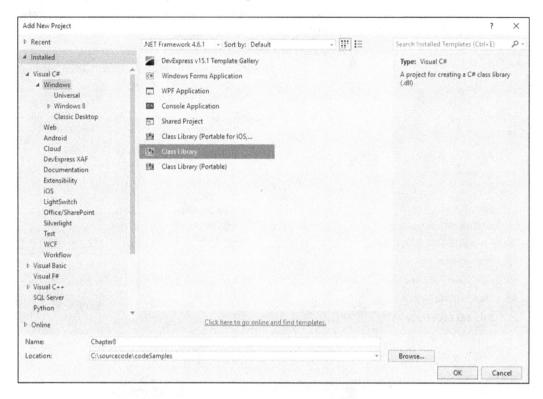

3. Your new class library will be added to your solution with a default name of Class1. cs, which we renamed to Recipes.cs in order to distinguish the code properly. You can, however, rename your class to whatever you like.

4. To rename your class, simply click on the class name in **Solution Explorer** and select **Rename** from the context menu:

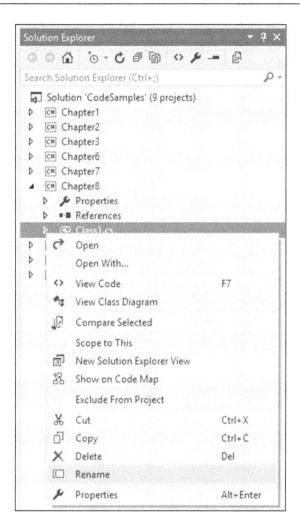

5. Visual Studio will ask you to confirm a rename of all references to the code element **Class1** in the project. Just click on **Yes**:

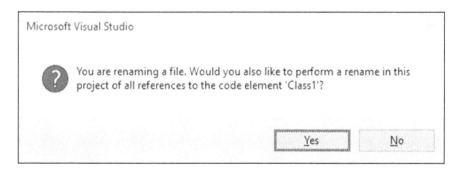

6. Next, click on the **Tools** menu and select **Extensions and Updates...**:

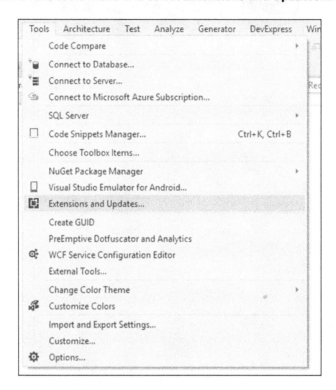

7. You will see the **Extensions and Updates** window appear. Be sure to click on the **Visual Studio Gallery** on the left-hand side and type Code Contracts as the search term. If you have not got the Code Contracts installer, you will see a download button appear on the **Code Contracts for .NET** result. Click on it to download and install code contracts:

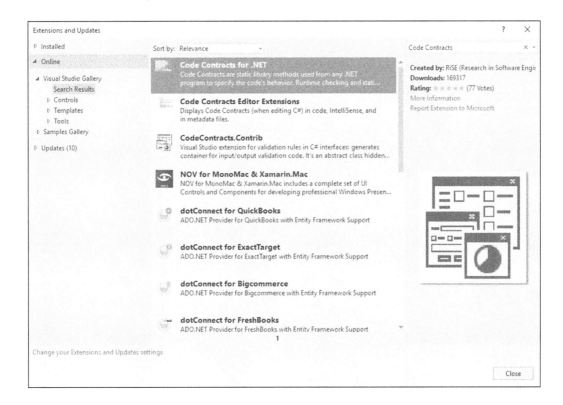

8. After code contracts have been installed, you might need to restart Visual Studio. After doing this, right-click on the `Chapter8` project and select **Properties** from the context menu:

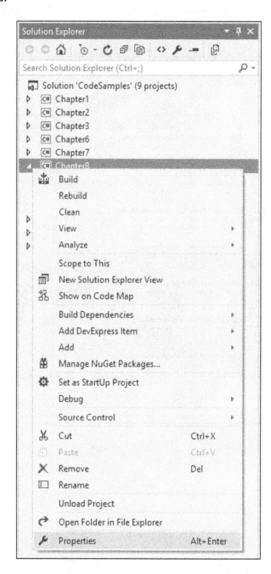

9. You will notice that a new **Code Contracts** tab has been added to the properties page for your `Chapter8` project. Click on this tab and make sure that **Perform Runtime Contract Checking** is checked. Then, save your changes and close the properties page:

10. Finally, add a reference to your `Chapter8` project in the console application created earlier. Do this by expanding your console application project and right-clicking on the **References** item. Select **Add Reference** from the context menu:

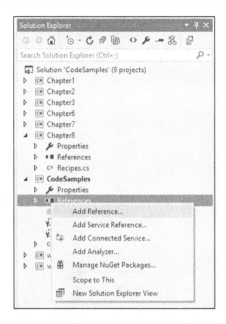

11. Make sure that you have selected `Chapter8` in the project references section and click on **OK**:

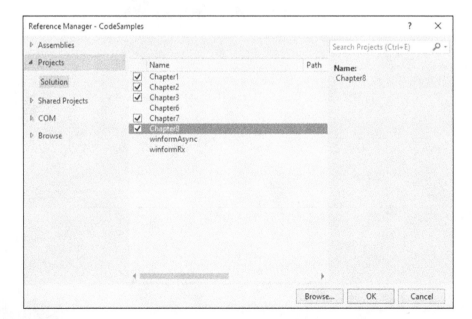

How it works...

You have now installed and configured the minimum requirements to enable code contracts in your `Chapter8` class. You can now go ahead and build your solution to make sure that everything builds successfully.

Creating code contract preconditions

Preconditions allow you to control exactly what the parameters need to look like before they are used in your method. This means that you can assume a lot of things about the data being sent to your method by the calling code. You can, for example, specify that a parameter should never be null or that a value must always be within a specific value range. Dates can be checked, and objects can be verified and vetted.

You have complete control over the data coming in to your method. It gives you the peace of mind to use that data once it has passed your contract without having to do additional checks.

Getting ready

Be sure that you have installed code contracts and that you have configured the settings correctly in the project properties, as described in the previous recipe.

How to do it...

1. In your `Recipes` class, create a new method called `ValueGreaterThanZero()` and have it take an integer as a parameter:

```
public static class Recipes
{
    public static void ValueGreaterThanZero(int
    iNonZeroValue)
    {

    }
}
```

2. In the `ValueGreaterThanZero()` method, type the start of the `Contract` declaration, and you will notice that the code is underlined with a red squiggly line. Hold down *Crtl +* . (period) to bring up the suggestions for potential fixes. Click on the suggestion to add the `using` statement for the code contracts to your class:

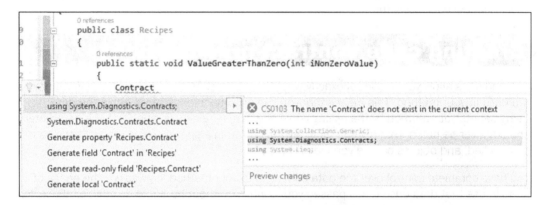

3. When you have done that, continue entering the precondition. Define that the parameter value must be greater than zero:

```
public static void ValueGreaterThanZero(int iNonZeroValue)
{
    Contract.Requires(iNonZeroValue >= 1, "Parameter
    iNonZeroValue not greater than zero");
}
```

4. If you go back to the console application, add the following `using` statements:

```
using static System.Console;
using static Chapter8.Recipes;
```

5. Since we have created a static class and brought it into scope with the `using` statement, you can just call the method name in the `Recipes` class directly. To see how code contracts work, pass a zero parameter to the method:

```
try
{
    ValueGreaterThanZero(0);
}
catch (Exception ex)
{
    WriteLine(ex.Message);
    ReadLine();
}
```

6. Finally, run your console application and see the exception generated:

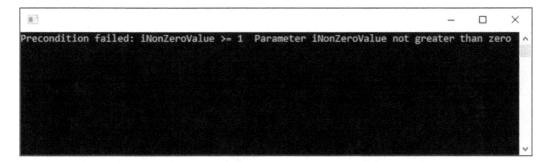

How it works...

The code contract has inspected the precondition and determined that the parameter value passed to the method under contract failed the precondition check. An exception is thrown and output to the console window.

Creating code contract postconditions

Just as code contract preconditions control what information is passed to the method under contract, code contract postconditions control what information the method under contract returns to the calling code. You can, therefore, specify that the method will never return a null value or an empty dataset, for example. The actual condition does not matter; this is something that will change on a case-by-case basis. The important thing to remember here is that this code contract allows you to have more control over the data returned by your code.

Getting ready

Assume that the method under contract needs to ensure that the value returned will always be greater than zero. Using a code contract postcondition, we can easily enforce this rule.

How to do it...

1. Before you start, make sure that you have added the following `using` statement to the top of your `Recipes` class:

```
using System.Diagnostics.Contracts;
```

2. In the `Recipes` class, add a method called `NeverReturnZero()` and pass an integer parameter to this method:

```
public static class Recipes
{
    public static int NeverReturnZero(int iNonZeroValue)
    {

    }
}
```

3. Inside the method, add your postcondition contract. As one could expect, the method in the contract class is called `Ensures`. This is quite descriptive of its function. The code contract ensures that a specific method result is never returned. You can see this in the signature of the `Contract.Ensures` method. The postcondition, therefore, ensures that the result of this method will never be zero:

```
public static int NeverReturnZero(int iNonZeroValue)
{
    Contract.Ensures(Contract.Result<int>() > 0, "The value
    returned was not greater than zero");

    return iNonZeroValue - 1;
}
```

4. Go back to the console application, and add the following `using` statements:

```
using static System.Console;
using static Chapter8.Recipes;
```

5. Since you have created a static class and brought it into scope with the `using` statement, you can just call the method name in the `Recipes` class directly. Pass the `NeverReturnZero()` method a value of 1:

```
try
{
    NeverReturnZero(1);
}
catch (Exception ex)
{
    WriteLine(ex.Message);
    ReadLine();
}
```

6. Finally, run your console application and review the output in the console window:

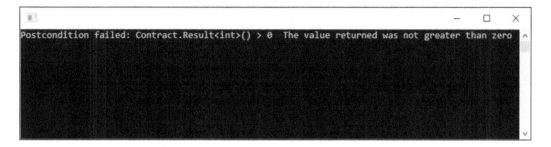

How it works...

When the value of 1 was passed to the method under contract, it resulted in a return value of zero being returned. We forced this by subtracting 1 from the parameter passed to the method. As the method ensures non-zero values, an exception was thrown with the message we defined.

Creating code contract invariant

Something that is defined as invariant tells us that it will never change. It will always be the same, no matter what. This brings up a vast array of use cases if we consider this in the context of code contracts. The invariant code contract is basically used to validate the internal state of a class. So, what do we mean by the "internal state?" Well, the properties of the class give that class a specific state. Let's assume that we wanted to guarantee that the properties of the class we are using only accept specific values, thereby assuring the internal state of that class. This is where the code contract invariant comes into play.

Getting ready

You can understand the use of the invariant better with the use of the following example. Assume that the class needs to store dates. We can't ever store a date in the past though. Any date used in the class must be a current or future date.

How to do it...

1. Before you go on, ensure that you have added the code contracts `using` statement to the top of your `Recipes.cs` class file:

    ```
    using System.Diagnostics.Contracts;
    ```

2. Next, we will add a new class called `InvariantClassState` to the `Recipes.cs` class file. This is so that we can create an instance class and not a static class:

```
public class InvariantClassState
{

}
```

3. Add the following `private` properties to your `InvariantClassState` class that will accept integer values for the year, month, and day:

```
private int _Year { get; set; }
private int _Month { get; set; }
private int _Day { get; set; }
```

4. We will now add a constructor to our `InvariantClassState` class. The constructor will accept parameters to set the properties created earlier:

```
public InvariantClassState(int year, int month, int day)
{
    _Year = year;
    _Month = month;
    _Day = day;
}
```

 If you create `public` properties, it is always a good practice to create them with `private` setters such as `public int Value { get; private set; }`.

5. The next method we need to add is the contract invariant method. You can call this method any name you like, and in this example, it is called `Invariants()`. You will read many developers stating that a commonly accepted practice is to call this method `ObjectInvariant()`. The naming of this method, however, has no impact on the invariant code contract. You will notice that we decorate this method with `[ContractInvariantMethod]`, and it is this that defines this method (whatever the name) as the invariant code contract. Another important thing to remember is that the invariant code contract method must be a `void` method and be specified as a `private` method.

Inside our code contract invariant method, we now specify which properties are invariant. In other words, those properties that can never be any other value than what we specify inside this code contract invariant method. For starters, we will specify that the year value cannot be in the past. We will also ensure that the month value is a valid value between 1 and 12. Finally, we will specify that the day value cannot be a value outside the days contained in the month supplied or a value less than 1:

```
[ContractInvariantMethod]
private void Invariants()
{
```

```
        Contract.Invariant(this._Year >= DateTime.Now.Year);
        Contract.Invariant(this._Month <= 12);
        Contract.Invariant(this._Month >= 1);
        Contract.Invariant(this._Day >= 1);
        Contract.Invariant(this._Day <=
        DateTime.DaysInMonth(_Year, _Month);
    }
```

6. You can further extend the `Contract.Invariant` methods by supplying an exception message. Your `Invariants()` method will then look like this:

```
[ContractInvariantMethod]
private void Invariants()
{
    Contract.Invariant(this._Year >= DateTime.Now.Year,
    "The supplied year is in the past");
    Contract.Invariant(this._Month <= 12, $"The value
    {_Month} is not a valid Month value");
    Contract.Invariant(this._Month >= 1, $"The value
    {_Month} is not a valid Month value");
    Contract.Invariant(this._Day >= 1, $"The value {_Day}
    is not a valid calendar value");
    Contract.Invariant(this._Day <=
    DateTime.DaysInMonth(_Year, _Month), $"The month given
    does not contain {_Day} days");
}
```

7. Finally, add another method that returns the date formatted as month/day/year:

```
public string ReturnGivenMonthDayYearDate()
{
    return $"{_Month}/{_Day}/{_Year}";
}
```

8. When you are finished, your `InvariantClassState` class will look like this:

```
public class InvariantClassState
{
    private int _Year { get; set; }
    private int _Month { get; set; }
    private int _Day { get; set; }

    public InvariantClassState(int year, int month, int
    day)
    {
        _Year = year;
        _Month = month;
        _Day = day;
```

```
        }

        [ContractInvariantMethod]
        private void Invariants()
        {
            Contract.Invariant(this._Year >= DateTime.Now.Year,
            "The supplied year is in the past");
            Contract.Invariant(this._Month <= 12, $"The value
            {_Month} is not a valid Month value");
            Contract.Invariant(this._Month >= 1, $"The value
            {_Month} is not a valid Month value");
            Contract.Invariant(this._Day >= 1, $"The value
            {_Day} is not a valid calendar value");
            Contract.Invariant(this._Day <=
            DateTime.DaysInMonth(_Year, _Month), $"The month
            given does not contain {_Day} days");
        }

        public string ReturnGivenMonthDayYearDate()
        {
            return $"{_Month}/{_Day}/{_Year}";
        }
    }
```

9. Head back to the console application and add the following using statement to your console application Program.cs file:

```
using Chapter8;
```

10. We will now add a new instance of our InvariantStateClass class and pass the values to the constructor. First, pass the current year less than 1 to the constructor. This will result in the last year being passed to the constructor:

```
try
{
    InvariantClassState oInv = new
    InvariantClassState(DateTime.Now.Year - 1, 13, 32);
    string returnedDate =
    oInv.ReturnGivenMonthDayYearDate();
    WriteLine(returnedDate);
}
catch (Exception ex)
{
    WriteLine(ex.Message);
}
ReadLine();
```

11. Running your console application will result in the code contract invariant throwing an exception because the year passed to the constructor is in the past:

```
Invariant failed: this.Year >= DateTime.Now.Year   The supplied year is in the past
```

12. Let's modify our code by passing a valid year value to the constructor, but keep the rest of the parameter values the same:

```
try
{
    InvariantClassState oInv = new
    InvariantClassState(DateTime.Now.Year, 13, 32);
    string returnedDate =
    oInv.ReturnGivenMonthDayYearDate();

    WriteLine(returnedDate);
}
catch (Exception ex)
{
    WriteLine(ex.Message);
}
ReadLine();
```

13. Running the console application will again result in an exception message stating that the month value cannot be greater then `12`:

```
Invariant failed: this._Month <= 12   The value 13 is not a valid Month value
```

14. Once again, modify the parameters passed to the method and supply a valid year and month value, but pass an invalid day value:

```
try
{
    InvariantClassState oInv = new
    InvariantClassState(DateTime.Now.Year, 11, 32);
    string returnedDate =
    oInv.ReturnGivenMonthDayYearDate();

    WriteLine(returnedDate);
}
catch (Exception ex)
{
    WriteLine(ex.Message);
}
ReadLine();
```

15. Running the console application again will result in the code contract invariant throwing an exception because the day is clearly wrong. No month contains 32 days:

```
Invariant failed: this._Day <= DateTime.DaysInMonth(_Year, _Month)   The month given does not contain 32 days
```

16. Modify the parameters passed to the constructor again, and this time, add valid values for year, month, and day:

```
try
{
    InvariantClassState oInv = new
    InvariantClassState(DateTime.Now.Year, 11, 25);
    string returnedDate =
    oInv.ReturnGivenMonthDayYearDate();

    WriteLine(returnedDate);
}
catch (Exception ex)
{
    WriteLine(ex.Message);
}
ReadLine();
```

17. Because November 25, 2016 is a valid date (because the current year is 2016), the formatted date is returned to the console application window:

18. Let's mix things up a little by passing 29 February, 2017 to the constructor:

```
try
{
    InvariantClassState oInv = new
    InvariantClassState(DateTime.Now.Year + 1, 2, 29);
    string returnedDate =
    oInv.ReturnGivenMonthDayYearDate();

    WriteLine(returnedDate);
}
catch (Exception ex)
{
    WriteLine(ex.Message);
}
ReadLine();
```

19. Again, the code contract invariant method throws an exception because 2017 is not a leap year:

How it works...

The code contract invariant method is a simple yet effective way to ensure that the state of your class is not modified. You can then assume that the properties you use inside your class are always correct and will never contain unexpected values. We like to think of the code contract invariant as a type of immutable (which it isn't). Strings are immutable, which means that the original value is never modified when the value changes. A new space in memory is always created when you change the value of a string. Similarly, this reminds me of the properties defined as invariant. These property values can never change to values other than those defined by our code contract invariant method.

Creating code contract Assert and Assume methods

The code contract `Assert` and `Assume` methods might seem confusing at first, but both provide a specific function. Where the previous code contract conditions had to appear at the beginning of the methods they were defined in, the `Assert` method can be placed somewhere inside a method. This means that it will have an effect on the code at that specific time in the compilation. If you, for example, perform a calculation somewhere in your method under contract and you need to check the value calculated, you can use `Assert` to perform a check in place to ascertain whether the calculated value passes the contract.

 Don't confuse `Debug.Assert` with `Contract.Assert`. They aren't the same thing. `Debug.Assert` will only have an effect if your code is run in the **Debug** mode. `Contract.Assert` will run in the **Debug** and **Release** modes.

With `Contract.Assume`, however, we are telling the code contract that it needs to assume that the condition it needs to check is true. This is only applicable when the static checker is switched on, and this will become clearer in this recipe.

Getting ready

We will use the same method under contract to illustrate the use of `Assert` and `Assume` methods with the static checker switched on.

How to do it...

1. Before you go on, ensure that you have added the code contracts `using` statement to the top of your `Recipes.cs` class file:

    ```
    using System.Diagnostics.Contracts;
    ```

2. Add a method called `ValueIsValid()` to the class, which accepts two integer parameters:

    ```
    public static int ValueIsValid(int valueForCalc, int
    valueToDivide)
    {

    }
    ```

3. To this method, add a calculation (it appears first in the method before the contract) that subtracts 1 from the `valueForCalc` parameter. The `Contract.Assert` method is placed after the calculation to check the value of the calculated value. We want to ensure that the value is not zero:

    ```
    public static int ValueIsValid(int valueForCalc, int
    valueToDivide)
    {
        int calculatedVal = valueForCalc - 1;
        Contract.Assert(calculatedVal >= 1, "Calculated value
        will result in divide by zero exception.");
        return valueToDivide / calculatedVal;
    }
    ```

4. In the console application, add the relevant `using` statement to the `Program.cs` class to bring the static class into scope:

    ```
    using static Chapter8.Recipes;
    ```

5. Call the `ValueIsValid()` method by passing two integer values to it. As you can see, the first parameter will result in a zero value being calculated inside the method under contract:

    ```
    try
    {
        int calcVal = ValueIsValid(1, 9);
    }
    catch (Exception ex)
    {
        WriteLine(ex.Message);
        ReadLine();
    }
    ```

6. Run your console application and inspect the output window. We can see that the `Assert` contract correctly threw an exception because the calculated value was zero:

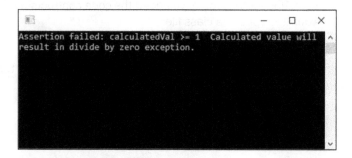

7. However, what if we want our code to be checked when we build our application? This is where the static checker comes into play. Right-click on the `Chapter8` project and select **Properties**:

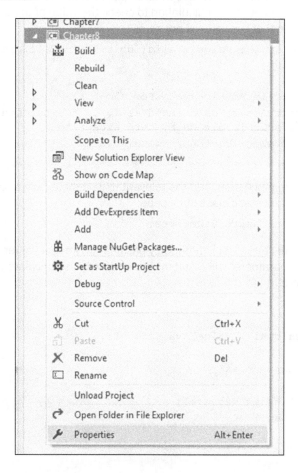

8. Click on the **Code Contracts** tab and select the checkbox next to **Perform Static Contract Checking**. Also, uncheck the **Check in background** box and select **Fail build on warnings**. Moreover, set **Warning Level** to **hi**:

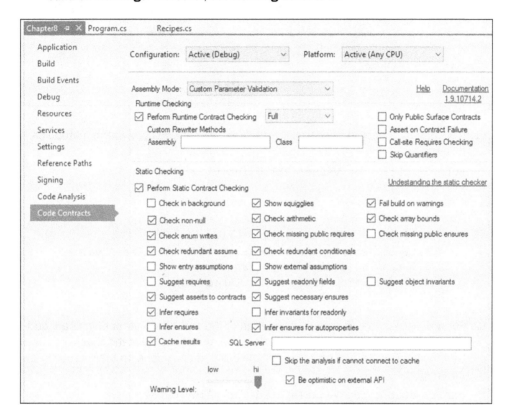

 We assume that the developers of Code Contracts meant to make the warning level between low and high. "Hi" is probably a typo in the code.

9. Save your code contract settings and run your console application. You will notice that your build fails:

10. If we have a look at the `ValueIsValid()` method, we can see that the static checker has identified that the method under contract needs an additional contract defined. The static checker has identified that we need to add `Contract.Requires` to our method to check whether the `valueForCalc` parameter is greater than zero:

```
1 reference
public static int ValueIsValid(int valueForCalc, int valueToDivide)
{
    int calculatedVal = valueForCalc - 1;
    CodeContracts: Missing precondition in an externally visible method. Consider adding Contract.Requires((valueForCalc - 1) >= 1); for parameter validation
}
```

11. If we had to correct this, we would add `Contract.Requires` to the method as follows:

```
public static int ValueIsValid(int valueForCalc, int
valueToDivide)
{
    Contract.Requires((valueForCalc - 1) >= 1);
    int calculatedVal = valueForCalc - 1;
    Contract.Assert(calculatedVal >= 1, "Calculated value
    will result in divide by zero exception.");
    return valueToDivide / calculatedVal;
}
```

12. For now, let's ignore the recommendation of the static checker and, instead, add `Contract.Assume` to our method. Here, we are telling the static checker to assume that the value will never be zero after the calculation is done on the `valueForCalc` parameter:

```
public static int ValueIsValid(int valueForCalc, int
valueToDivide)
{
    Contract.Assume((valueForCalc - 1) >= 1);
    int calculatedVal = valueForCalc - 1;
    Contract.Assert(calculatedVal >= 1, "Calculated value
    will result in divide by zero exception.");
    return valueToDivide / calculatedVal;
}
```

13. If we run our console application again, we will get a clean build, because the static checker assumes that you know best and that the value will never equal zero after the calculation. If, however, the calculated value turns out to be zero, `Assume` still checks the value at runtime and will throw an exception if the value equals zero:

How it works...

You might be wondering what the use of `Assume` in code contracts is. As it turns out, this is quite useful when working with code that you have no control over. If you implement code that you can't edit or that does not contain code contracts, you can tell the static checker to ignore specific portions of the code that produce errors based on the check it does.

Creating code contract ForAll method

If this code contract sounds like it is validating some or the other collection, then you would be correct. The code contract `ForAll` will perform validation of `IEnumerable` collections. This is very handy, because as a developer, you do not need to do any kind of iteration over the collection and writing validation logic. This contract does it for you.

Getting ready

We will create a simple list of integers and populate the list with values. Our code contract will validate that the list does not contain any zero values.

How to do it...

1. Before you go on, ensure that you have added the code contracts `using` statement to the top of your `Recipes.cs` class file:

    ```
    using System.Diagnostics.Contracts;
    ```

2. Add a method called `ValidateList()` to your class and pass a `List<int>` collection to it:

    ```
    public static void ValidateList(List<int> lstValues)
    {

    }
    ```

3. Inside the `ValidateList()` method, add the `Contract.ForAll` contract. Interestingly, you will notice that we are using `Contract.Assert` here to check whether this list passes our contract conditions. The `Contract.ForAll` will use a lambda expression to check that none of the values contained in our list of integers equals zero:

```
public static void ValidateList(List<int> lstValues)
{
    Contract.Assert(Contract.ForAll(lstValues, n => n !=
    0), "Zero values are not allowed");
}
```

4. In the console application, add the relevant `using` statement to the `Program.cs` class to bring the static class into scope:

```
using static Chapter8.Recipes;
```

5. You can then add a simple list of integers containing at least one zero value and pass it to the `ValidateList()` method:

```
try
{
    List<int> intList = new List<int>();
    int[] arr;
    intList.AddRange(arr = new int[] { 1, 3, 2, 6, 0, 5});
    ValidateList(intList);
}
catch (Exception ex)
{
    WriteLine(ex.Message);
    ReadLine();
}
```

6. Run the console application and inspect the results in the output:

How it works...

We can see that the `ForAll` contract has worked exactly as we had expected. This is an extremely useful code contract to use, especially since you need not add copious amounts of boilerplate code to check the collection for various invalid values.

Creating code contract ValueAtReturn method

The best example we can think of when using the code contract `ValueAtReturn` is `out` parameters. Personally, I do not use `out` parameters often, but there are times when you need to use them. Code contracts make provision for this, and you can check the value at the time it is returned.

Getting ready

We will create a simple method that subtracts a value from a parameter. The `out` parameter will be validated by the code contract, and the result will be output to the console window.

How to do it...

1. Before you go on, ensure that you have added the code contracts `using` statement to the top of your `Recipes.cs` class file:

```
using System.Diagnostics.Contracts;
```

2. In the `Recipes` class, create a new method called `ValidOutValue()` and pass an `out` parameter called `secureValue` to it:

```
public static void ValidOutValue(out int secureValue)
{

}
```

3. Finally, add `Contract.ValueAtReturn` to the method. Interestingly, you will note that this needs to be contained in `Contract.Ensures`. This actually makes sense, because the code contract ensures that the value that we will return will adhere to a specific condition:

```
public static void ValidOutValue(out int secureValue)
{
    Contract.Ensures(Contract.ValueAtReturn<int>(out
    secureValue) >= 1, "The secure value is less or equal
    to zero");
    secureValue = secureValue - 10;
}
```

4. In the console application, add the relevant `using` statement to the `Program.cs` class to bring the static class into scope:

    ```
    using static Chapter8.Recipes;
    ```

5. Then, add some code to call the `ValidOutValue()` method and pass an `out` parameter to it:

    ```
    try
    {
        int valueToCheck = 5;
        ValidOutValue(out valueToCheck);
        WriteLine("The value is not zero");
    }
    catch (Exception ex)
    {
        WriteLine(ex.Message);
    }
    ReadLine();
    ```

6. Run the console application and inspect the results in the output window:

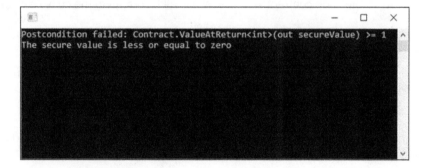

```
Postcondition failed: Contract.ValueAtReturn<int>(out secureValue) >= 1
The secure value is less or equal to zero
```

How it works...

We can see that the `out` parameter has been successfully validated. As soon as the condition was not met, the code contract threw an exception that we were able to catch.

Creating code contract Result method

Sometimes, we simply want a way to validate the result of a method. We want to be able to check what is returned and validate it against some or the other condition. It is here that the code contract `Result` can be used. It will inspect the value returned by the method under contract against the contract specified, and then it will succeed or fail.

How to do it...

1. Before you go on, ensure that you have added the code contracts `using` statement to the top of your `Recipes.cs` class file:

```
using System.Diagnostics.Contracts;
```

2. In the `Recipes` class, add a new method called `ValidateResult()` that takes two integer values as parameters:

```
public static int ValidateResult(int value1, int value2)
{


}
```

3. To this method, add the code contract `Result` that checks the resultant value of the method. It has to be mentioned that the code contract `Result` can never be used in a `void` method. This is obvious, because the very purpose of this code contract is to examine and validate the result of a method. You will also notice that the code contract `Result` method is used in conjunction with the `Contract.Ensures` method. The format of `Contract.Result` is made up of the return type `<int>()` and the condition `>= 0` that the return value needs to adhere to:

```
public static int ValidateResult(int value1, int value2)
{
    Contract.Ensures(Contract.Result<int>() >= 0, "Negative
    result not allowed");
    return value1 - value2;
}
```

4. In the console application, add the relevant `using` statement to the `Program.cs` class to bring the static class into scope:

```
using static Chapter8.Recipes;
```

5. Add the call to the static method under contract and pass to it parameters that will cause the code contract to throw an exception. In this case, we are passing `10` and `23`, which will result in a negative result being returned from the `ValidateResult()` method:

```
try
{
    WriteLine(ValidateResult(10, 23));
}
catch (Exception ex)
{
    WriteLine(ex.Message);
}
ReadLine();
```

6. Finally, run the console application and inspect the result returned to the console output window:

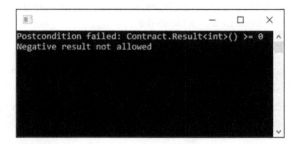

How it works...

You will see that the code contract has inspected the resultant value of the `ValidateResult()` method and found that it contravenes the contract. An exception is then thrown and displayed in the console window.

Using code contracts on abstract classes

If you use abstract classes in your code, you will know that being able to control how they are used with code contracts will result in more robust code. But how exactly can we use code contracts with abstract classes? Especially since abstract classes are supposed to contain no implementation? Well, it is definitely possible, and here is how we do it.

Getting ready

If you have not worked with abstract classes before, we advise you to first read *Chapter 2, Classes and Generics*, to familiarise yourself with how abstract classes are used and created.

How to do it...

1. Before you go on, ensure that you have added the code contracts `using` statement to the top of your `Recipes.cs` class file:

   ```
   using System.Diagnostics.Contracts;
   ```

2. Create an abstract class called `Shape` that defines two methods called `Length()` and `Width()` which each take an integer value as a parameter. Remember that abstract classes contain no implementation:

   ```
   public abstract class Shape
   {
   ```

```
        public abstract void Length(int value);
        public abstract void Width(int value);
    }
```

3. Create another abstract class called `ShapeContract` that inherits the `Shape` abstract class. It is here that our code contracts will reside:

```
public abstract class ShapeContract : Shape
{

}
```

4. Override the `Length()` and `Width()` methods of the `Shape` abstract class and ensure that they require a non-zero parameter:

```
public abstract class ShapeContract : Shape
{
    public override void Length(int value)
    {
        Contract.Requires(value > 0, "Length must be
        greater than zero");
    }

    public override void Width(int value)
    {
        Contract.Requires(value > 0, "Width must be greater
        than zero");
    }
}
```

5. We now need to associate the `ShapeContract` contract class to the `Shape` abstract class. We will do this via the use of attributes. Add the following attribute to the top of your `Shape` abstract class:

```
[ContractClass(typeof(ShapeContract))]
```

6. After doing this, your `Shape` abstract class will look like this:

```
[ContractClass(typeof(ShapeContract))]
public abstract class Shape
{
    public abstract void Length(int value);
    public abstract void Width(int value);
}
```

7. We also need to associate the `Shape` abstract class to the `ShapeContract` abstract class as a means of telling the compiler which class the contracts need to act upon. We will do this by adding the following attribute to the top of the `ShapeContract` class:

```
[ContractClassFor(typeof(Shape))]
```

8. When you have done this, your `ShapeContract` class will look like this:

```
[ContractClassFor(typeof(Shape))]
public abstract class ShapeContract : Shape
{
    public override void Length(int value)
    {
        Contract.Requires(value > 0, "Length must be
        greater than zero");
    }

    public override void Width(int value)
    {
        Contract.Requires(value > 0, "Width must be greater
        than zero");
    }
}
```

9. We are now ready to implement the `Shape` abstract class. Create a new class called `Rectangle` and inherit the `Shape` abstract class:

```
public class Rectangle : Shape
{

}
```

10. You will notice that Visual Studio underlines the `Rectangle` class with a red squiggly line. This is because no implementation of the `Shape` class exists yet. Hover your mouse cursor over the red squiggly line and look at the lightbulb pop-up suggestion provided by Visual Studio:

11. By holding down *Ctrl + .* (period), you will see the suggested fixes that you can implement to correct the error that Visual Studio is warning you about. In this instance, there is only a single fix that Visual Studio suggests we implement, which is to implement the abstract class:

```
class Rectangle : Shape
    💡 ▾
        Implement Abstract Class        ▸    ⊗ CS0534 'Rectangle' does not implement inherited abstract member
                                                 'Shape.Width(int)'
                                             ...
                                             {
                                                 public override void Length(int value)
                                                 {
                                                     throw new NotImplementedException();
                                                 }

                                                 public override void Width(int value)
                                                 {
                                                     throw new NotImplementedException();
                                                 }
                                             }
                                             ...

                                             Preview changes
                                             Fix all occurrences in: Document | Project | Solution
```

12. After you have clicked on the **Implement Abstract Class** suggestion in the lightbulb suggestion, Visual Studio will insert the implementation of the `Shape` abstract class. You will notice that the methods inserted for you still don't contain any implementation and will throw `NotImplementedException` if you don't add any implementation to the `Length()` and `Width()` methods:

```
0 references
public class Rectangle : Shape
{
    3 references
    public override void Length(int value)
    {
        throw new NotImplementedException();
    }

    3 references
    public override void Width(int value)
    {
        throw new NotImplementedException();
    }
}
```

13. To add implementation to our `Rectangle` class, create two properties for the `Length()` and `Width()` methods and set these properties equal to the value of the supplied parameter value:

```
public class Rectangle : Shape
{
    private int _length { get; set; }
    private int _width { get; set; }
    public override void Length(int value)
    {
        _length = value;
    }

    public override void Width(int value)
    {
        _width = value;
    }
}
```

14. In the console application, add the relevant `using` statement to the `Program.cs` class to bring the `Chapter8` class into scope:

```
using Chapter8;
```

15. Create a new instance of the `Rectangle` class and pass some values to the `Length()` and `Width()` methods of the `Rectangle` class:

```
try
{
    Rectangle oRectangle = new Rectangle();
    oRectangle.Length(0);
    oRectangle.Width(1);
}
catch (Exception ex)
{
    WriteLine(ex.Message);
}
ReadLine();
```

16. Finally, run the console application and inspect the output window:

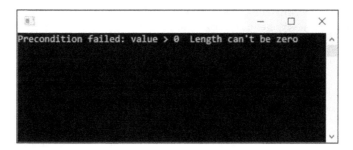

How it works...

As we have added a zero value to the `Length()` method, the code contract on the abstract class has correctly thrown an exception. Being able to implement code contracts on abstract classes allows developers to create better code, especially when working in teams where you need to convey implementation limitations based on certain business rules.

Using contract abbreviator methods

Abbreviator methods are a great addition to the features of code contracts. They allow us to create a single abbreviator method that contains often used or grouped code contracts. This means that we can simplify our code and make it more readable.

Getting ready

We will create two methods with the same code contract requirements. We will then simplify the methods under contract by implementing an abbreviator method to contain the code contracts.

How to do it...

1. Before you go on, ensure that you have added the code contracts `using` statement to the top of your `Recipes.cs` class file:

   ```
   using System.Diagnostics.Contracts;
   ```

2. Consider the following methods before you add them. We have two methods here, and each method requires that the parameter passed to it is not equal to zero and that the result is also not zero. The implementation within each method is different, but the code contracts applied are identical. To avoid a situation where code contracts are unnecessarily repeated, we can use abbreviator methods:

   ```
   public static int MethodOne(int value)
   {
   ```

```
        Contract.Requires(value > 0, "Parameter must be greater
        than zero");
        Contract.Ensures(Contract.Result<int>() > 0, "Method
        result must be greater than zero");

        return value - 1;
    }

    public static int MethodTwo(int value)
    {
        Contract.Requires(value > 0, "Parameter must be greater
        than zero");
        Contract.Ensures(Contract.Result<int>() > 0, "Method
        result must be greater than zero");

        return (value * 10) - 10;
    }
```

3. Add a new method called `StandardMethodContract()` to your `Recipes` class. This method's name can be anything you like, but the signature needs to match the methods it abbreviates. Inside this method, add the required code contracts defined earlier in `MethodOne()` and `MethodTwo()`:

```
private static void StandardMethodContract(int value)
{
    Contract.Requires(value > 0, "Parameter must be greater
    than zero");
    Contract.Ensures(Contract.Result<int>() >= 1, "Method
    result must be greater than zero");
}
```

4. Add the following attribute to the top of the `StandardMethodContract()` method to identify it as an abbreviator method:

```
[ContractAbbreviator]
```

5. Once you have done this, your abbreviator method should look like this:

```
[ContractAbbreviator]
private static void StandardMethodContract(int value)
{
    Contract.Requires(value > 0, "Parameter must be greater
    than zero");
    Contract.Ensures(Contract.Result<int>() >= 1, "Method
    result must be greater than zero");
}
```

6. You can now go ahead and simplify `MethodOne()` and `MethodTwo()` by simply referencing the abbreviator method in place of the code contracts:

```
public static int MethodOne(int value)
{
    StandardMethodContract(value);

    return value - 1;
}

public static int MethodTwo(int value)
{
    StandardMethodContract(value);

    return (value * 10) - 10;
}
```

7. In the console application, add the relevant `using` statement to the `Program.cs` class to bring the static class into scope:

```
using static Chapter8.Recipes;
```

8. First, call the two methods using the following parameters:

```
try
{
    MethodOne(0);
    MethodTwo(1);
}
catch (Exception ex)
{
    WriteLine(ex.Message);
}
ReadLine();
```

9. If you run your console application, you will notice that the code contract throws an exception in the abbreviator contract, telling us that the supplied parameter can't be zero:

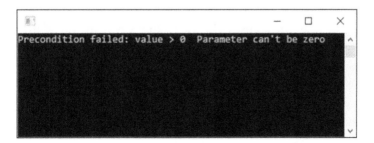

10. Then, modify your calling code and pass a valid value for `MethodOne()`, but leave the call to `MethodTwo()` as is. Run your console application again:

```
try
{
    MethodOne(200);
    MethodTwo(1);
}
catch (Exception ex)
{
    WriteLine(ex.Message);
}
ReadLine();
```

11. This time, you will see that the code contract in the abbreviator method throws an exception on the return value that can't be zero:

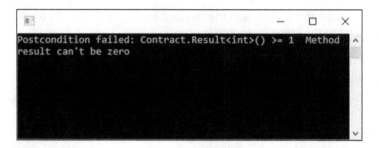

How it works...

Abbreviator methods allow us to create more readable code and to group often used code contracts in a common method decorated with the `[ContractAbbreviator]` attribute. Abbreviator methods are a powerful feature of code contracts that developers can utilize to produce better code.

Creating tests using IntelliTest

IntelliTest allows developers to create and run tests against their code contracts. This allows developers to create the most robust code possible by creating additional code contracts to pass the test failures reported by IntelliTest. One thing to note, however, is that IntelliTest is included in the Visual Studio Enterprise only.

Getting ready

You will need to use Visual Studio Enterprise 2015 to be able to create and run IntelliTests.

How to do it...

1. Before you go on, ensure that you have added the code contracts `using` statement to the top of your `Recipes.cs` class file:

```
using System.Diagnostics.Contracts;
```

2. Add a new class called `CodeContractTests` to your `Recipes.cs` file:

```
public class CodeContractTests
{

}
```

3. Then, add a method called `Calculate()` to the `CodeContractTests` class and pass two integer values as parameters to the `Calculate()` method. Inside the `Calculate()` method, add a code contract to ensure that the result from this method is never equal to zero:

```
public class CodeContractTests
{
    public int Calculate(int valueOne, int valueTwo)
    {
        Contract.Ensures(Contract.Result<int>() >= 1, "");

        return valueOne / valueTwo;
    }
}
```

4. Select the `Calculate()` method and right-click on it. From the context menu, click on the **Create IntelliTest** menu item:

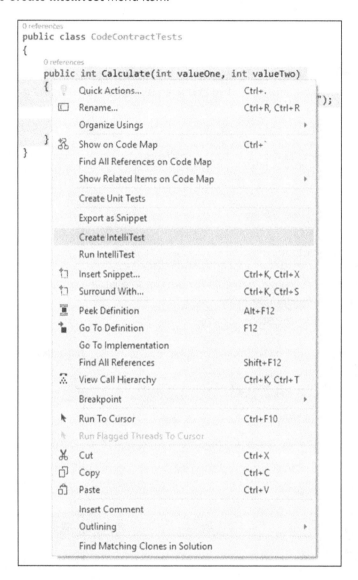

5. Visual Studio will then show the **Create IntelliTest** window. Here, you can define several settings for your IntelliTest. One thing to note is that you can use a different test framework than **MSTest**. For our purposes, however, we will use **MSTest** and keep the rest of the settings set to their defaults:

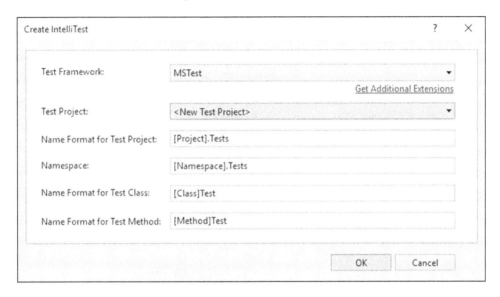

6. When you click on the **OK** button, Visual Studio will continue to create a new test project for you:

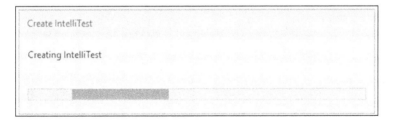

7. When the project creation is complete, you will see the new test project created in the **Solution Explorer**. In this case, because we kept the default settings in the **Create IntelliTest** window, our new test project will be called `Chapter8.Tests`:

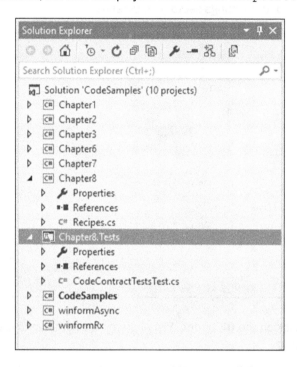

8. Go ahead and expand the `Chapter8.Tests` project and then click on the `CodeContractTestsTest.cs` file created for you. You will see the following code created for you by Visual Studio:

```
/// <summary>This class contains parameterized unit tests
for CodeContractTests</summary>
[PexClass(typeof(CodeContractTests))]
[PexAllowedExceptionFromTypeUnderTest(typeof(InvalidOperati
onException))]
[PexAllowedExceptionFromTypeUnderTest(typeof(ArgumentExcept
ion), AcceptExceptionSubtypes = true)]
[TestClass]
public partial class CodeContractTestsTest
{
    /// <summary>Test stub for Calculate(Int32,
    Int32)</summary>
    [PexMethod]
    public int CalculateTest(
        [PexAssumeUnderTest]CodeContractTests target,
        int valueOne,
        int valueTwo
```

```
        )
        {
            int result = target.Calculate(valueOne, valueTwo);
            return result;
            // TODO: add assertions to method
            CodeContractTestsTest.CalculateTest
            (CodeContractTests,
            Int32, Int32)
        }
    }
```

9. Back in the `CodeContractTests` class, right-click on the `Calculate()` method and select **Run IntelliTest** from the context menu:

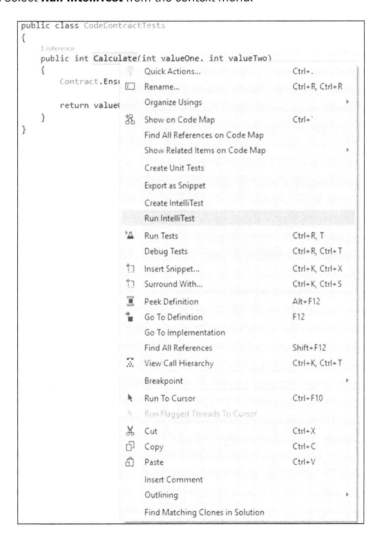

10. IntelliTest will jump into action and open the **IntelliTest Exploration Results** window:

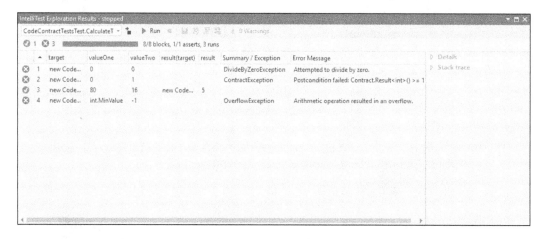

11. From the test results we ran for the `Calculate()` method, we can see that we have three failed tests and one successful test. The test failures reported are `DivideByZeroException`, `ContractException`, and `OverflowException`. Clicking on individual test failures allows you to view the test details as well as the **Stack trace**:

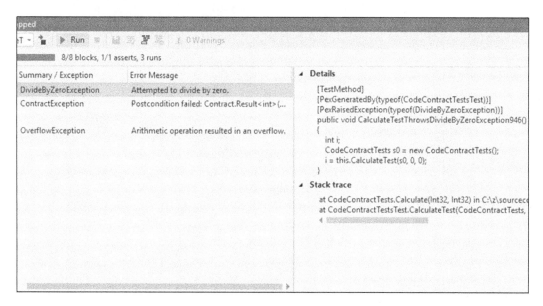

12. Let's modify the `Calculate()` method by adding the following additional code contracts:

```
public int Calculate(int valueOne, int valueTwo)
{
    Contract.Requires(valueOne > 0, "Parameter must be
    greater than zero");
    Contract.Requires(valueTwo > 0, "Parameter must be
    greater than zero");
    Contract.Requires(valueOne > valueTwo, "Parameter
    values will result in value <= 0");
    Contract.Ensures(Contract.Result<int>() >= 1, "");

    return valueOne / valueTwo;
}
```

13. From the additional code contracts, we can see that by requiring the `valueTwo` parameter to be greater than zero, we have resolved the `DivideByZeroException`. We can also see that the code contract that requires `valueOne` is always greater than `valueTwo`. Thus, we have resolved the `ContractException`. Finally, by requiring that both parameters be greater than zero, we have automatically resolved the `OverflowException`:

ts, 3 runs		
result	Summary / Exception	Error Message
	DivideByZeroException	Attempted to divide by zero.
	ContractException	Postcondition failed: Contract.Result<int>() >= 1
5		
	OverflowException	Arithmetic operation resulted in an overflow.

14. Right-click on the `Calculate()` method and run the IntelliTest again. This time, you will see that all the tests have passed, and our method under contract is now ready for use in production code:

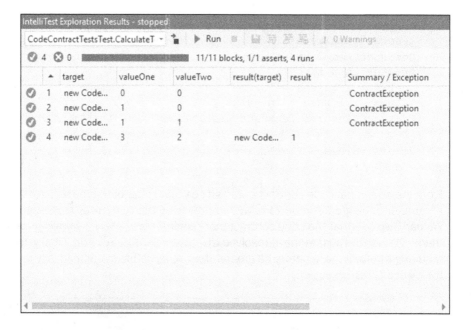

How it works...

IntelliTest allows developers to quickly and efficiently create tests for your code contracts with a few clicks of your mouse.

Using code contracts in extension methods

The previous recipes illustrated how a developer might create various code contracts to secure your code from unexpected input and output, but let's look at how a developer could leverage code contracts. The idea of extension methods come to mind, where we create code that can be used throughout your project to perform actions that are often used.

Let's use the code contract `ForAll` method. This has an impact on a collection, so naturally, its use in extension methods leads us to a possible implementation. In this recipe, we will create an extension method that uses a code contract to validate the list we have just created.

Getting ready

We will create a static class for our extension method and then use the `ForAll` code contract to validate the `List` collection.

How to do it...

1. Before you go on, ensure that you have added the code contracts `using` statement to the top of your `Recipes.cs` class file:

   ```
   using System.Diagnostics.Contracts;
   ```

2. Create a new static class called `ExtensionMethods` and add it to your `Recipes.cs` class file:

   ```
   public static class ExtensionMethods
   {

   }
   ```

3. Next, add an extension method called `ContainsInvalidValue()` that takes the given list of anonymous type `T` and an invalid value to check as type `T` as parameters:

   ```
   public static bool ContainsInvalidValue<T>(this List<T> value, T
   invalidValue)
   {

   }
   ```

4. Inside our extension method, add code contract `ForAll` wrapped in a `try` `catch` statement that checks the existence of the given parameter in the list:

   ```
   try
   {
       Contract.Assert(Contract.ForAll(value, n => !value.
   Contains(invalidValue)), "Zero values are not allowed");
       return false;
   }
   catch
   {
       return true;
   }
   ```

5. Once you have added all the code to your extension method, it should look like this:

```
public static class ExtensionMethods
{
    public static bool ContainsInvalidValue<T>(this List<T> value,
T invalidValue)
    {
        try
        {
            Contract.Assert(Contract.ForAll(value, n =>
            !value.Contains(invalidValue)),
            "Zero values are not allowed");
            return false;
        }
        catch
        {
            return true;
        }
    }
}
```

6. In the console application, add the relevant `using` statement to the `Program.cs` class to bring the `Chapter8` class into scope:

```
using Chapter8;
```

7. As we did earlier, create a simple list, but this time, call the extension method that is exposed via the static extension methods class on the list. We will now be able to directly validate our list via the use of extension methods and code contracts:

```
List<int> intList = new List<int>();
int[] arr;
intList.AddRange(arr = new int[] { 1, 3, 2, 6, 0, 5 });

if (intList.ContainsInvalidValue(4))
    WriteLine("Invalid integer Value");
else
    WriteLine("Valid integer List");
```

8. Running the application will result in the following output:

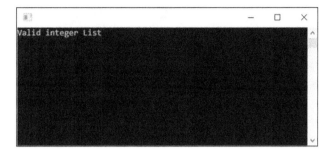

9. As we are using an anonymous type here, we can easily call this extension method on lists containing different types. Here is an example of an implementation on a list of strings:

```
List<string> strList = new List<string>();
string[] arr2;
strList.AddRange(arr2 = new string[] { "S", "A", "Z" });

if (strList.ContainsInvalidValue("G"))
    WriteLine("Invalid string Value");
else
    WriteLine("Valid string List");
```

10. Running the application again will result in the following output:

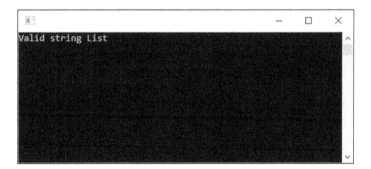

How it works...

We can see that using code contracts along with other powerful features of C# allows us to utilize very powerful code checking and validation techniques. The extension methods can be used throughout your project to perform frequent validation or other code logic specific to your project.

9
Regular Expressions

Regular Expressions (**regex**) are somewhat of a mystery for many developers. We admit that they are something that we use often enough to warrant a deeper understanding of how they work. On the flip side, there are so many tried and tested regex patterns on the Internet that just reusing one that already exists is most times easier than trying to create one yourself. The subject of regex is much larger than what can be explained in a single chapter in this book.

Therefore, in this chapter, we will merely introduce some of the concepts of regex. For a deeper understanding of regex, further study is needed. For the purpose of this book, however, we will take a closer look at how regex are created and how they can be applied to some common programming problems. In this chapter, we will cover the following recipes:

- ▸ Getting started with regex
- ▸ Matching a valid date
- ▸ Sanitizing input
- ▸ Dynamic regex matching

Introduction

A regex is a pattern that describes a string through the use of special characters that denote a specific bit of text to match. The use of regex is not a new concept in programming. For regex to work, they need to use a regex engine that does all the heavy lifting.

In the .NET Framework, Microsoft has provided for the use of regex. To use regex, you will need to import the `System.Text.RegularExpressions` assembly to your project. This will allow the compiler to use your regex pattern and apply it to the specific text you need to match.

Secondly, regex have a specific set of metacharacters that hold special meaning to the Regex engine. These characters are [ ], { }, ( ), *, +, \, ?, |, $, . and, ^.

The use of the curly brackets { }, for example, enables developers to specify the number of times a specific set of characters need to occur. Using square brackets, on the other hand, defines exactly what needs to be matched.

If we, for example, specified [abc], the pattern would look for lowercase As, Bs, and Cs. Regex, therefore, also allows you to define a range, for example, [a-c], which is interpreted in exactly the same way as the [abc] pattern.

Regex then also allow you to define characters to exclude by using the ^ character. Therefore, typing [^a-c] would find lowercase D through Z because the pattern is telling the regex engine to exclude lowercase As, Bs, and Cs.

Regex also define \d and \D as types of shortcut for [0-9] and [^0-9], respectively. Therefore, \d matches all numeric values, and \D matches all non-numeric values. Another shortcut is \w and \W, which match any character from lowercase A to Z, irrespective of the case, all numeric values from 0 to 9, and the underscore character. Therefore, \w is [a-zA-Z0-9_], while \W is [^a-zA-Z0-9_].

The basics of regex are rather easy to understand, but there is a lot more that you can do with regex.

Getting started with regex

We will be create a new class in C# called Chapter9. Here, we will create various methods to illustrate the use of regex.

Getting ready

For the purpose of this book, we will create a simple console application to illustrate the use of regex. In reality, you would probably not have this logic mixed in with your production code, because this would result in code being rewritten. The best place to add something like regex is in a helper class within an extension method.

How to do it...

1. Start by right-clicking the solution, going to **Add**, and then to **New Project** from the context menu:

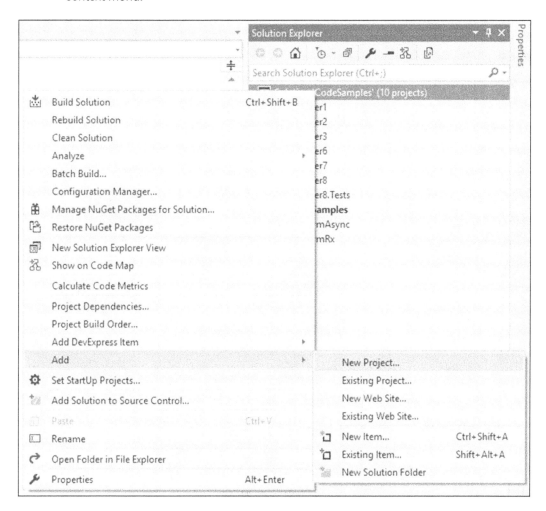

2. The **Add New Project** window opens up. Select the **Class Library** project type and call the project Chapter9:

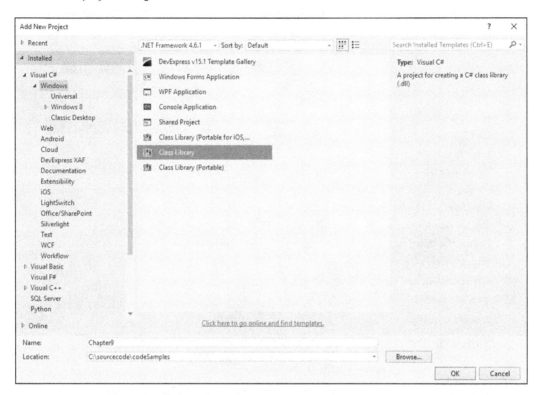

3. After the new class file has been added, your **Solution Explorer** should look like this:

4. Right-click the `Class1.cs` file and select **Rename** from the context menu:

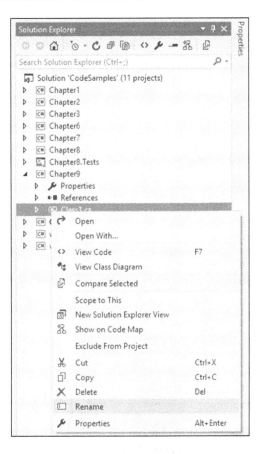

5. Rename the `Class1.cs` file to `Recipes.cs` and select **Yes** from the confirmation dialog:

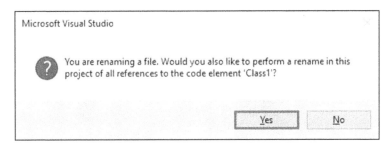

6. In the console application, click on the **References** section and select **Add Reference** from the context menu:

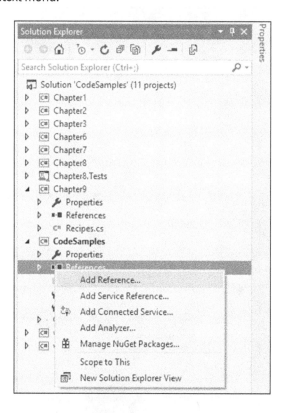

7. In **Reference Manager** for the console application, select Chapter9 and click on **OK** to add it as a reference to the console application:

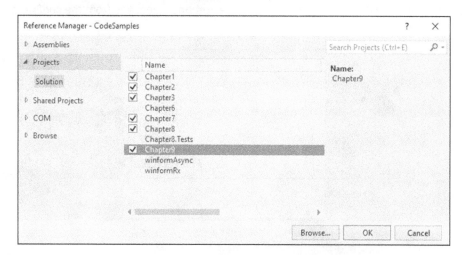

8. In the `Recipes` class, add the following `using` statement so that we can use the regex assembly in .NET:

```
using System.Text.RegularExpressions;
```

9. After you have done all this, your `Chapter9` class should look like this:

```
using System.Text.RegularExpressions;
namespace Chapter9
{
    public class Recipes
    {
    }
}
```

How it works...

We have added a basic class file that will be used to validate regex patterns, which is called from our console application.

Matching a valid date

We will create a regex to validate a date pattern of yyyy-mm-dd, yyyy/mm/dd, or yyyy.mm.dd. At first, the regex will look daunting, but bear with me. When you have completed the code and run the application, we will dissect the regex. Hopefully, the expression logic will become clear.

Getting ready

Ensure that you have added the correct assembly to your class. At the top of your code file, add the following line of code if you haven't already done so:

```
using System.Text.RegularExpressions;
```

How to do it...

1. Create a new method called `ValidDate()` that takes a string as the parameter. This string will be the date pattern we want to validate:

```
public void ValidDate(string stringToMatch)
{

}
```

2. Add the following regex pattern to your method, to a variable in the method:

```
string pattern = $@"^(19|20)\d\d[-./](0[1-9]|1[0-2])[-
./](0[1-9]|[12][0-9]|3[01])$";
```

3. Finally, add the regex to match the supplied string parameter:

```
if (Regex.IsMatch(stringToMatch, pattern))
    Console.WriteLine($"The string {stringToMatch} contains
    a valid date.");
else
    Console.WriteLine($"The string {stringToMatch} DOES NOT
    contain a valid date.");
```

4. When you have done this, your method should look like this:

```
public void ValidDate(string stringToMatch)
{
    string pattern = $@"^(19|20)\d\d[-./](0[1-9]|1[0-2])[-
    ./](0[1-9]|[12][0-9]|3[01])$";

    if (Regex.IsMatch(stringToMatch, pattern))
        Console.WriteLine($"The string {stringToMatch}
        contains a valid date.");
    else
        Console.WriteLine($"The string {stringToMatch} DOES
        NOT contain a valid date.");
}
```

5. Going back to your console application, add the following code and debug your application by clicking on Start:

```
Chapter9.Recipes oRecipe = new Chapter9.Recipes();
oRecipe.ValidDate("1912-12-31");
oRecipe.ValidDate("2018-01-01");
oRecipe.ValidDate("1800-01-21");
            oRecipe.ValidDate($"{DateTime.Now.Year}.{DateTime.Now.
Month
}.{DateTime.Now.Day}");
oRecipe.ValidDate("2016-21-12");
Read();
```

> You will notice that Read() is used in the preceding code example
> instead of Console.Read(). This is because using static
> System.Console; is added to the console application's using
> statements. Doing this will allow you to omit the Console keyword.

6. The date strings are passed to the regex, and the pattern is matched against the date string in the parameter. The output is displayed in the console application:

```
The string 1912-12-31 contains a valid date.
The string 2018-01-01 contains a valid date.
The string 1800-01-21 DOES NOT contain a valid date.
The string 2016.4.10 DOES NOT contain a valid date.
The string 2016-21-12 DOES NOT contain a valid date.
```

7. If you look at the output carefully, you will notice that there is a mistake. We are validating the date string in the format yyyy-mm-dd, yyyy/mm/dd, and yyyy.mm.dd. If we use this logic, our regex has incorrectly flagged a valid date as invalid. This is the date 2016.4.10, which is 10 April, 2016, and is in fact quite valid.

 We will explain shortly why the date 1800-01-21 is invalid.

8. Go back to your ValidDate() method and change the regular expression to read as follows:

```
string pattern = $@"^(19|20)\d\d[-./](0[1-9]|1[0-2]|[1-
9])[-./](0[1-9]|[12][0-9]|3[01])$";
```

9. Run the console application again and look at the output:

```
The string 1912-12-31 contains a valid date.
The string 2018-01-01 contains a valid date.
The string 1800-01-21 DOES NOT contain a valid date.
The string 2016.4.10 contains a valid date.
The string 2016-21-12 DOES NOT contain a valid date.
```

This time the regex worked for all the given date strings. But what exactly did we do? This is how it works.

How it works...

Let's take a closer look at the two expressions used in the previous code example. Comparing them with each other, you can see the change we made in yellow:

```
string pattern = $@"^(19|20)\d\d[-./](0[1-9]|1[0-2])[-./](0[1-9]|[12][0-9]|3[01])$";
string pattern = $@"^(19|20)\d\d[-./](0[1-9]|1[0-2]|[1-9])[-./](0[1-9]|[12][0-9]|3[01])$";
```

Before we get to what that change means, let's break up the expression and view the individual components. Our regex is basically saying that we must match all string dates that start with 19 or 20 and have the following separators:

- Dash (-)
- Decimal (.)
- Forward slash (/)

To understand the expression better, we need to understand the following format of the expression *<Valid Years><Valid Separators><Valid Months><Valid Separators><Valid Days>*.

We also need to be able to tell the regex engine to consider one OR another pattern. The word OR is symbolised by the | metacharacter. To make the regex engine consider the word OR without splitting up the whole expression, we wrap it in parenthesis ().

Here are the symbols used in the regex:

The conditional OR	
|	This denotes the OR metacharacter.
The year portion	
(19|20)	Only allow 19 or 20.
\d\d	Match two single digits between 0 and 9. To match only one digit between 0 and 9, you would use \d.
The valid separator character set	
[-./]	Match any of the following characters in the character set. These are our valid separators. To match a space date separator, you would change this to [- ./], where you add a space anywhere in the character set. We added the space between the dash and the decimal.
Valid digits for months and days	
0[1-9]	Match any part starting with zero followed by any digit between 1 and 9. This will match 01, 02, 03, 04, 05, 06, 07, 08, and 09.

1[0-2]	Match any part starting with 1 followed by any digit between 0 and 2. This will match 10, 11, or 12.
[1-9]	Match any digit between 1 and 9.
[12][0-9]	Match any part starting with 1 or 2, followed by any digit between 0 and 9. This will match all number strings between 10 and 29.
3[01]	Match any part starting with 3 and followed by 0 or 1. This will match 30 or 31.
Start and end of string	
^	Tells the regex engine to start at the beginning of the given string to match.
$	Tells the regex engine to stop at the end of the given string to match.

The first regex we created, interprets as follows:

▶ ^: Start at the beginning of the string to match

▶ (19|20): Check whether the string starts with 19 or 20

▶ \d\d: After the check, follows two single digits between 0 and 9

▶ [-./]: The year portion ends followed by a date separator

▶ (0[1-9]|1[0-2]): Find the month logic by looking for digits starting with 0, followed by any digit between 1 and 9, or digits starting with 1, followed by any digit between 0 and 2

▶ [-./]: The month logic ends, followed by a date separator

▶ (0[1-9]|[12][0-9]|3[01]): Then, find the day logic by looking for digits starting with 0, followed by a digit between 1 and 9, or digits starting with 1 or 2, followed by any digit between 0 and 9, or a digit matching 3, followed by any digit between 0 and 1

▶ $: Do this until the end of the string

Our first regex was incorrect because our month logic was incorrect. Our month logic dictates to find the month logic by looking for digits starting with a 0 followed by any digit between 1 and 9, or digits starting with a 1 followed by any digit between 0 and 2 (0[1-9]|1[0-2]).

This will then find 01, 02, 03, 04, 05, 06, 07, 08, 09 or 10, 11, 12. The date that it didn't match was 2016.4.10 (the date separators don't make a difference here). This is because our month came through as a single digit, and we were looking for months where the single digits started with a zero. To fix this, we had to modify the expression of the month logic to include single digits between 1 and 9. We did this by adding [1-9] to the expression at the end.

The modified regex then reads as follows:

- ▸ `^`: Start at the beginning of the string to match.
- ▸ `(19|20)`: Check whether the string starts with 19 or 20.
- ▸ `\d\d`: After the check, follows two single digits between 0 and 9.
- ▸ `[-./]`: The year portion ends, followed by a date separator
- ▸ `(0[1-9]|1[0-2])`: Find the month logic by looking for digits starting with 0, followed by any digit between 1 and 9, or digits starting with 1, followed by any digit between 0 and 2, or any single digits between 1 and 9
- ▸ `[-./]`: The month logic ends, followed by a date separator
- ▸ `(0[1-9]|[12][0-9]|3[01])`: Then, find the day logic by looking for digits starting with 0, followed by a digit between 1 and 9, or digits starting with 1 or 2, followed by any digit between 0 and 9, or a digit matching 3, followed by any digit between 0 and 1
- ▸ `$`: Do this until the end of the string

This is a basic regex, and we say basic because there is a lot more we can do to make the expression better. We can include logic to consider alternative date formats such as mm-dd-yyyy or dd-mm-yyyy. We can add logic to check February and validate that it contains only 28 days, unless it is a leap year, in which case we need to allow the twenty-ninth day of February. Furthermore, we can also extend the regex to check that January, March, May, July, August, October, and December have 31 days while April, June, September, and November contain only 30 days.

Sanitizing input

Sometimes, you will need to sanitize input. This could be to prevent SQL injections or ensure that an entered URL is valid. In this recipe, we will look at replacing the bad words in a string with asterisks. We are sure that there are more elegant and code-efficient methods of writing sanitation logic using regex (especially when we have a large collection of blacklist words), but we want to illustrate a concept here.

Getting ready

Ensure that you have added the correct assembly to your class. At the top of your code file, add the following line of code if you haven't done so already:

```
using System.Text.RegularExpressions;
```

How to do it...

1. Create a new method in your `Recipes.cs` class called `SanitizeInput()` and let it accept a string parameter:

```
public string SanitizeInput(string input)
{

}
```

2. Add a list of type `List<string>` to the method that contains the bad words we want to remove from the input:

```
List<string> lstBad = new List<string>(new string[] {
"BadWord1", "BadWord2", "BadWord3" });
```

 In reality, you might make use of a database call to read the blacklisted words from a table in the database. You would usually not hardcode them in a list like this.

3. Start constructing the regex that we will use to look for the blacklisted words. Concatenate the words with the | (OR) metacharacter so that the regex will match any of the words. When the list is complete, you can append the \b expression to either side of the regex. This denotes a word boundary and, therefore, will only match whole words:

```
string pattern = "";
foreach (string badWord in lstBad)
    pattern += pattern.Length == 0 ? $"{badWord}" :
$"|{badWord}";

pattern = $@"\b({pattern})\b";
```

4. Finally, we will add the `Regex.Replace()` method that takes the input and looks for the occurrence of the words defined in the pattern, while ignoring case and replacing the bad words with *****:

```
return Regex.Replace(input, pattern, "*****",
RegexOptions.IgnoreCase);
```

5. When you have completed this, your `SanitizeInput()` method will look like this:

```
public string SanitizeInput(string input)
{
    List<string> lstBad = new List<string>(new string[] {
    "BadWord1", "BadWord2", "BadWord3" });
    string pattern = "";
    foreach (string badWord in lstBad)
```

```
            pattern += pattern.Length == 0 ? $"{badWord}" :
            $"|{badWord}";

       pattern = $@"\b({pattern})\b";

       return Regex.Replace(input, pattern, "*****",
       RegexOptions.IgnoreCase);
}
```

6. In the console application, add the following code to call the `SanitizeInput()` method and run your application:

```
string textToSanitize = "This is a string that contains a
badword1, another Badword2 and a third badWord3";
Chapter9.Recipes oRecipe = new Chapter9.Recipes();
textToSanitize = oRecipe.SanitizeInput(textToSanitize);
WriteLine(textToSanitize);
Read();
```

7. When you run your application, you will see the following in the console window:

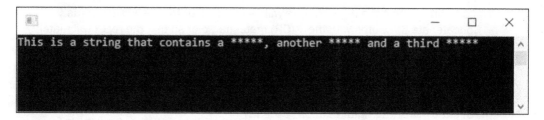

Let's take a closer look at the regular expression generated.

How it works...

Let's step through the code to understand what is happening. We need to get a regex that looks like this: `\b(wordToMatch1|wordToMatch2|wordToMatch3)\b`.

What this basically says is find me any of the words and only whole words that are denoted by `\b`. When we look at the list we created, we will see the words we want to remove from the input string:

```
1 reference
public string SanitizeInput(string input)
{
    List<string> lstBad = new List<string>(new string[] { "BadWord1", "BadWord2", "BadWord3" });
    string pattern ⊿ ● lstBad  Count = 3  ⊟
    foreach (string b    ● [0]        Q ▾ "BadWord1"
        pattern += pa    ● [1]        Q ▾ "BadWord2"  ord}" : $"|{badWord}";
                         ● [2]        Q ▾ "BadWord3"
    pattern = $@"\b({ ▷ ● Raw View

    return Regex.Replace(input, pattern, "*****", RegexOptions.IgnoreCase);
}
```

We then created a simple loop that will create the list of words to match using the OR metacharacter. We ended up with a BadWord1|BadWord2|BadWord3 pattern after the foreach loop has completed. However, this is still not a valid regex:

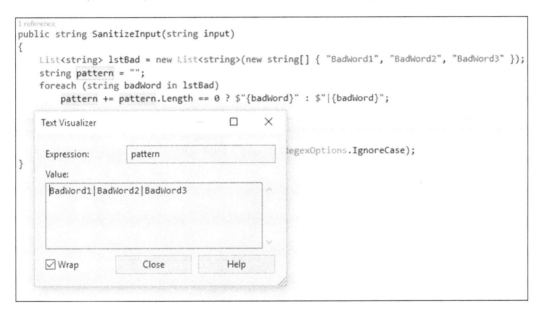

To complete the pattern resulting in the valid regex, we need to add the \b expression on either side of the pattern to tell the regex engine to only match whole words. As you can see, we are using string interpolation. String interpolation is covered in detail in *Chapter 1, New Features in C#6*.

It is here, however, that we need to be very careful. Start off by writing the code to complete the pattern without the @ sign, as follows:

```
pattern = $"\b({pattern})\b";
```

If you run your console application, you will see that the bad words are not matched and filtered out. This is because we have not escaped the \ character before b. The compiler, therefore, interprets this line of code:

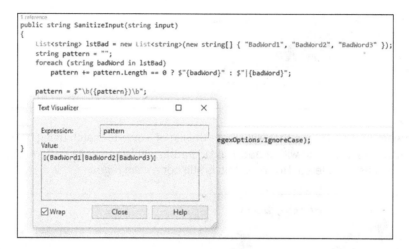

The generated expression [] (BadWord1| BadWord2| BadWord3) [] is not a valid expression and will therefore not sanitize the input string.

To correct this, we need to add the @ symbol before the string to tell the compiler to treat the string as a literal. This means any escape sequences are ignored. The correctly formatted line of code looks like this:

```
pattern = $@"\b({pattern})\b";
```

Once you do this, the string for the pattern is interpreted literally by the compiler, and the correct regex pattern generated:

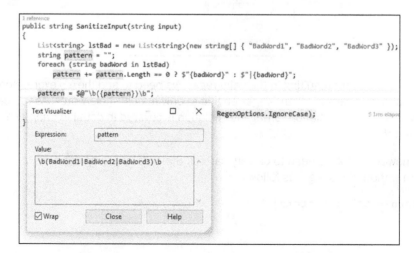

With our correct regex pattern, we called the `Regex.Replace()` method. It takes the input to check, the regex to match, the text to replace the matched words with, and optionally allows for the ignoring of case:

```
1 reference
public string SanitizeInput(string input)
{
    List<string> lstBad = new List<string>(new string[] { "BadWord1", "BadWord2", "BadWord3" });
    string pattern = "";
    foreach (string badWord in lstBad)
        pattern += pattern.Length == 0 ? $"{badWord}" : $"|{badWord}";

    pattern = $@"\b({pattern})\b";

    return Regex.Replace(input, pattern, "*****", RegexOptions.IgnoreCase);        ≤ 1ms elapse
}
```

Text Visualizer   □   ✕

Expression: input

Value:
This is a string that contains a
badword1, another Badword2 and a third
badWord3

☑ Wrap   Close   Help

When the string returns to the calling code in the console application, the string will be sanitized properly:

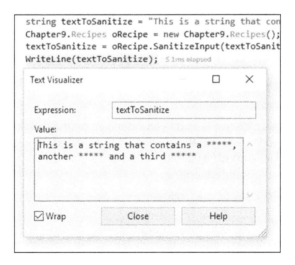

```
string textToSanitize = "This is a string that con
Chapter9.Recipes oRecipe = new Chapter9.Recipes();
textToSanitize = oRecipe.SanitizeInput(textToSanit
WriteLine(textToSanitize);  ≤ 1ms elapsed
```

Text Visualizer   □   ✕

Expression: textToSanitize

Value:
This is a string that contains a *****,
another ***** and a third *****

☑ Wrap   Close   Help

Regex can become quite complex and can be used to perform a multitude of tasks to format and validate input and other text.

Dynamic regex matching

What does dynamic regex matching even mean? Well, it isn't an official term, but it is a term we use to explain a Regex that uses variables at runtime to generate a specific expression. Assume for a minute that you are working on a document-management system that needs to implement versioning of documents for a company called Acme Corporation. To do this, the system validates that the document has a valid file name.

A business rule states that the file name of any file uploaded on a specific day must be prefixed with acm (for Acme) and today's date in the yyyy-mm-dd format. There can be only text files, Word documents (only `.docx`), and Excel documents (only `.xlsx`). Any documents not conforming to this file format are processed by another method that takes care of archive and invalid documents.

The only task that your method needs to perform is to process fresh documents as version one documents.

In a production system, further logic will probably be needed to determine whether the same document has been uploaded previously on the same day. This, however, is beyond the scope of this chapter. We are just trying to set the scene.

Getting ready

Ensure that you have added the correct assembly to your class. At the top of your code file, add the following line of code if you haven't already done so:

```
using System.Text.RegularExpressions;
```

How to do it...

1. A really nice way to do this is to use an extension method. This way, you can call the extension method directly on the file name variable and have it validated. In your `Recipes.cs` file, start off by adding a new class called `CustomRegexHelper` with the `public static` modifier:

```
public static class CustomRegexHelper
{


}
```

2. Add the usual extension method code to the `CustomRegexHelper` class and call the `ValidAcmeCompanyFilename` method:

```
public static bool ValidAcmeCompanyFilename(this String
value)
{

}
```

3. Inside your `ValidAcmeCompanyFilename` method, add the following regex. We will explain the makeup of this regex in the *How it works...* section of this recipe:

```
return Regex.IsMatch(value,
$@"^acm[_]{DateTime.Now.Year}[_]({DateTime.Now.Month}|0[{Da
teTime.Now.Month}])[_]({DateTime.Now.Day}|0[{DateTime.Now.D
ay}])(.txt|.docx|.xlsx)$");
```

4. When you have completed this, your extension method should look like this:

```
public static class CustomRegexHelper
{
    public static bool ValidAcmeCompanyFilename(this String
    value)
    {
        return Regex.IsMatch(value,
        $@"^acm[_]{DateTime.Now.Year}[_]
        ({DateTime.Now.Month}|0[{DateTime.Now.Month}])
        [_]({DateTime.Now.Day}|0[{DateTime.Now.Day}])
        (.txt|.docx|.xlsx)$");
    }
}
```

5. Back in the `Recipes` class, create a method with the `void` return type called `DemoExtendionMethod()`:

```
public void DemoExtendionMethod()
{

}
```

6. Add some output text to show the current date and the valid file name types:

```
Console.WriteLine($"Today's date is: {DateTime.Now.Year}-
{DateTime.Now.Month}-{DateTime.Now.Day}");
Console.WriteLine($"The file must match:
acm_{DateTime.Now.Year}_{DateTime.Now.Month}_{DateTime.Now.
Day}.txt including leading month and day zeros");
Console.WriteLine($"The file must match:
acm_{DateTime.Now.Year}_{DateTime.Now.Month}_{DateTime.Now.
Day}.docx including leading month and day zeros");
Console.WriteLine($"The file must match:
acm_{DateTime.Now.Year}_{DateTime.Now.Month}_{DateTime.Now.
Day}.xlsx including leading month and day zeros");
```

7. Then, add the file name checking code:

```
string filename = "acm_2016_04_10.txt";
if (filename.ValidAcmeCompanyFilename())
    Console.WriteLine($"{filename} is a valid file name");
else
    Console.WriteLine($"{filename} is not a valid file
    name");


filename = "acm-2016_04_10.txt";
if (filename.ValidAcmeCompanyFilename())
    Console.WriteLine($"{filename} is a valid file name");
else
    Console.WriteLine($"{filename} is not a valid file
    name");
```

8. You will notice that the `if` statement contains the call to the extension method on the variable that contains the file name:

```
filename.ValidAcmeCompanyFilename()
```

9. If you have completed this, your method should look like this:

```
public void DemoExtendionMethod()
{
    Console.WriteLine($"Today's date is:
    {DateTime.Now.Year}-{DateTime.Now.Month}-
    {DateTime.Now.Day}");
    Console.WriteLine($"The file must match:
    acm_{DateTime.Now.Year}_{DateTime.Now.Month}_
    {DateTime.Now.Day}.txt including leading month and day
    zeros");
    Console.WriteLine($"The file must match:
    acm_{DateTime.Now.Year}_{DateTime.Now.Month}_
    {DateTime.Now.Day}.docx including leading month and day
    zeros");
    Console.WriteLine($"The file must match:
    acm_{DateTime.Now.Year}_{DateTime.Now.Month}
    _{DateTime.Now.Day}.xlsx including leading month and
    day zeros");

    string filename = "acm_2016_04_10.txt";
    if (filename.ValidAcmeCompanyFilename())
```

```
        Console.WriteLine($"{filename} is a valid file
        name");
    else
        Console.WriteLine($"{filename} is not a valid file
        name");

    filename = "acm-2016_04_10.txt";
    if (filename.ValidAcmeCompanyFilename())
        Console.WriteLine($"{filename} is a valid file
        name");
    else
        Console.WriteLine($"{filename} is not a valid file
        name");
}
```

10. Going back to the console application, add the following code that simply just calls the `void` method. This is just to simulate the versioning method talked about earlier:

```
Chapter9.Recipes oRecipe = new Chapter9.Recipes();
oRecipe.DemoExtendionMethod();
Read();
```

11. When you are done, run your console application:

```
Today's date is: 2016-4-10
The file must match: acm_2016_4_10.txt including leading month and day zeros
The file must match: acm_2016_4_10.docx including leading month and day zeros
The file must match: acm_2016_4_10.xlsx including leading month and day zeros
acm_2016_04_10.txt is a valid file name
acm-2016_04_10.txt is not a valid file name
```

How it works...

Let's have a closer look at the regex generated. The line of code we are looking at is the `return` statement in the extension method:

```
return Regex.IsMatch(value,
$@"^acm[_]{DateTime.Now.Year}[_]({DateTime.Now.Month}|0[{DateTime.
Now.Month}])[_]({DateTime.Now.Day}|0[{DateTime.Now.Day}])(.txt|.do
cx|.xlsx)$");
```

To appreciate what is happening, we need to break this expression up into the different components:

The conditional OR	
|	This denotes the OR metacharacter.
The file prefix and separator	
acm	The file must begin with the text acm.
[_]	The only valid separator between the date components and the prefix in the file name is an underscore.
The date parts	
{DateTime.Now.Year}	The interpolated year part of the date for the file name.
{DateTime.Now.Month}	The interpolated month part of the date for the file name.
0[{DateTime.Now.Month}]	The interpolated month part of the date with a leading zero for the file name.
{DateTime.Now.Day}	The interpolated day part of the date for the file name.
0[{DateTime.Now.Day}]	The interpolated day part of the date with a leading zero for the file name.
Valid file formats	
(.txt|.docx|.xlsx)	Match any of these file extensions for text documents, Word documents, or Excel documents.
Start and end of string	
^	Tells the regex engine to start at the beginning of the given string to match.
$	Tells the regex engine to stop at the end of the given string to match.

Creating the regex in this manner allows us to always have it stay up to date. As we have to always match the current date to the file being validated, this creates a unique challenge that is easily overcome using string interpolation, DateTime, and regex OR statements.

Having a look at some of the more useful bits of regex, you will see that this chapter has not even begun to scratch the surface of what can be accomplished. There is a whole lot more to explore and learn. There are many resources on the Internet, as well as some free (some online) and commercial tools that will assist you in creating regex.

10

Choosing and Using a Source Control Strategy

Source control is an essential part of every developer's toolkit. It doesn't matter whether you are a hobbyist or professional programmer; when you get up from your desk to go home you better be sure your code is safe. In this chapter, we will be looking at choosing and using a source control strategy. Some of the topics we will be taking a look at are:

▸ Setting up Visual Studio account management and determining which source control solution is best for you

▸ Setting up Visual Studio GitHub integration, checking in code for the first time, and checking in changes

▸ Working as a team using GitHub, and handling and resolving conflicts in code

Introduction

During my career, I have used Visual SourceSafe, SVN, VSTS, Bitbucket, and GitHub. It really does not matter how you approach it, the important thing is that you keep your source code safe and versioned.

Setting up Visual Studio account management and determining which source control solution is best for you

Visual Studio allows developers to create an account and sign in. This is particularly beneficial if you hot desk often or work in multiple locations on different machines (think work and home PCs), because Visual Studio will then automatically sync your settings between the machines you're signed in to.

Getting ready

This recipe will assume that you have just completed installing Visual Studio 2015 on your machine. It doesn't matter whether you have installed the trial or licensed version of Visual Studio 2015.

How to do it...

1. After installation completes, open up Visual Studio:

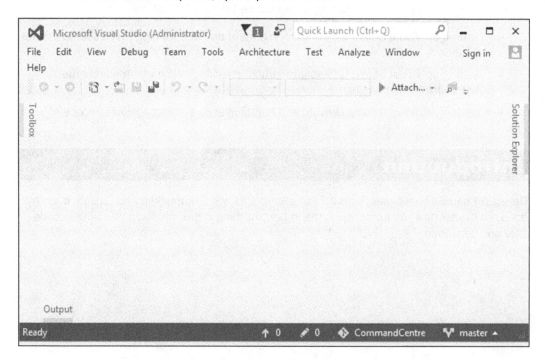

2. At the top right of Visual Studio, you will see that there is a **Sign in** link:

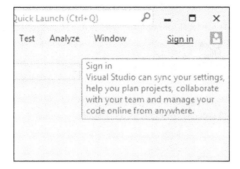

3. Clicking on the **Sign in** link, you will be allowed to enter your e-mail address here. I find it useful to just use my Outlook e-mail address. In my opinion, it is one of the best web e-mails available.

 Please note, I'm not endorsing Outlook for any reason other than I really think it is a great product. I also have a Gmail account as well as an iCloud e-mail account.

4. After adding your e-mail account, Visual Studio will redirect you to a sign-in page:

5. Because I already have an Outlook account, Visual Studio simply allows me to sign in with it. If you don't have an account, you can create one here:

6. Visual Studio will now ask you to enter some additional information. One part to note is that you can already link your Team Services account here if you have one. For now, leave it blank, as this will be dealt with in a later recipe:

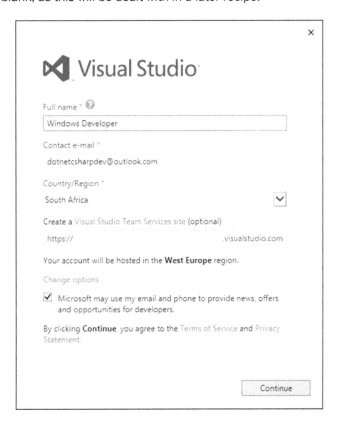

7. After your account is created, you can see that you have been signed in by looking at the account selected in the right-hand corner of the Visual Studio IDE:

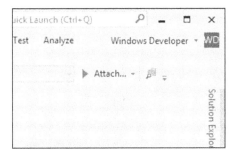

8. Clicking on the down arrow next to your account name, you can view your **Account settings...**

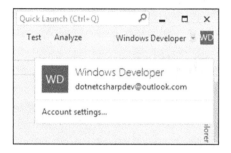

9. This will show you a summary of your account, from where you can further personalize your account:

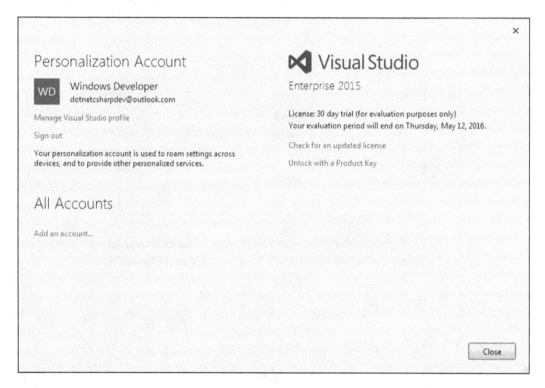

The choice of source control is a topic every developer has a strong opinion about. Unfortunately, if you work for a boss, that decision might not even be up to you. Many companies have already set up their source control system just the way they like it, and you will need to fall in with company procedure. That is just the way it is. It is however good to know about the options available to you as an indie developer.

All good developers should be writing code on their own time too. You are not only a developer while you sit at work. We eat, breathe, sleep, and live code. It is part of who and what we are. I will say that in order for you to become better at your job as a developer, you must play with code on your own time. Start a pet project, get some friends together, and decide to write some software together. Not only will this make you all better at what you do, but you will learn a lot from each other.

If you are a remote developer that does not commute to, and work in, an office every day, you can still connect with the developer community. There are so many resources available to developers, and the developer community is more than happy to rally around newbies and help them grow. Starting a solo or pet project is useless if you don't commit (pun intended) to keeping your code safe. To do this, you don't have to pay a single dollar either. Visual Studio Online (now called Team Services) and GitHub both provide developers with a fantastic platform to keep your code safe.

Let us start by looking at Team Services. The site can be found by pointing your browser to `https://www.visualstudio.com/en-us/products/what-is-visual-studio-online-vs`.

Here you will see that Microsoft has given developers a fantastic opportunity to use Team Services. It is absolutely free for up to five users. This means that you and your mates can collaboratively work on the next big thing while ensuring that your code remains secure. Signing up is as simple as clicking on the **Get started for free** link:

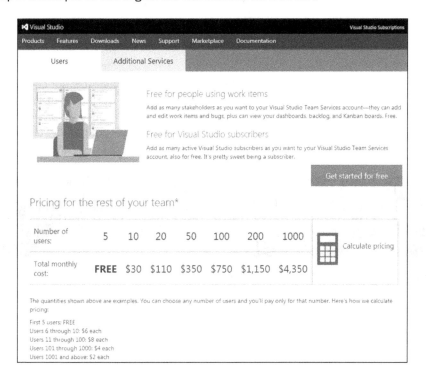

The second excellent option is GitHub. It differs slightly in its free offering by requiring developers to using a public repository on the free account. If you don't mind your code being essentially open source, then GitHub is a great choice. With GitHub though, you can have unlimited collaborators and public repositories:

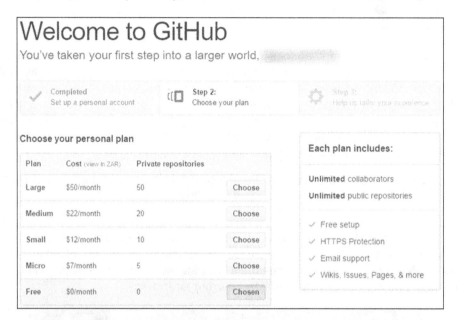

How it works...

The choice of source control essentially comes down to the openness of your code. If you can afford to let other developers see and download your code, then GitHub is a great choice. If you need your code to remain private and only shared between specific people, then a paid GitHub account will be better suited. If you don't want to fork out money yet, then Team Services will be your best bet.

Setting up Visual Studio GitHub integration, checking in code for the first time, and checking in changes

GitHub has been a tour de force for so many years. There are developers that swear by it. In fact, it is the default option when using Apple's Xcode IDE. For whatever reason you decide to use GitHub, rest assured that you and your code are in good hands.

Getting ready

The following recipe will assume that you have already signed up for GitHub and that you have enabled **Two-factor authentication**. If you have not signed up for a GitHub account, you can do so by going to www.github.com and creating a new account. To enable **Two-factor authentication** on your GitHub account (something I personally strongly advise), do the following:

1. Click on the down arrow next to your profile image, and select **Settings**:

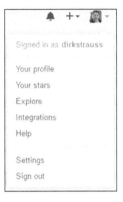

2. From the **Personal settings** menu that appears on the left of the next web page, select **Security**:

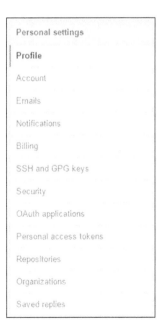

3. The first section on the security page will be your **Two-factor authentication** status. To get started with setting it up, click on the **Set up two-factor authentication** button:

4. You will then be presented with a brief overview of what **Two-factor authentication** is and you will be given the choice of **Set up using an app** (which I recommend) or **Set up using SMS**. Using an app is by far the easiest, and if you have a smartphone or tablet you can download an authenticator application from the applicable app store. From there on, follow the prompts that GitHub gives you to complete the **Two-factor authentication** setup:

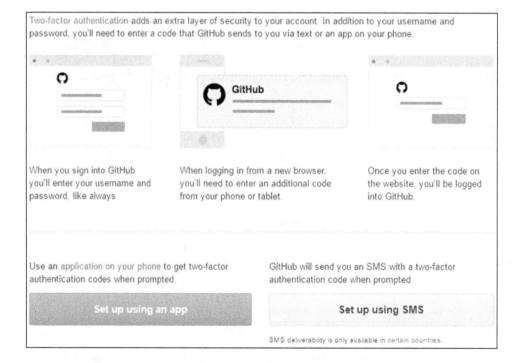

How to do it...

1. If you are installing Visual Studio 2015 for the first time, have a look at the **Custom** installation option. Under **Common Tools**, when expanded you will see the option to add GitHub to your Visual Studio installation. After you have selected that and other options to install, click **Next** and finish the installation window wizard. Visual Studio 2015 will now begin to install. You can now take a break, and go have a cup of coffee because the installation can take a while, depending on the hardware of your machine and speed of your Internet connection:

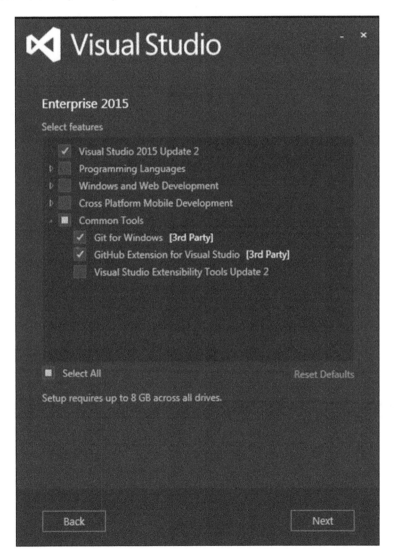

2. If you have already installed Visual Studio 2015 without adding the GitHub extension, you can easily just download it from the following link and install it: `https://visualstudio.github.com/downloads/GitHub.VisualStudio.vsix`.

3. Assuming that you have an existing application you want to add to GitHub, the process of adding it to a new repository is quite simple. I have simply created a console application with nothing but the template code, but you can add any project type and size to GitHub:

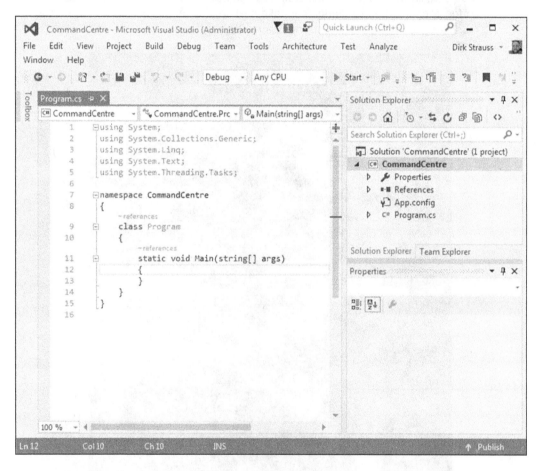

4. On the **View** menu in Visual Studio 2015, select the **Team Explorer** option:

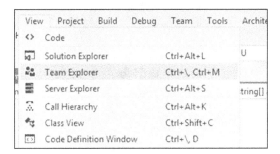

5. You will be presented with two options under the **Hosted Service Providers** section. For now, we will select **GitHub** and, seeing as we already have an account, we will click on **Connect...**

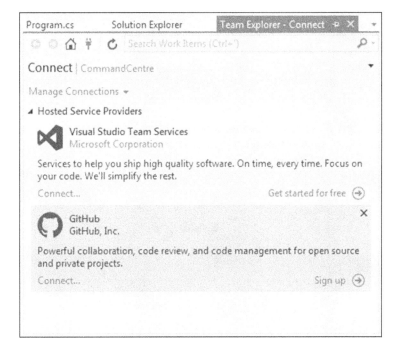

6. You will now be presented with the GitHub login page. You are also offered the chance to sign up from here if you do not have an existing GitHub account:

7. Because I have **Two-factor authentication** set up on my GitHub account, I am prompted to use my authenticator application to enter the generated authentication code and authenticate myself:

8. After you have been authenticated, you will return to the **Manage Connections** screen:

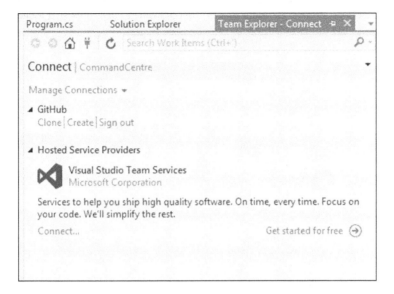

9. Next, you will want to click on the Home icon, which is a picture of a little house at the top of the **Team Explorer** window. From the **Home** screen, click on the **Sync** button:

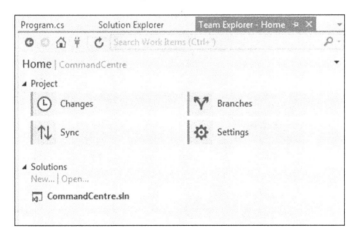

10. This will display the **Publish** window to you. Under GitHub, click on the **Get Started** link. This is going to publish your project to a new repository on GitHub.

Remember, if you are using the free GitHub, all your repositories are public. If you are writing code that can't be made public (is not open source), then sign up for one of the paid GitHub accounts that include private repositories.

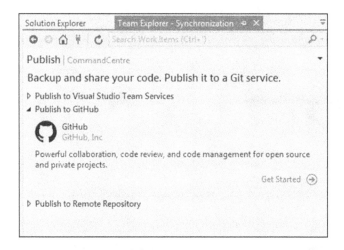

11. GitHub will then prompt you to add in the details for this publish. Because you connected to GitHub earlier, your username will already be selected in the drop-down menu. When you are ready, click **Publish**:

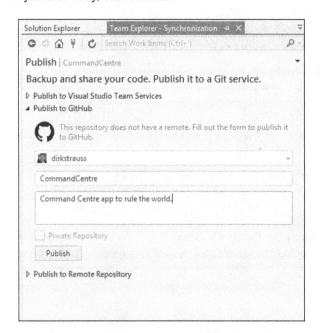

12. When the project has been published to GitHub, you will automatically be returned to the **Home** screen:

13. Looking at your GitHub account online, you will see that the project has been added:

14. Next, let us go and make some changes to the `CommandCentre` application. Just go ahead and add a new class to your project. I called mine `Dominion.cs`, but you can call yours whatever you like:

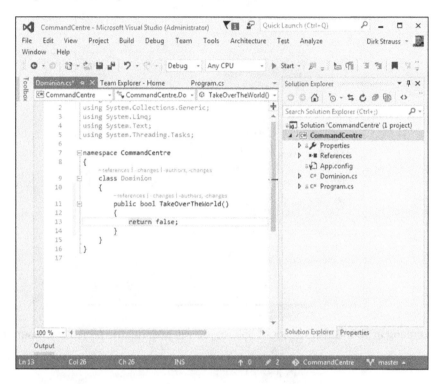

15. You will notice that as soon as a change is made to your project, that the solution will mark the changed items with a red tick:

16. To add the changes to your GitHub repository, you can follow two routes. The first option is to go to the **Team Explorer - Home** window and click on the **Changes** button:

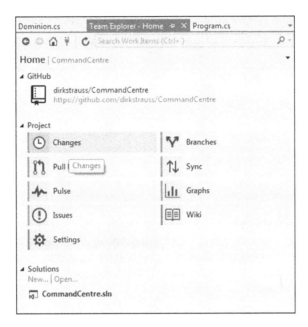

17. The second (and in my opinion more convenient) option, is to right-click the solution in **Solution Explorer** and click on the **Commit...** menu item from the context menu:

18. GitHub might ask you for your user information the first time you perform a commit:

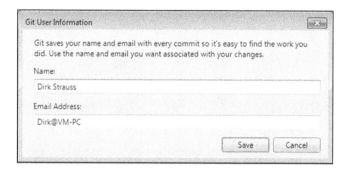

19. Before you are allowed to commit your changes, you must fill in the required commit message. In a real team project, be as descriptive as possible in your commit message. Consider using task item code (or backlog codes) to uniquely identify the code being added. This will save your (or another developer's) bacon sometime in the future, I guarantee it:

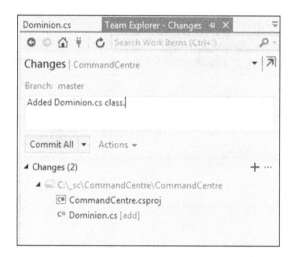

20. One important thing to note is that you have three commit options available to you if you click on the down arrow next to the **Commit All** button. The **Commit All** button will just record the changes you make on your local machine. In other words, the change will not be reflected in the remote repository. The **Commit All and Push** button will record the changes on your local machine and push those changes to your remote GitHub repository. The **Commit All and Sync** button will record the changes on your local machine, then it will pull any changes from the remote repository, and finally it will do the push. You will want to do this if you are working in a team. For this recipe, however, I will just do a **Commit All and Push**, seeing as I am the only developer working on this repo:

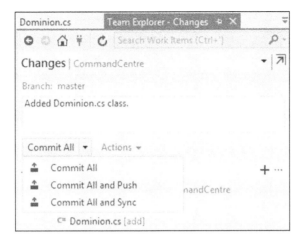

21. When the commit has completed, the **Team Explorer** window will notify you of the successful commit:

22. Heading over to GitHub online, you will see the newly pushed changes reflected in your GitHub repository, along with the commit message:

23. GitHub is a fantastic source control solution for any developer. Consider creating an open source project. It is more beneficial than you might imagine.

How it works...

The free GitHub account allows you to create public repositories. This means that anyone is able to search for, view, and clone your project from GitHub to their own desktop. This is the central idea behind GitHub. This is obviously a key factor for indie developers and corporates that don't want to spend money. Corporates can afford it more though than an indie developer, but I think that some companies prefer to roll their own than use a service provider hosted in the cloud somewhere. This means that they prefer to keep the source control under their control by setting up a source control system on their own corporate servers. Having GitHub as an option for indie developers is an awesome solution. For those that require private repos, the fee isn't a stumbling block either.

Working as a team using GitHub, and handling and resolving conflicts in code

GitHub and Team Services really come into their own when working in teams. The effect of collaborative effort is quite powerful. Sometimes though, it can be a bit challenging. Let us have a look at using GitHub to work in a team setup.

Getting ready

We will be using the existing `CommandCentre` app checked in to GitHub. Before you can let other developers push code to your branch, you need to add them as a collaborator. To do this, log in to GitHub and click on the down arrow next to the plus sign. Click on **New collaborator** in the menu:

You can then search for collaborators to add by entering their GitHub username, full name, or e-mail address:

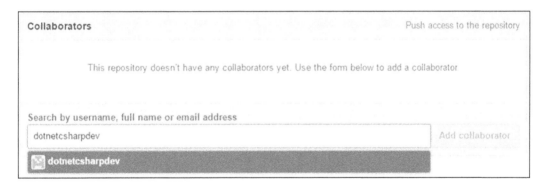

When you are done, click on the **Add collaborator** button to add that user as a collaborator to your project:

How to do it...

1. Let us assume that a new developer (let's call him John) has joined the team. You have already added the developer as a collaborator to your project. John goes about setting up his Visual Studio environment, including getting connected to GitHub. Click on **Team** in the menu and click on **Manage Connections...**

2. Presented with the options for the **Hosted Service Providers**, select **Connect...** under the GitHub service:

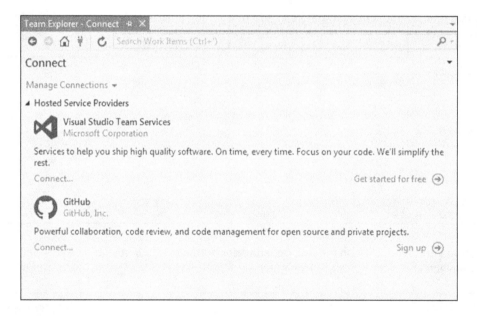

3. Log in to GitHub with your e-mail address and password.

Take note that if you have just signed up to GitHub, you will need to click on a verification e-mail sent to the e-mail address you specified when signing up. Without verifying your e-mail address, you will not be able to log in from Visual Studio.

4. When you have connected, you will see your GitHub details loaded:

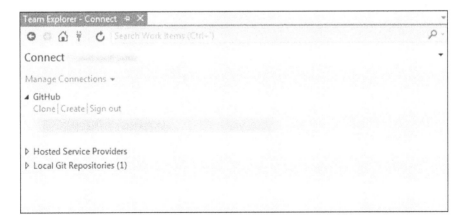

5. We now want to work on the `CommandCentre` application. You can find it on GitHub by searching for it by name:

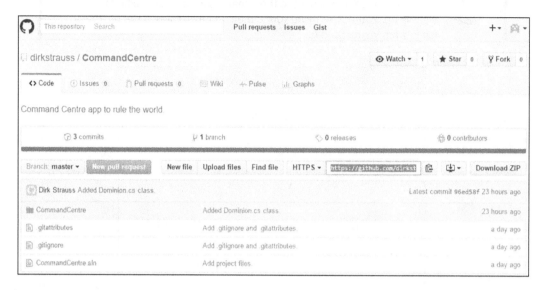

6. When you have found the correct project, copy the URL from the **HTTPS** text box on the page:

7. Back in Visual Studio, expand the **Local Git Repositories** and click on **Clone**. Paste the copied URL to the Git Repository path and specify where the code should be cloned to on your hard drive. When you are ready, click on **Clone**:

8. When the code is cloned, you will see it in the folder path you specified earlier:

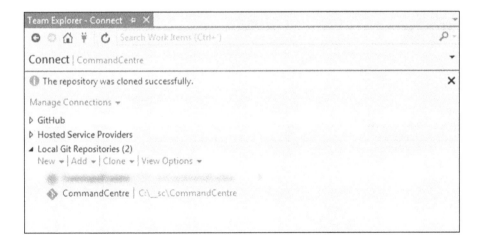

9. Time to make some changes to the code. Open the project in Visual Studio as normal. John decided to work on the `Dominion.cs` class and added a new function that returns a countdown integer:

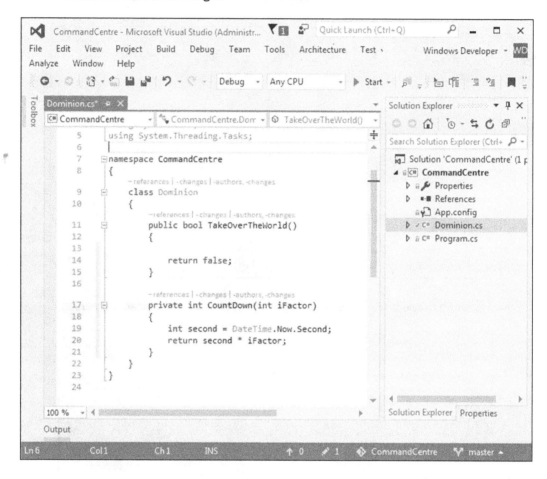

10. After the code change is complete, John commits the code he just added to the GitHub repository:

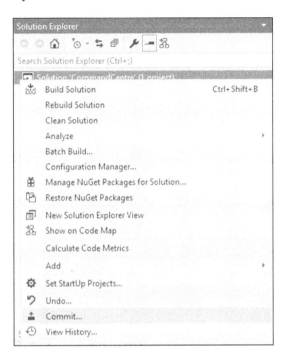

11. GitHub then asks for John's name and e-mail address for this commit:

12. John adds a meaningful commit message to describe the change he made:

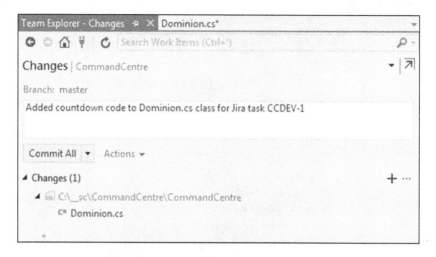

13. He then clicks on **Commit All and Sync**.

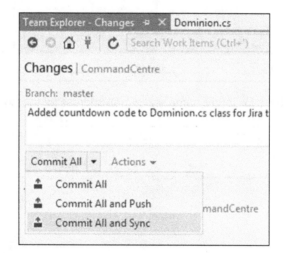

14. John's changes are committed to the GitHub repository:

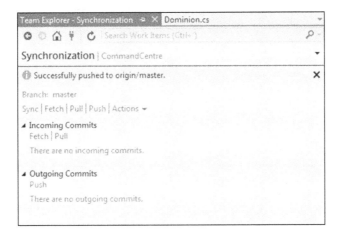

15. On the other side of the office, I am working on the same bit of code. The only problem is that I have added the same method with my own implementation of the CountDown logic:

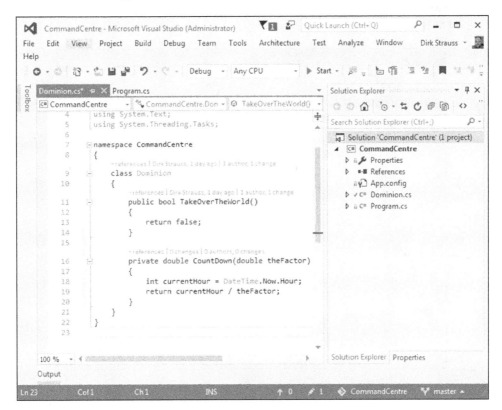

16. I get ready and commit my changes to GitHub:

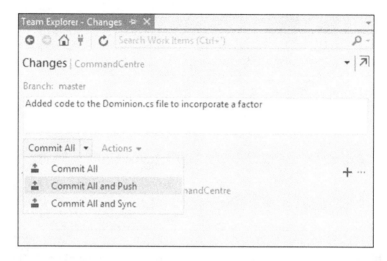

17. GitHub immediately prevents me from doing this. This is because if my code is pushed, the earlier commit by John will be lost. GitHub has a great help file on the subject in GitHub Help here: `https://help.github.com/articles/dealing-with-non-fast-forward-errors/`.

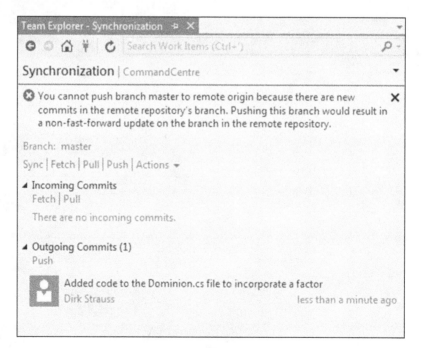

18. To resolve this, click on **Pull** to get the latest commit that John did. Your code will then be in a conflicted state. This sounds bad, but it isn't. It is putting you in control of the decision on which code will be used. You can see that the pull shows that there are conflicted files and also the incoming commit message that John added:

19. To view the conflicts, click on the **Resolve the conflicts** link in the message pop-up:

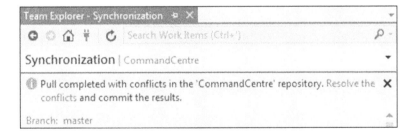

20. You will then see the **Resolve Conflicts** screen listing the conflicted files. Clicking on a file will expand it into a short summary and action options screen. It is always prudent to click on the **Compare Files** link to see the difference between the files in conflict:

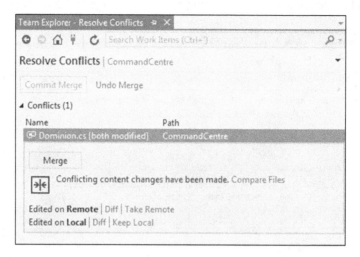

21. The differences in code are immediately evident. The process you follow from here on is subject to how you work together as a team. Usually, the conflict can be quite complex, and it is always a good idea to speak to the developer concerned about the way forward:

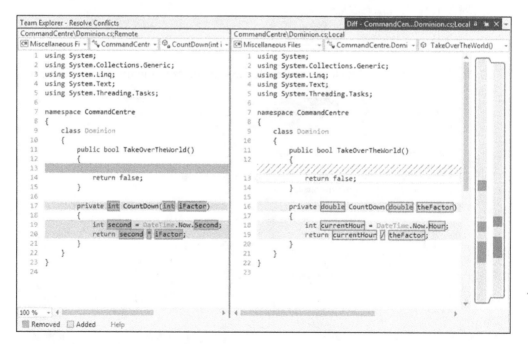

22. In this case, John and I decided that his code was simply better and more concise. So the decision was made to simply click on **Take Remote** and use John's code. When you have clicked on the link, you need to click on **Commit Merge**:

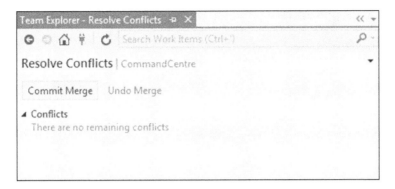

23. After adding a commit message, you can then push your code to the repo. In this case, I simply replaced all my code with John's, but there might be situations when you will be using some of your code and some of another developer's code. GitHub allows us to easily handle these conflicts:

24. After pushing the code to the remote, GitHub notifies you that the code has successfully been synchronised:

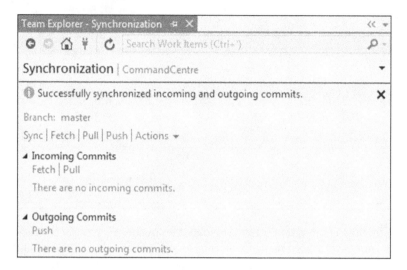

How it works...

GitHub takes the pain out of committing, resolving conflicts, and merging code. It is without a doubt an essential tool in any developer's toolkit and essential for development teams.

11

Creating a Mobile Application in Visual Studio

Visual Studio is the tour de force of **integrated development environments** (**IDEs**). There is no doubt about that. You as a developer are able to be as versatile as you like by creating applications for a wide range of platforms. One of these platforms is mobile development. Developers are starting to create mobile applications, but don't want to use a different IDE. With Visual Studio 2015, you don't have to. It will allow you to create Android and (now with **Xamarin**) iOS applications too. This chapter will therefore take a look at the following concepts:

- ▶ Installing Xamarin and other required components
- ▶ Creating an Android Visual Studio project using Apache Cordova
- ▶ Creating an iOS application using Xamarin Forms

Introduction

If you have not heard about Xamarin, we encourage you to do a Google search for this tool. Traditionally, developers needed to use **Xcode** or **NetBeans** to create iOS and Android applications. The challenge for developers was that it meant learning a new programming language. If you, for example, created an application that you wanted to deploy to iOS, Android, and Windows, you needed to know Objective-C or Swift, Java, and a .NET language.

This also created additional challenges for development, because it meant having to maintain multiple code bases. If a change was to be made in the Windows version of the application, it also had to be made to the iOS and Android code base. Sometimes companies would manage different development teams for each platform. You can imagine the complications involved in managing a change across multiple teams on multiple platforms. This is especially true if you are dealing with a large code base.

Xamarin solves this problem by allowing .NET developers to use standard .NET libraries to create iOS and Android applications using Visual Studio. You, as a .NET developer, can now use the skills you already have to accomplish this. In a nutshell, you would create a shared library for your applications and then have different facades for the different platforms. A second option is to use Xamarin Forms to create one Visual Studio project and target all three platforms. This makes it very easy for developers to target multiple platforms.

Installing Xamarin and other required components

Xamarin can be installed during custom Visual Studio installation. For now, let's assume that Xamarin has not been installed and that you need to do that now, after you have installed Visual Studio.

Getting ready

One thing to be aware of if you want to target iOS is that you will need to use a Mac to build your iOS applications.

How to do it...

1. In the **Control Panel**, click on **Programs and Features**. Right-click on your Visual Studio installation and click on **Change**:

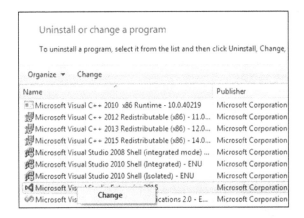

2. This will display the Visual Studio installer for you. Here you can modify your current Visual Studio installation by adding and removing components at will. Notice that we have selected **C#/.NET (Xamarin v4.0.3)** and **HTML/JavaScript (Apache Cordova) Update 8.1** to install. If you have no interest in using Xamarin, then leave off the Xamarin component and just keep the Apache Cordova option selected. This will still allow you to create Android applications using Apache Cordova instead of using Xamarin. Similarly, if you have no interest in Apache Cordova and simply want to create Android applications and iOS applications using Visual Studio, select the Xamarin component to install. The rest of the installation is straightforward:

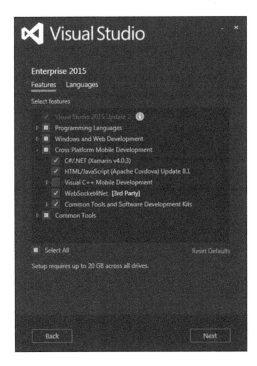

3. There is also a second step we need to take if we want to use Xamarin to target iOS applications. We have to install the required software on a Mac. Head on over to Xamarin's website on your Mac. The URL is `https://www.xamarin.com/`. Click on the **Products** dropdown and select **Xamarin Platform** from the list:

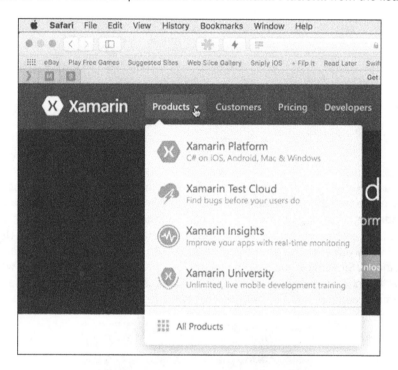

4. You can also access the required page by going to `https://www.xamarin.com/platform`. Clicking on the **Download now for free** button will install something called Xamarin Studio on your Mac. You need to be aware that when installed on a Mac, Xamarin Studio cannot create Windows Apps. It will only allow you to create iOS and Android apps on a Mac. Along with Xamarin Studio, you will also get the Xamarin Mac Agent (previously called the Xamarin Build Host). This is a required component so that you can link your PC to your Mac in order to build your iOS application. Lastly, the PC and Mac must also be able to connect to each other over a network (more on this later):

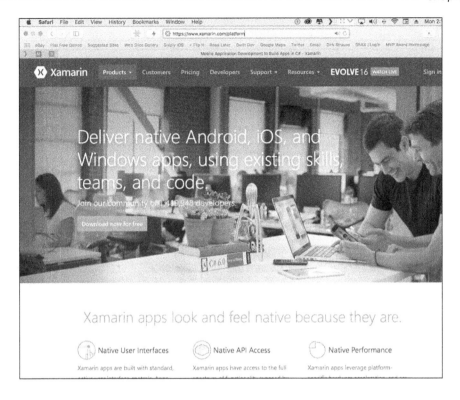

5. After downloading the installer on the Mac, the installation is straightforward. Just follow the screen prompts to complete the installation:

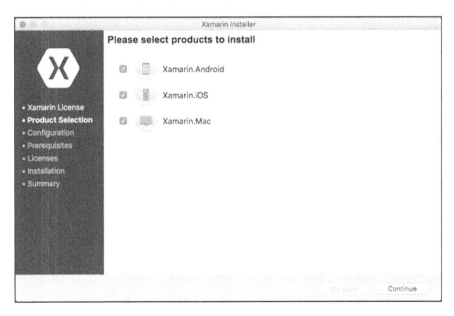

How it works...

The steps we took previously when installing Xamarin and Apache Cordova will allow us to do the following:

- **Install Apache Cordova**: If you only want to target Android, iOS, and Windows but don't want to use Xamarin
- **Install Xamarin**: If you want to target Android, iOS, Windows, or all three and use a single solution to do so

Visual Studio is extremely flexible and offers developers a wide variety of choice.

Creating an Android Visual Studio project using Apache Cordova

Creating an Android application using Apache Cordova is extremely easy. This recipe, however, will only show you how to get started.

Getting ready

You will need to have Apache Cordova installed as part of the custom installation options during Visual Studio setup. To see how to do this, refer to the *Installing Xamarin and other required components* recipe in this chapter.

How to do it...

1. From the **New Project** dialog screen, select **Apache Cordova Apps** and select the **Blank App (Apache Cordova)** as the template to use. Choose a location for your project and click on the **OK** button:

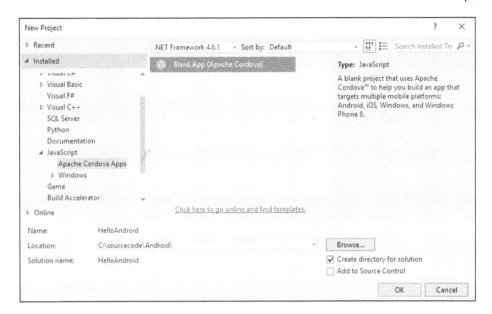

2. Once Visual Studio has created your application, you will notice that it has a very specific structure to it. From the project, you will notice that you can target Android, iOS, Windows, or Windows Phone 8.1. This is the framework you will be using to create your Android application:

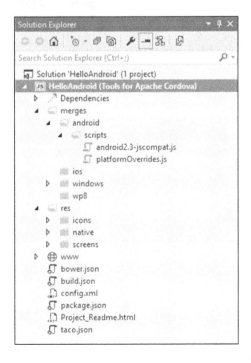

3. When you are ready to debug, you can choose an emulator from the **Debug** menu. This will deploy your application to the selected emulator and allow you to test your application:

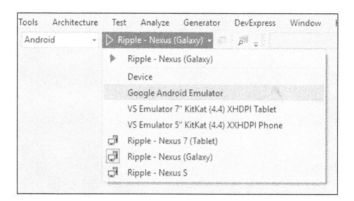

How it works...

Being able to target different mobile devices from a single solution using Visual Studio allows developers the freedom to experiment and find what solution fits them and their development style the best.

Creating an iOS application using Xamarin Forms

Many developers want to try their hand at writing an iOS application. The big drawback has always been learning a new programming language and a new IDE. For some, it is probably not an issue as they want to learn something new. But for many .NET developers, being able to stick to an IDE and programming language they know is immensely empowering. Well, this is exactly what Xamarin Forms and Visual Studio achieve. It gives .NET developers the ability to use Visual Studio to write applications that can be run cross-platform easily, without having a separate code base for each.

Getting ready

You will need to have a Mac running OS X. You will only need this for debugging iOS applications.

How to do it...

1. In Visual Studio 2015, create a new project. From the installed templates, choose **Cross-Platform** and select **Blank App (Xamarin.Forms.Portable)**. This will allow us to create an application that will be cross-platform and not specific to a single platform (Android or iOS, for example):

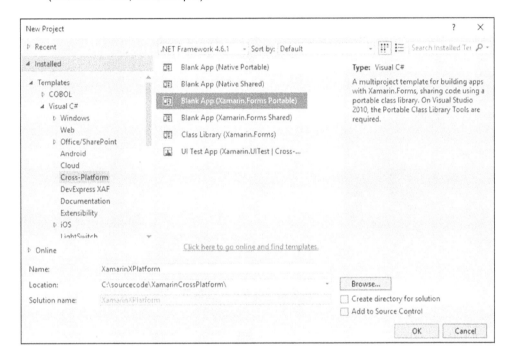

2. Project creation can take a few minutes to complete. Along the way, you might see a message telling you that **Developer Mode** is not enabled for Windows 10 (assuming you are running Windows 10):

3. Enabling this is easy enough. You can click on the **settings for developers** link in the message that popped up, or you can type in `Developer mode` in the **Find a setting** search box in Windows 10 **Settings**:

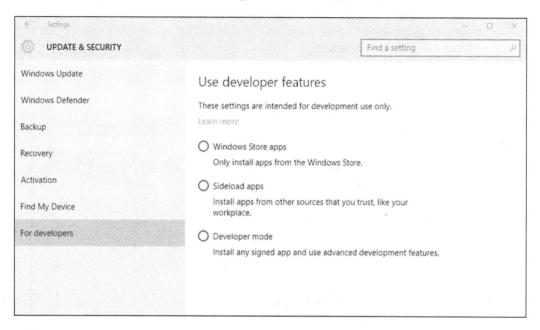

4. Clicking on the **Developer mode** option will display the **Use developer features** confirmation dialog. Just click on **Yes** to continue:

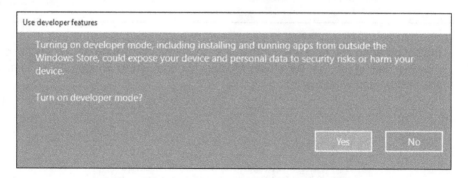

5. After the project is created, you will be presented with a **Get started with Xamarin. Forms** screen:

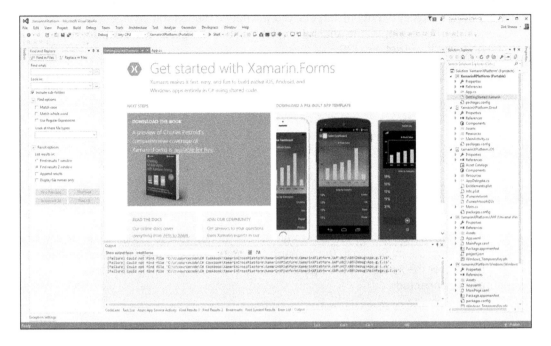

6. Looking at your **Solution Explorer** you will notice that several projects have been created. We will only focus on the iOS project:

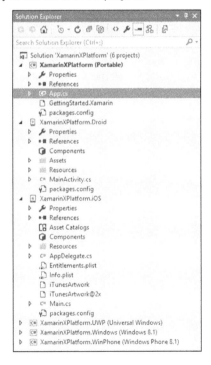

7. Taking a look at the debug targets, you will notice that as you change your target to Droid, for example, the Android project is set as the start-up project. The same happens if you set it to iOS:

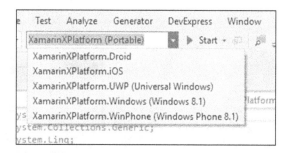

8. As it stands now, before you can go ahead and debug your iOS application, you need to connect Visual Studio to the Xamarin Mac Agent on your Mac. In Visual Studio, hover over the **Xamarin Mac Agent** button on the iOS toolbar. It will show as disconnected:

 See the *Installing Xamarin and other required components* recipe earlier in this chapter for how to install the Xamarin Mac Agent.

9. To connect to the Xamarin Mac Agent, click on this button. The **Xamarin Mac Agent Instructions** window will be displayed. You can follow the instructions on this screen, which are as follows:

10. On your Mac, open up **System Preferences**. Look for and click on the **Sharing** icon:

11. This will display the **Sharing** window. Select **Remote Login** from the menu on the left and, under **Only these users**, select or add your current Mac user to this list:

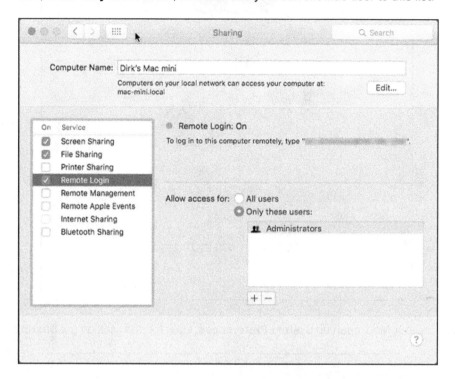

12. When you have added your current Mac user to the **Remote Login** list, click the back button to return to the previous screen. Then look for and click on **Network**:

13. This will open up the **Network** screen. Look where it shows the current status as **Connected**. Underneath that, you will see an IP address. Make a note of the IP address displayed, because you will need to use it to connect Visual Studio to the Xamarin Mac Agent:

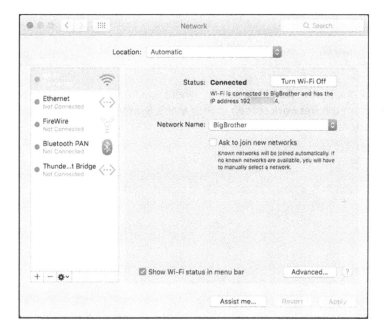

[Just note that I have purposefully masked my IP address in the screenshot.]

14. Back in Windows, in Visual Studio click **OK** to dismiss the **Xamarin Mac Agent Instructions** screen. The **Xamarin Mac Agent** screen will now be visible. At the bottom of this screen, click on the **Add Mac...** button:

15. This will display the **Add Mac** screen, where you need to enter the IP address you noted from the **Network** screen in your Mac's **System Preferences**. Click on the **Add** button:

 Just note that I have purposefully masked my IP address in the screenshot.

16. You will now be asked to provide the username and password for the Mac user you added on the **Remote Login** screen earlier. Click on the **Login** button:

Just note that I have purposefully masked IP addresses and GUID in the screenshot.

17. After clicking **Login**, you should automatically be connected to your Xamarin Mac Agent from Visual Studio:

18. You can now select the iOS device you want to debug on. As you can see, there are a wide variety of iOS devices to choose from:

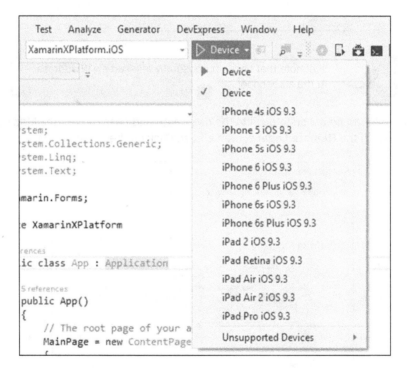

19. For the purposes of this recipe, we have just chosen an **iPhone 4S iOS 9.3**. Click on the **Debug** button to start the app:

20. This will now build your application and send that information over the network connection to the Xamarin Mac Agent. This will then fire up the simulator on your Mac. The first time you do this, it might take a few minutes to spin up the simulator, but once it is done, successive debug sessions will go much quicker:

21. After the simulator is started on the Mac, the Xamarin application will be launched:

22. When the Xamarin splash screen closes, you will see the **Welcome to Xamarin Forms!** text:

23. Back in Visual Studio, stop debugging. You will notice that the app closes in the simulator app on the Mac, and that debugging stops in Visual Studio. The simulator, however, remains open on your Mac.

Now let's change some text. Look at the portable project in your Visual Studio solution. This is the shared project that all the other projects in the solution will use. In the portable project, click on the `App.cs` file:

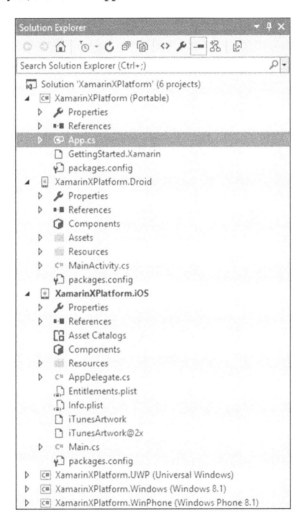

24. The default code is displayed. Here you can see the `Welcome to Xamarin Forms!` text we saw in the application we debugged earlier:

```
namespace XamarinXPlatform
{
    6 references
    public class App : Application
    {
        5 references
        public App()
        {
            // The root page of your application
            MainPage = new ContentPage
            {
                Content = new StackLayout
                {
                    VerticalOptions = LayoutOptions.Center,
                    Children = {
                        new Label { HorizontalTextAlignment = TextAlignment.Center,
                            Text = "Welcome to Xamarin Forms!"
                        }
                    }
                }
            };
        }
    }
}
```

25. Change the code to look as follows. All we are doing is adding the date and time. A few things to note here are:

   ❑ We are using the standard .NET `DateTime` library here

   ❑ We are using string interpolation to create our text to display on the form:

```
MainPage = new ContentPage
{
    Content = new StackLayout
    {
        VerticalOptions = LayoutOptions.Center,
        Children = {
            new Label { HorizontalTextAlignment =
            TextAlignment.Center,
                Text = $"Welcome to Xamarin Forms! The date
                is {DateTime.Now}"
            }
        }
    }
};
```

26. When you have done that, debug your application again. When the simulator displays your iOS application on the Mac, you will see that the date and time are shown:

How it works...

One thing to note is that we are not doing anything different here than we would do in any other standard .NET application. We are writing C# code and compiling it to run on an iOS operating system. We can also easily change the application to debug on any iOS device. We didn't need to learn Objective-C or Swift (although Swift is an awesome language and well worth learning). We also didn't need to get to grips with learning a new IDE (Xcode, which is used to develop iOS and Mac applications). We didn't have to tweak any constraints, modify any playground elements, or learn how to use any new controls. Xamarin Forms and Visual Studio take care of all of this for us out of the box. Best of all, Xamarin is now free with Visual Studio. There is no reason why you shouldn't try your hand at writing an iOS application.

12
Writing Secure Code and Debugging in Visual Studio

In this chapter, we will have a look at some examples of being more efficient as a developer when it comes to debugging your code. We will also be looking at how to write secure code. Writing secure code can be a challenge, but consider the following: if part of your code security involves making sure that passwords are securely stored, why write that code over and over between projects? Write the code once and implement it in every new project you create. The concepts we will be looking at are as follows:

- ▸ Encrypting and storing passwords correctly
- ▸ Using `SecureString` in code
- ▸ Securing sensitive parts of `App.config/web.config`
- ▸ Preventing SQL injection attacks
- ▸ Using **Diagnostic Tools** and **Historical Debugging**
- ▸ Setting conditional breakpoints
- ▸ Using **PerfTips** to identify bottlenecks in code

Introduction

Something that many developers tend to miss is the need to write secure code. Development deadlines and other project-related pressures cause developers to put delivering code above doing it the right way. Many of you might not agree with me, but believe me when I say that I have heard the excuse of "We do not have budget for this" once too many times. This is usually when the development budget has been determined by other stakeholders and the developer not consulted.

Consider a situation where a consultant tells the developer that they have sold a system to a customer. That system now needs to be developed. Furthermore, the developer is told that they have *x* amount of hours to complete the development. A document outlining the requirements is given to the developer and the developer is given the go-ahead to begin, and to complete development in the required time.

This scenario is the reality many developers face. You might think that this scenario can't possibly exist, or perhaps you are reading this and relate to the scenario as being how the process currently works in your company. Whatever the case may be, this is something that happens today in software development.

So how do developers combat project suicide? (I call these projects this because projects approached like this rarely succeed.) Start by creating reusable code. Think of processes you repeat often enough to warrant writing a reusable DLL for. Did you know that you can create Visual Studio templates? If you have a standard project structure you use, create a template from it and re-use it for each new project, thereby speeding up delivery and cutting down on bugs.

A few considerations for project templates are database layers, security layers, common validation code (does this data table contain any data), common extension methods, and so on.

Encrypting and storing passwords correctly

One thing I have often seen is badly stored passwords. Just because the password is stored in a database on your server, does not make it secure. So what do badly stored passwords look like?

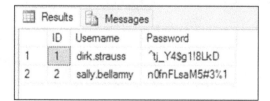

Secure passwords stored badly are no longer secure. The passwords in the previous screenshot are the actual user passwords. Entering the first password, `^tj_Y4$g1!8LkD` at the login screen will give the user access to the system. Passwords should be stored securely in the database. In fact, you need to employ salted password hashing. You should be able to encrypt the user's password, but never decrypt it.

So how do you decrypt the password to match it to the password the user enters at the login screen? Well, you don't. You always hash the password the user enters at the login screen. If it matches the hash of their real password stored in the database, you give them access to the system.

Getting ready

The SQL tables in this recipe are for illustration only and are not written to by the code in the recipe. The database can be found in the `_database scripts` folder that accompanies the source code for this book.

How to do it...

1. Create a new class library by right-clicking on your solution, and selecting **Add** and then **New Project** from the context menu:

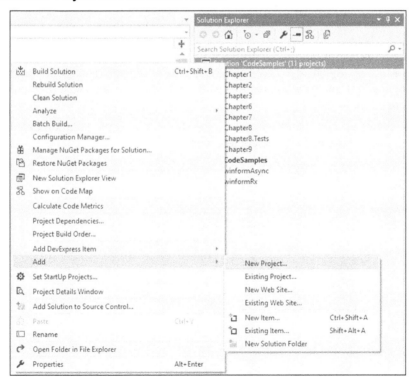

2. From the **Add New Project** dialog screen, select **Class Library** from the installed templates and call your class `Chapter12`:

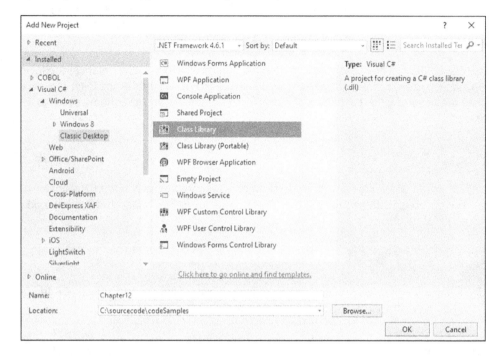

3. Your new class library will be added to your solution with a default name of `Class1.cs`, which we renamed `Recipes.cs` in order to distinguish the code properly. You can, however, rename your class whatever you like if that makes more sense to you.

4. To rename your class, simply click on the class name in the **Solution Explorer** and select **Rename** from the context menu:

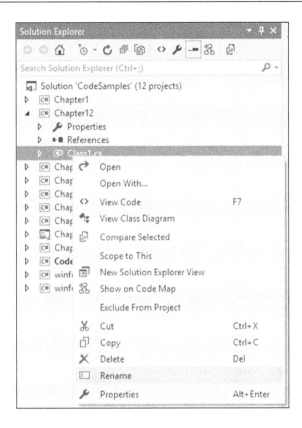

5. Visual Studio will ask you to confirm a rename of all references to the code element **Class1** in the project. Just click **Yes**:

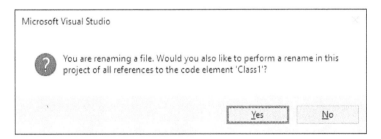

6. The following class is added to your `Chapter12` library project:

```
namespace Chapter12
{
    public class Recipes
    {

    }
}
```

7. Add the following `using` statement to your class:

```
using System.Security.Cryptography;
```

8. Next, you need to add two properties to the class. These properties will store the salt and the hash. Usually you will write these values to the database along with the username, but for the purposes of this recipe we will simply add them to the static properties. Also add two methods to the class called `RegisterUser()` and `ValidateLogin()`. Both methods take as parameters the `username` and `password` variables:

```
public static class Recipes
{
    public static string saltValue { get; set; }
    public static string hashValue { get; set; }

    public static void RegisterUser(string password, string
    username)
    {

    }

    public static void ValidateLogin(string password,
    string username)
    {

    }
}
```

9. Starting with the `RegisterUser()` method, here we do a number of things. To list the steps in the method:

    1. We generate a truly random, cryptographically strong salt value using `RNGCryptoServiceProvider`

    2. Add the salt to the password and hash the salted password using `SHA256`.

 It doesn't matter if you add the salt before or after the password. Just remember to be consistent each time you do it.

    3. Store the salt value and the hash value along with the username in the database.

In order to cut down on code, I have not actually added code to write the hash and salt values to the database. I simply added them to the properties created earlier. In a real-world situation, you would always write these to the database.

This is a very secure way to handle user passwords in your application:

```
public static void RegisterUser(string password, string
username)
{
    // Create a truly random salt using
    RNGCryptoServiceProvider.
    RNGCryptoServiceProvider csprng = new
    RNGCryptoServiceProvider();
    byte[] salt = new byte[32];
    csprng.GetBytes(salt);

    // Get the salt value
    saltValue = Convert.ToBase64String(salt);
    // Salt the password
    byte[] saltedPassword =
    Encoding.UTF8.GetBytes(saltValue + password);

    // Hash the salted password using SHA256
    SHA256Managed hashstring = new SHA256Managed();
    byte[] hash = hashstring.ComputeHash(saltedPassword);

    // Save both the salt and the hash in the user's
    database record.
    saltValue = Convert.ToBase64String(salt);
    hashValue = Convert.ToBase64String(hash);
}
```

10. The next method we need to create is the `ValidateLogin()` method. Here we take the username and validate that first. If the user entered the username incorrectly, do not tell them so. This would alert someone trying to compromise the system that they have the wrong username and that as soon as they get a wrong password notification, they know that the username is correct. The steps in this method are as follows:

    1. Get the salt and hash values for the entered username from the database.

    2. Salt the password the user entered at the login screen with the salt read from the database.

    3. Hash the salted password using the same hashing algorithm as when the user registered.

4.   Compare the hash value read from the database to the hash value generated in the method. If the two hashes match, then the password is correctly entered and the user validated.

Note that we never decrypt the password from the database. If you have code decrypting user passwords and matching that to the password entered, you need to reconsider and rewrite your password logic. A system should never be able to decrypt user passwords.

```
public static void ValidateLogin(string password, string username)
{
    // Read the user's salt value from the database
    string saltValueFromDB = saltValue;

    // Read the user's hash value from the database
    string hashValueFromDB = hashValue;

    byte[] saltedPassword = Encoding.UTF8.GetBytes(saltValueFromDB
+
    password);

    // Hash the salted password using SHA256
    SHA256Managed hashstring = new SHA256Managed();
    byte[] hash = hashstring.ComputeHash(saltedPassword);

    string hashToCompare = Convert.ToBase64String(hash);

    if (hashValueFromDB.Equals(hashToCompare))
        Console.WriteLine("User Validated.");
    else
        Console.WriteLine("Login credentials incorrect. User not
        validated.");
}
```

11. To test the code, add a reference to the `Chapter12` class in your `CodeSamples` project:

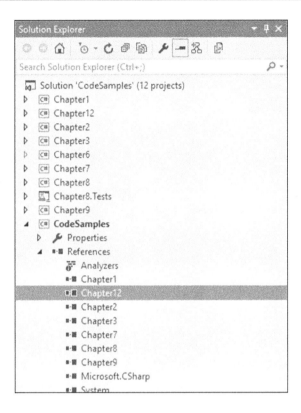

12. Because we created a static class, you can add the new `using static` to your `Program.cs` file:

```
using static Chapter12.Recipes;
```

13. Test the code by calling the `RegisterUser()` method and pass it the `username` and `password` variable. After that, call the `ValidateLogin()` method and see whether the password matches the hash. This would obviously not happen at the same time in a real production system:

```
string username = "dirk.strauss";
string password = "^tj_Y4$g1!8LkD";
RegisterUser(password, username);

ValidateLogin(password, username);
Console.ReadLine();
```

14. When you debug the code, you will see the user has been validated:

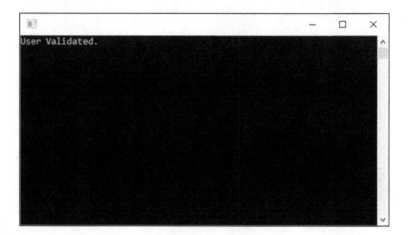

15. Lastly, modify the code slightly and set the `password` variable to something else. This will mimic a user entering an incorrect password:

```
string username = "dirk.strauss";
string password = "^tj_Y4$g1!8LkD";
RegisterUser(password, username);

password = "WrongPassword";
ValidateLogin(password, username);
Console.ReadLine();
```

16. When you debug the application, you will see that the user is not validated:

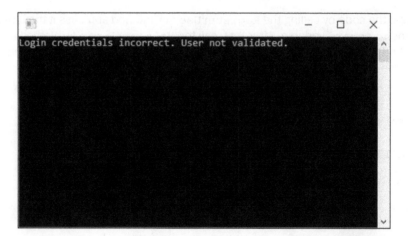

How it works...

Nowhere in the code did we decrypt the password. In fact, the password is never stored anywhere. We always worked with the hash of the password. Here are the important points to take away from this recipe:

- Never use the `Random` class in C# to generate your salt. Always use the `RNGCryptoServiceProvider` class.

- Never re-use the same salt in your code. So don't create a constant with your salt and use it to salt all the passwords in your system.

- Never tell the user that the password is incorrect if the password didn't match. Also, never tell the user that they entered an incorrect username. This prevents someone trying to compromise the system from knowing that they got one of the two login credentials correct. If either the username or password has been entered incorrectly, rather notify the user that their login credentials are incorrect. This could mean that either the username or password (or both) have been entered incorrectly.

- You can't get the passwords from the hash or salt stored in the database. Therefore, if the database was compromised, the password data stored within it would not be at risk. The encryption of the user's password is a one-way operation, meaning that it can never be decrypted. Also important to note is that even if the source code was compromised and stolen by someone with malicious intent, you would not be able to use the code to decipher the encrypted data in the database.

- Combine the previous methods with a strong password policy (because even in 2016, there are still users that think using `'l3tm31n'` for a password is good enough), and you have a very good password encryption routine.

When we look at the user access table, the correct way to store user credentials would look something like this:

	ID	Username	Salt	Hash
1	1	dirk.strauss	KxZH/jO8OFbNBvAiUJDnTHwG&iMJ384+Tlq1JbKnKYY=	Togax/WIna6Y8wblyiSvX7GFiQBf4MQ+foBfobSlLzo=
2	2	sally.bellarmy	9qSLUCH+VLQYa5DIlwlclpQoadyiVKIlxqqsuabN3k0=	vOBzPiM2Z+qxed7n8gVIKGfnm3o6lvqXIRkrWR2hM9k=

The salt and hash are stored alongside the username, and are secure because they can't be decrypted to expose the actual password.

> If you sign up for a service on the Internet and they send you a confirmation either via email or text message and display your password in this message in plain text, then you should seriously consider closing your account. If a system can read your password and send it to you in plain text, then so can anybody else. Never use the same password for all your logins.

Using SecureString in code

Securing your application against malicious attacks is not an easy task. It is the constant struggle between writing secure code while minimizing bugs (which hackers usually exploit) and black hats writing more and more sophisticated methods to compromise systems and networks. I personally believe that higher learning institutions need to teach IT students two things:

- How to use and integrate with a popular ERP system
- Proper software security principles

In fact, I believe that secure programming 101 must not simply be a module or topic in a given IT course, but a whole course on its own. It needs to be handled with the seriousness and respect it deserves and needs to preferably be taught by someone that can actually hack a system or network.

White hats teaching students how to compromise systems, exploit vulnerable code, and infiltrate networks will make a big difference in changing the way future software developers approach programming. It comes down to developers knowing what not to do when programming defensively. It is quite possible that some of those students might go on to become black hats themselves, but they would have done that irrespective of whether they took a class on hacking secure programming or not.

Getting ready

The code might look a little funny in some places. This is because SecureString is using unmanaged memory to store the sensitive information. Rest assured that SecureString is well supported and used within the .NET Framework, as can be seen from the instantiation of the SqlCredential object used in creating connections to a database:

```
SqlCredential cred = new SqlCredential()
        SqlCredential(string userId, SecureString password)
        Creates an object of type SqlCredential.
        userId: The user id.
```

How to do it...

1. Start by adding a new Windows Forms project to your solution:

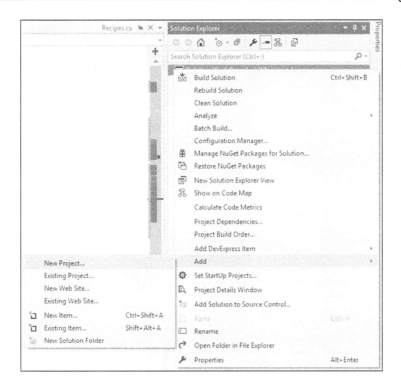

2. Call the project `winformSecure` and click on the **OK** button:

3. In the **Toolbox**, search for the **TextBox** control and add it to your form:

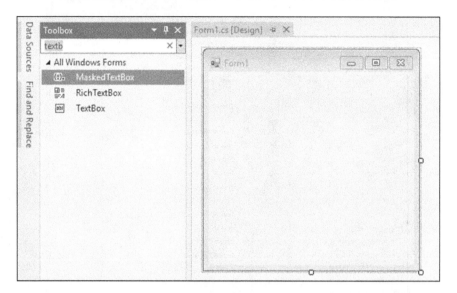

4. Lastly, add a button control to your form. You can resize this form however you like to look more like a login form:

5. With the text box control selected on the Windows Forms, open up the **Properties** panel and click on the Events button (it looks like a lightning bolt). In the **Key** group, double-click on the **KeyPress** event to create the handler in the code behind:

The code that is created for you is the **KeyPress** event handler for the text box control. This will fire whenever a user presses a key on the keyboard:

```
private void textBox1_KeyPress(object sender,
KeyPressEventArgs e)
{

}
```

6. Back in the **Properties** panel, expand the **Behavior** group and change the value of **UseSystemPasswordChar** to true:

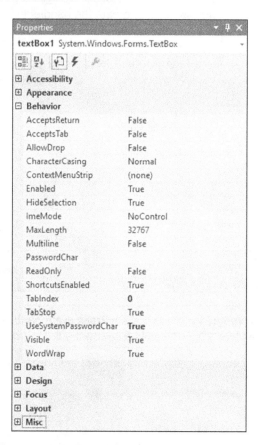

7. In the code behind, add the following using statement:

```
using System.Runtime.InteropServices;
```

8. Add the SecureString variable as a global variable to your Windows Forms:

```
SecureString secure = new SecureString();
```

9. Then in the KeyPress event, append the KeyChar value to the SecureString variable every time the user presses a key. You might want to add code to ignore certain key presses, but this is beyond the scope of this recipe:

```
private void textBox1_KeyPress(object sender,
KeyPressEventArgs e)
{
    secure.AppendChar(e.KeyChar);
}
```

10. Then in the **Login** button's event handler, add the following code to read the value from the SecureString object. Here we are working with unmanaged memory and unmanaged code:

```
private void btnLogin_Click(object sender, EventArgs e)
{
    IntPtr unmanagedPtr = IntPtr.Zero;

    try
    {
        if (secure == null)
            throw new ArgumentNullException("Password not
            defined");
        unmanagedPtr =
        Marshal.SecureStringToGlobalAllocUnicode(secure);
        MessageBox.Show($"SecureString password to validate
        is {Marshal.PtrToStringUni(unmanagedPtr)}");
    }
    catch(Exception ex)
    {
        MessageBox.Show(ex.Message);
    }
    finally
    {
        Marshal.ZeroFreeGlobalAllocUnicode(unmanagedPtr);
        secure.Dispose();
    }
}
```

11. Run your Windows Forms application and type in a password:

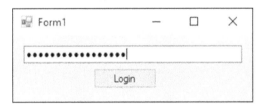

12. Then click on the **Login** button. You will then see the password you typed in displayed in the message box:

How it works...

It has become almost a habit for many developers to use `System.String` to store sensitive information such as passwords. The problem with this approach is that `System.String` is immutable. This means that the object created in memory by `System.String` can't be changed. If you modify the variable, a new object is created in memory. You also cannot determine when the object created by `System.String` will be removed from memory during garbage collection. Conversely, by using the `SecureString` object, you will encrypt sensitive information and when that object is no longer needed, it is deleted from memory. `SecureString` encrypts and decrypts your sensitive data in unmanaged memory.

Now I need to be clear regarding one thing here. `SecureString` is by no means foolproof. If your system contains a virus with the sole purpose of compromising the `SecureString` operations, using it doesn't help much (be sure to use proper anti-virus software anyway). At some point during the code execution, the string representation of your password (or sensitive information) is visible. Secondly, if a hacker somehow found a way to inspect your heap or log your key strokes, the password might be visible. The use of `SecureString`, however makes this window of opportunity for a hacker much smaller. The window of opportunity reduces because there are less attack vectors (points of entry for a hacker), thereby reducing your attack surface (sum of all points of attack by a hacker).

The bottom line is this: `SecureString` is there for a reason. As a software developer concerned about security, you should be using `SecureString`.

Securing sensitive parts of App.config/web.config

As a developer, you will undoubtedly work with sensitive information such as passwords. How you handle this information during development is very important. In the past, I have received copies of a client's live database to use for testing. This does pose a very real security risk for your client.

Often, we keep settings in a `web.config` file (when working with web applications). For this example, though, I will be demonstrating a console application that uses an `App.config` file. The same logic can be applied to a `web.config` file too.

Getting ready

Creating a console application is the quickest way to demonstrate this recipe. If, however, you want to follow along using a web application (and securing a `web.config` file), you can do so.

How to do it...

1. In the console application, locate the `App.config` file. This is the file that contains the sensitive data:

2. If you open the `App.config` file, you will see that within the `appSettings` tag there is a key added called `Secret`. This information should probably not be in the `App.config` to start off with. The problem here is that it might be checked into your source control. Imagine that on GitHub?

```xml
<?xml version="1.0" encoding="utf-8"?>
<configuration>
    <startup>
        <supportedRuntime version="v4.0"
        sku=".NETFramework,Version=v4.6.1"/>
    </startup>
    <appSettings>
      <add key="name" value="Dirk"/>
      <add key="lastname" value="Strauss"/>
      <add key="Secret" value="letMeIn"/>
    </appSettings>
</configuration>
```

3. To overcome this vulnerability, we need to move the sensitive data out of the `App.config` file into another file. To do this, we specify a path to a file that will contain the sensitive data we want to remove from the `App.config` file:

```
<appSettings file="C:\temp\secret\secret.config">
```

> You might be wondering, why not simply just encrypt the information? Well, that is a given really. The reason this value is in plain text is just to demonstrate a concept here. You would probably encrypt this value anyway in a real-world situation. You would not, however, want this sensitive information sitting on a server in a code repository somewhere, even if it is encrypted. Be safe, move it out of your solution.

4. When you have added the path to the secure file, remove the key containing the sensitive information:

```
1    <?xml version="1.0" encoding="utf-8"?>
2    <configuration>
3        <startup>
4            <supportedRuntime version="v4.0" sku=".NETFramework,Version=v4.6.1"/>
5        </startup>
6        <appSettings file="C:\temp\secret\secret.config">
7            <add key="name" value="Dirk"/>
8            <add key="lastname" value="Strauss"/>
9        </appSettings>
10   </configuration>
```

5. Navigate to the path you specified in the `App.config` file property. Create your `secret.config` file and open it up for editing:

6. Inside this file, repeat the `appSettings` section and add the `Secret` key to it. What happens now is that when your console application runs, it reads the `appSettings` section in your solution and finds the reference to the secret file. It then looks for the secret file and merges it with the `App.config` in your solution:

7. To see that this merge works, add a reference to your console application:

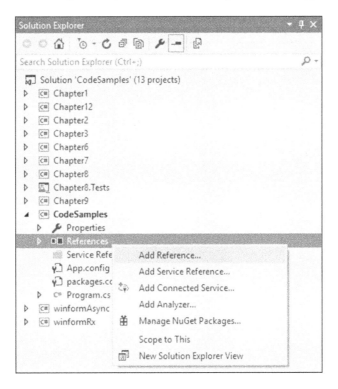

8. Search for and add `System.Configuration` to your references:

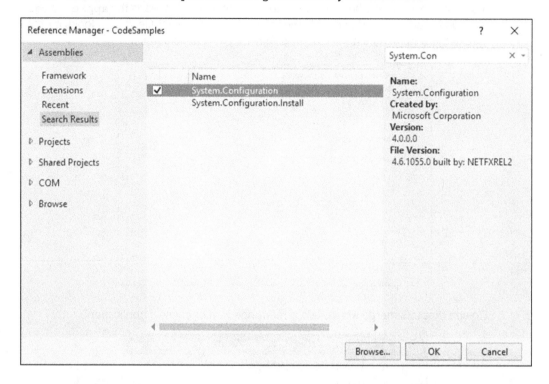

9. When you have added the reference, your solution references should look something like this:

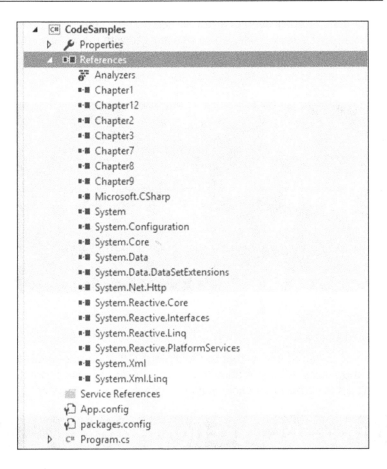

10. To the top of your `Program.cs` file, add the following `using` statement:

```
using System.Configuration;
```

11. Add the following code to read the `Secret` key setting from your `App.config` file. Only this time, it will read the merged file, which is made up of your `App.config` and your `secret.config` file:

```
string sSecret =
ConfigurationManager.AppSettings["Secret"];
Console.WriteLine(sSecret);
Console.ReadLine();
```

12. Run your console application and you will see that the sensitive data has been read from the `secret.config` file, which was merged with the `App.config` file at runtime:

```
letMeIn
```

How it works...

Something I need to point out here is that this technique will also work for `web.config` files. If you need to remove sensitive information from your configuration file, move it to another file so that it doesn't get included in your source control check-in or deployment.

Preventing SQL injection attacks

SQL injection attacks are a very real problem. There are too many applications that still make themselves vulnerable to this kind of attack. If you develop a web application or website, you should be vigilant of bad database operations. Vulnerable in-line SQL exposes the database to a SQL injection attack. A SQL injection attack is where an attacker modifies SQL statements via a web form input box to produce a different result than originally intended. This is usually attempted on a form where the web application is supposed to access the database to authenticate the user login. By not sanitizing the user input, you are exposing your data to exploits such as this.

The accepted solution to mitigate SQL injection attacks is to create a parametrized stored procedure and call that from your code.

Getting ready

You need to create the `CookbookDB` database in your SQL Server before continuing this recipe. You will find the script in the `_database scripts` folder in the accompanying source code.

How to do it...

1. For this recipe, I am using SQL Server 2012. The concept is the same if you are using an older version of SQL Server. After you have created the CookbookDB database, you will see that there is a table called UserDisplayData under the Tables folder:

2. The UserDisplayData table is simply used to illustrate the concept of querying using a parameterized stored procedure. It would not have any real benefit in a production database, because it only returns a screen name:

3. We need to create a stored procedure to select data from this table for a specific ID (user ID). Click on the `Programmability` node to expand it:

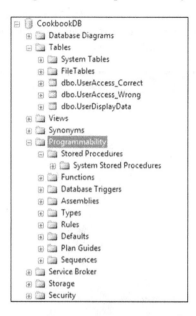

4. Next, right-click on the `Stored Procedures` node and select **New Stored Procedure...** from the context menu:

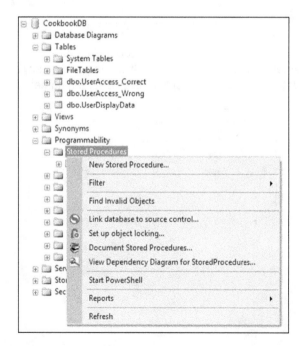

5. SQL Server will create the following stored procedure template for you. This template consists of a section where you can comment on the particular stored procedure, as well as a section to add parameters you might need, and obviously a section that you need to add the actual SQL statement to:

```
SET ANSI_NULLS ON
GO
SET QUOTED_IDENTIFIER ON
GO
-- =============================================
-- Author:           <Author,,Name>
-- Create date:      <Create Date,,>
-- Description:      <Description,,>
-- =============================================
CREATE PROCEDURE <Procedure_Name, sysname, ProcedureName>
    -- Add the parameters for the stored procedure here
    <@Param1, sysname, @p1> <Datatype_For_Param1, , int> =
    <Default_Value_For_Param1, , 0>,
    <@Param2, sysname, @p2> <Datatype_For_Param2, , int> =
    <Default_Value_For_Param2, , 0>
AS
BEGIN
    -- SET NOCOUNT ON added to prevent extra result sets
    from
    -- interfering with SELECT statements.
    SET NOCOUNT ON;

    -- Insert statements for procedure here
    SELECT <@Param1, sysname, @p1>, <@Param2, sysname, @p2>
END
GO
```

6. Give the stored procedure a suitable name that will describe the action or intent of the stored procedure:

```
CREATE PROCEDURE cb_ReadCurrentUserDisplayData
```

There are many people that do prefix their stored procedures, and I'm one of those. I like to keep my stored procedures grouped. I therefore name my stored procedures in the format *[prefix]_[tablename_or_ module]_[stored_procedure_action]*. Having said that, I generally avoid using `sp_` as a prefix to my stored procedures. There are a lot of opinions on the Internet as to why this is a bad idea. It is generally believed that using `sp_` as a stored procedure prefix impacts on performance because it is used as the stored procedure prefix in the master database.

For the purposes of this recipe, I have just kept to a simple name for the stored procedure.

7. Define a parameter for this stored procedure. By doing this, you are telling the database that when this stored procedure is called, it will pass through a value of type integer that is stored in a parameter caller `@userID`:

```
@userID INT
```

8. You now define the SQL statement to be used by this stored procedure. We are just going to do a straightforward `SELECT` statement:

```
SELECT
    Firstname, Lastname, Displayname
FROM
    dbo.UserDisplayData
WHERE
    ID = @userID
```

You will notice that my `SELECT` statement contains the specific column names instead of a `SELECT * FROM`. Doing a `SELECT *` is considered bad practice. You would usually not want to return all the column values from a table. If you want all the column values, then it is better to explicitly list the columns by name instead of just getting all.

Using `SELECT *` returns unnecessary columns and increases the overhead on the server. This does make a difference in the bigger scheme of things, especially when the database starts getting a lot of traffic.

The thought of having to type out the column names for a large table is definitely not something I would look forward to. You can however use the following tricks to make it easy for you to add the column names to your SQL `SELECT` statement. You can right-click on the database table and select **Script Table As** to create one of several SQL statements. Secondly, you can expand the `Table` node and expand the table you wish to write the statement for. You will then see a node called `Columns`. Drag the `Columns` node onto the query editor. That will insert all the column names into the query editor for you.

9. When you have completed adding the code to your stored procedure, it will look like this:

```
SET ANSI_NULLS ON
GO
SET QUOTED_IDENTIFIER ON
GO
-- ============================================
-- Author:          <Dirk Strauss>
-- Create date:     <2 April 2016>
-- Description:     <Read the user data for the specific user ID supplied as parameter>
-- ============================================
CREATE PROCEDURE cb_ReadCurrentUserDisplayData
    @userID INT
AS
BEGIN
    -- SET NOCOUNT ON added to prevent extra result sets from
    -- interfering with SELECT statements.
    SET NOCOUNT ON;

    SELECT
        Firstname, Lastname, Displayname
    FROM
        dbo.UserDisplayData
    WHERE
        ID = @userID
END
GO
```

10. To create the stored procedure, you need to click on the **Execute** button. Be certain that you have the correct database selected when clicking on the **Execute** button:

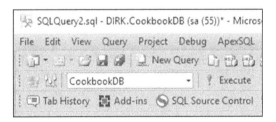

11. The stored procedure will then be created under the `Stored Procedures` node in SQL Server:

12. We have now got to halfway through this task. It is time to construct the code that we will use in our application to query the database. We will be adding this code directly to the `Program.cs` file of your console application. While this code isn't considered best practice (hardcoding the server credentials), it serves merely to illustrate the concept of calling a parameterized stored procedure from C#.

13. To start, add the following `using` statement to the top of your console application:

```
using System.Data.SqlClient;
```

14. We then add the variables to contain the credentials we need to log on to the server:

```
int intUserID = 1;
int cmdTimeout = 15;
string server = "DIRK";
string db = "CookbookDB";
string uid = "dirk";
string password = "uR^GP2ABG19@!R";
```

15. We now use `SecureString` to store the password and add it to a `SqlCredential` object:

```
SecureString secpw = new SecureString();
if (password.Length > 0)
{
    foreach (var c in password.ToCharArray())
    secpw.AppendChar(c);
}
secpw.MakeReadOnly();

string dbConn = $"Data Source={server};Initial
Catalog={db};";
6SqlCredential cred = new SqlCredential(uid, secpw);
```

 For more on `SecureString`, see the *Using SecureString in code* recipe of this chapter.

16. We now create a `SqlConnection` object inside a `using` statement. This ensures that the SQL connection is closed when the `using` statement moves out of scope:

```
using (SqlConnection conn = new SqlConnection(dbConn,
cred))
{
    try
    {

    }
    catch (Exception ex)
    {
        Console.WriteLine(ex.Message);
    }
}
Console.ReadLine();
```

17. Inside the `try`, add the following code to open the connection string and create a `SqlCommand` object that takes the open connection and name of the stored procedure as parameters. You can use the shortcut method of creating the actual SQL parameter to pass to the stored procedure:

```
cmd.Parameters.Add("userID", SqlDbType.Int).Value = intUserID;
```

Because I'm just passing a parameter of type integer to the stored procedure, I'm not defining a length for this parameter:

```
cmd.Parameters.Add("userID", SqlDbType.Int).Value = intUserID;
▲ 3 of 4 ▼  SqlParameter SqlParameterCollection.Add(string parameterName, SqlDbType sqlDbType, int size)
            Adds a SqlParameter to the SqlParameterCollection, given the specified parameter name, SqlDbType and size.
            sqlDbType: The SqlDbType of the SqlParameter to add to the collection.
uubata.Luau(recuiiivata),
```

If, however, you ever need to define a parameter of type `VarChar (MAX)`, you would need to define the size of the parameter type by adding `-1`. Let's say, for example you need to store a student's essay in the database, the code would then look as follows for the `VarChar (MAX)`:

```
cmd.Parameters.Add("essay", SqlDbType.VarChar, -1).Value =
essayValue;
```

18. After we have added our parameter with its value to the `SqlCommand` object, we specify a timeout value, execute the `SqlDataReader`, and load it into a `DataTable`. The value is then output to the console application:

```
conn.Open();
SqlCommand cmd = new SqlCommand("cb_ReadCurrentUserDisplayData",
conn);
cmd.CommandType = CommandType.StoredProcedure;
cmd.Parameters.Add("userID", SqlDbType.Int).Value = intUserID;
cmd.CommandTimeout = cmdTimeout;
var returnData = cmd.ExecuteReader();
var dtData = new DataTable();
dtData.Load(returnData);

if (dtData.Rows.Count != 0)
    Console.WriteLine(dtData.Rows[0]["Displayname"]);
```

19. After you have added all the code to your console application, the correct completed code will look as follows:

```
int intUserID = 1;
int cmdTimeout = 15;
string server = "DIRK";
string db = "CookbookDB";
string uid = "dirk";
string password = "uR^GP2ABG19@!R";
```

```
SecureString secpw = new SecureString();
if (password.Length > 0)
{
    foreach (var c in password.ToCharArray())
    secpw.AppendChar(c);
}
secpw.MakeReadOnly();

string dbConn = $"Data Source={server};Initial
Catalog={db};";

SqlCredential cred = new SqlCredential(uid, secpw);
using (SqlConnection conn = new SqlConnection(dbConn,
cred))
{
    try
    {
        conn.Open();
        SqlCommand cmd = new
        SqlCommand("cb_ReadCurrentUserDisplayData", conn);
        cmd.CommandType = CommandType.StoredProcedure;
        cmd.Parameters.Add("userID", SqlDbType.Int).Value =
        intUserID;
        cmd.CommandTimeout = cmdTimeout;
        var returnData = cmd.ExecuteReader();
        var dtData = new DataTable();
        dtData.Load(returnData);
        if (dtData.Rows.Count != 0)
        Console.WriteLine(dtData.Rows[0]["Displayname"]);

    }
    catch (Exception ex)
    {
        Console.WriteLine(ex.Message);
    }
}
Console.ReadLine();
```

20. Run your console application and you will see the display name output to the screen:

How it works...

By creating a parameterized SQL query, the compiler correctly substitutes the arguments before running the SQL statement against the database. It will prevent malicious data changing your SQL statement in order to exact a malicious result. This is because the SqlCommand object does not directly insert the parameter values into the statement.

To sum it all up, using parameterized stored procedures means no more Little Bobby Tables.

Using Diagnostic Tools and Historical Debugging

The trusty old bug has been the bane of software developers and engineers for more than 140 years. Yes, you read that right. It was in fact Thomas Edison that coined the term "bug" in the late 1870s. It appeared in many of his notebook entries where he describes for example that the incandescent lightbulb still had many "bugs left."

His efforts to debug his inventions are quite legendary. Consider the true grit and determination it took for a man already in his mid-sixties to work 112-hour working weeks. He and his seven-person team (it is a common misconception that there were only six because the seventh member didn't appear in the group photograph) became known as the insomnia squad during a 5-week stint that resulted in very little sleep.

These days, thanks to advances in technology, software developers have a vast array of debugging tools (inside and outside of Visual Studio) at their disposal. So does debugging really matter? Of course it does. It is part of what we as software developers do. If we don't debug, well, here are some examples:

- In 2004, the **Electronic Data Systems** (**EDS**) Child Support System in the UK overpaid almost 2 million people, underpaying almost a million and resulted in billions of dollars in uncollected child support payments. The incompatibility between EDS and another system it relied on resulted in taxpayers losing money and negatively affecting the lives of so many single parents.

- The initial release of Apple Maps in 2012. Enough said. While bemusing for many, I still find myself using Google Maps for turn-by-turn directions when in an unfamiliar city or area.

- The Therac-25 radiation therapy machine used electrons to target tumors in patients. Unfortunately, a race condition in the software caused the machine to deliver lethal overdoses of radiation in several patients.

Examples of software bugs affecting the lives of millions of people can be found all over the Internet. We're not simply talking about the run-of-the-mill bugs either. Sometimes we're faced with seemingly insurmountable issues. It is the comfort of knowing how to use some of the tools available that makes the difference between a stable application and one that is totally unusable.

Getting ready

As of writing this, IntelliTrace is only available in Visual Studio 2015 Enterprise. IntelliTrace is, however, not a new feature in Visual Studio. It has evolved over time, since Visual Studio 2010, into what we have available today.

How to do it...

1. First off, go to **Tools | Options**:

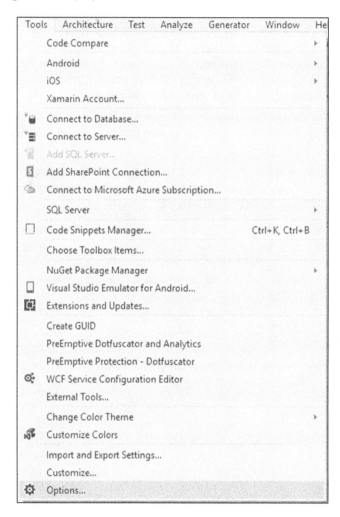

2. Expand the **IntelliTrace** node and click on **General**. Ensure that **Enable IntalliTrace** is checked. Also, make sure that the **IntelliTrace events and call information** option is selected. Click on **OK**:

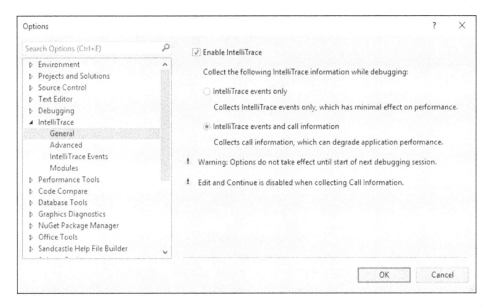

3. In the `Recipes.cs` file, you might need to add the following `using` statements:

```
using System.Diagnostics;
using System.Reflection;
using System.IO;
```

4. Add a method called `ErrorInception()` to the `Recipes` class. Also, add the code to read the base path and assume that there is a folder called `log`. Do not create this folder on your hard drive. We want an exception to be thrown. Lastly, add another method called `LogException()` that does nothing:

```
public static void ErrorInception()
{
    string basepath =
    Path.GetDirectoryName
    (Assembly.GetEntryAssembly().Location);
    var full = Path.Combine(basepath, "log");
}

private static void LogException(string message)
{

}
```

5. Add the following code to your `ErrorInception()` method after the full path has been determined. Here we are trying to open the log file. This is where the exception will occur:

```
try
{
    for (int i = 0; i <= 3; i++)
    {
        // do work
        File.Open($"{full}\\log.txt", FileMode.Append);
    }
}
catch (Exception ex)
{
    StackTrace st = new StackTrace();
    StackFrame sf = st.GetFrame(0);
    MethodBase currentMethodName = sf.GetMethod();
    ex.Data.Add("Date", DateTime.Now);
    LogException(ex.Message);
}
```

6. When you have added all your code, your code should look like this:

```
public static void ErrorInception()
{
    string basepath =
    Path.GetDirectoryName(Assembly.GetEntryAssembly().Location);
    var full = Path.Combine(basepath, "log");

    try
    {
        for (int i = 0; i <= 3; i++)
        {
            // do work
            File.Open($"{full}\\log.txt", FileMode.Append);
        }
    }
    catch (Exception ex)
    {
```

```
        StackTrace st = new StackTrace();
        StackFrame sf = st.GetFrame(0);
        MethodBase currentMethodName = sf.GetMethod();
        ex.Data.Add("Date", DateTime.Now);
        LogException(ex.Message);
    }
}

private static void LogException(string message)
{

}
```

7. In the `Program.cs` file, call the `ErrorInception()` method. Right after that, do a `Console.ReadLine()` so that our console application will pause there. Do not add any breakpoints anywhere to your code:

```
ErrorInception();
Console.ReadLine();
```

8. Start debugging your application. The exception is thrown and the application continues running, a condition often experienced with much more complex applications. At this point, you would expect a log file to be appended with the fictitious data of the app, but nothing happened. It is at this point that you stop your application and start adding breakpoints all over your code in a hit and miss-type exercise. I say hit and miss because you probably will not know exactly where the error is. This is especially true if your code file contains a few thousand lines of code.

Well now, with IntelliTrace and Historical Debugging, you just need to click on the **Break All** button:

9. Your application is now essentially paused. If you don't see the **Diagnostic Tools** window, go to **Debug** and click on **Show Diagnostic Tools** (or *Ctrl + Alt + F2*):

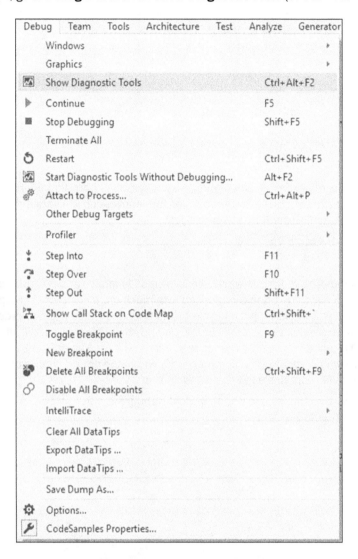

10. Visual Studio now displays the **Diagnostic Tools** window. Immediately you can see that there is a problem indicated by the red diamond icon on the **Events** section. In the **Events** tab at the bottom, you can click on the exception:

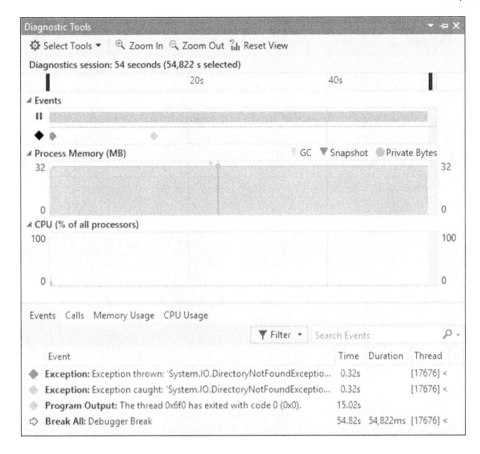

11. Doing this expands the exception details, where you can see that the log file was not found. Visual Studio, however, goes one step further with Historical Debugging:

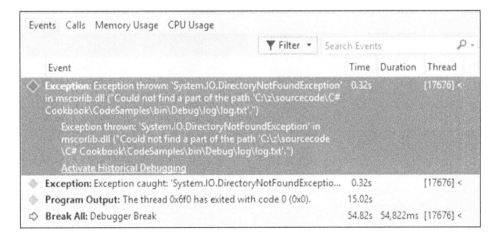

12. You will see a link at the bottom of the exception details that says **Activate Historical Debugging**. Click on this link. This allows you to see the actual line of code that caused this exception in the code editor. It also allows you to view the history of the application's state in the **Locals** window, call stack, and other windows. You now can see the specific line of code that caused the exception in your code editor. In the **Locals** window, you can also see what the path was that the application used to look for the log file. This kind of debugging experience is immensely powerful and allows developers to go straight to the source of the error. This leads to increased productivity and better code:

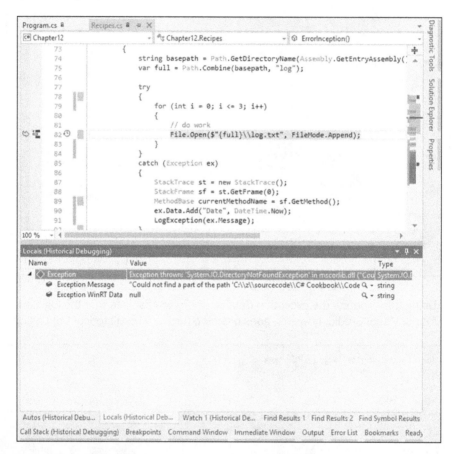

How it works...

So what is the takeaway here? If you only remember one thing, remember this. Once the users of your system lose faith in the abilities and potential of that system due to bugs, that confidence is almost impossible to regain. Even if you resurrect your system from the ashes, after it was laid low by bugs and other issues, to produce a flawless product, your users will not be easily swayed. This is because in their mind, the system is buggy.

I once had to take over a system partially developed by a senior developer who was leaving the company. She had an excellent specification and a well presented prototype shown to the customer. The only problem was that she left the company shortly after the system's phase one was implemented. When the bugs came popping up, the client naturally asked for her assistance.

Telling the client that the developer (who has been solely responsible for building a relationship with the client) has left the company did not bode well to instil a sense of confidence. Having a single developer involved was the first mistake of this particular project anyway.

Secondly, phase two was about to be developed by yours truly, who was also the only developer assigned to this client. This had to be done while building on top of the buggy phase one. So I was fixing bugs while developing new features for the system. Luckily this time round, I had a fantastic project manager called Rory Shelton as my wingman. Together we were dumped in the deep end and Rory did a fantastic job managing the client's expectations while being totally transparent with the client regarding the challenges we were facing.

The users were unfortunately already disillusioned with the provided system and didn't trust the software. This trust was never fully regained. If we had IntelliTrace and Historical Debugging back in 2007, I definitely would have been able to track down the issues in a code base that was unfamiliar to me.

Always debug your software. When you find no more bugs, debug it again. Then give the system to my mom (love you mom). You as the developer of that system know which buttons to click and what data to enter, and in which order things need to happen. My mom doesn't and I can assure you that a user unfamiliar with a system can break it quicker than you can brew a fresh cup of coffee.

Visual Studio provides developers with a very powerful and feature rich set of debugging tools. Use them.

Setting conditional breakpoints

Conditional breakpoints are another hidden gem when it comes to debugging. These allow you to specify one or several conditions. When one of these conditions are met, the code will stop at the breakpoint. Using conditional breakpoints is really easy.

Getting ready

There is nothing you specifically need to prepare to use this recipe.

How to do it...

1. Add the following code to your `Program.cs` file. We are simply creating a list of integers and looping through that list:

```
List<int> myList = new List<int>() { 1, 4, 6, 9, 11 };
foreach(int num in myList)
{
    Console.WriteLine(num);
}
Console.ReadLine();
```

2. Next, place a breakpoint on the `Console.WriteLine(num)` line of code inside the loop:

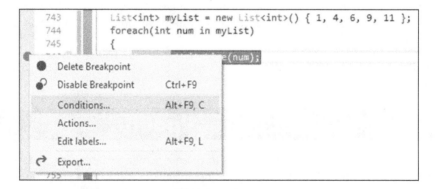

3. Right-click on the breakpoint and select **Conditions...** from the context menu:

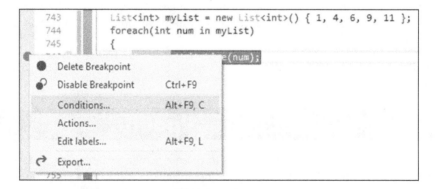

4. You will now see that Visual Studio opens a **Breakpoint Settings** window. Here we specify that the breakpoint needs to be hit only when the value of `num` is 9. You can add several conditions and specify different conditions. The condition logic is really flexible:

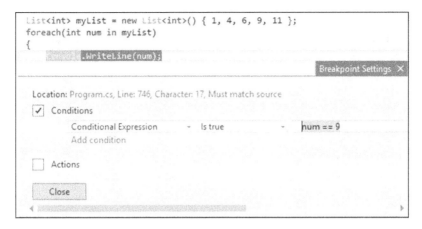

```
List<int> myList = new List<int>() { 1, 4, 6, 9, 11 };
foreach(int num in myList)
{
        .WriteLine(num);
```

Breakpoint Settings ✕

Location: Program.cs, Line: 746, Character: 17, Must match source

☑ Conditions

Conditional Expression   ▾   Is true   ▾   num == 9
Add condition

☐ Actions

Close

5. Debug your console application. You will see that when the breakpoint is hit, the value of num is 9:

```
743        List<int> myList = new List<int>() { 1, 4, 6, 9, 11 };
744        foreach(int num in myList)
745        {
746            Console.WriteLine(num);
747        }
748        Console.ReadLine();
749
```

100 % ▾

Autos

Name	Value
▷ ● myList	Count = 5
● num	9

How it works...

The condition is evaluated on every loop. When the condition is true, the breakpoint will be hit. In the example illustrated in this recipe, the true benefit of a conditional breakpoint is somewhat lost because it is a very small list. Consider this though. You are binding a data grid. Items on the grid are given specific icons based on the status of the item. Your grid contains hundreds of items, because this is a hierarchical grid. You identify the primary ID of the item which is bound to the grid. This primary ID is then passed to other code logic to determine the status, which determines the icon displayed.

To debug and press the *F10* key through hundreds of loops is not productive in any event. With conditional breakpoints, you can specify a value for the primary ID, and only break when the loop hits that value. You can then go straight to the item that is being displayed incorrectly.

Using PerfTips to identify bottlenecks in code

PerfTips are definitely one of my favorite features of Visual Studio 2015. Explaining what they do doesn't do them justice. You have to see them in action.

Getting ready

Do not confuse PerfTips with CodeLens. PerfTips is a separate option from CodeLens in Visual Studio.

How to do it...

1. PerfTips are enabled by default. But just in case you are not seeing any PerfTips, go to **Tools | Options**, and expand the **Debugging** node. Under **General**, to the bottom of the settings page, you will see an option called **Show elapsed time PerfTip while debugging**. Ensure that this option is checked:

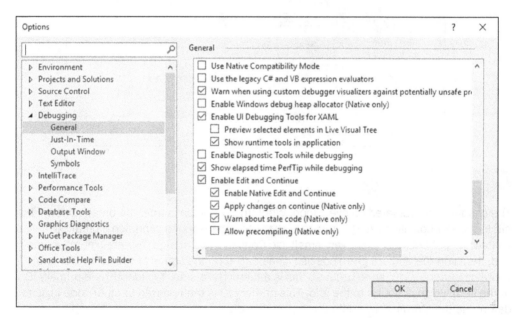

2. We will create a few simple methods that mimic long-running tasks. To do this, we will just sleep the thread for a couple of seconds. In the `Recipes.cs` file, add the following code:

```
public static void RunFastTask()
{
    RunLongerTask();
}

private static void RunLongerTask()
{
    Thread.Sleep(3000);
    BottleNeck();
}

private static void BottleNeck()
{
    Thread.Sleep(8000);
}
```

3. In your console application, call the static method `RunFastTask()` and place a breakpoint on this line of code:

```
RunFastTask();
Thread.Sleep(1000);
```

4. Start debugging your console application. Your breakpoint will stop on the `RunFastTask()` method. Hit *F10* to step over this method:

```
RunFastTask();

Thread.Sleep(1000);
}
```

5. You will notice that 11 seconds later, the next line will be highlighted and the PerfTip will be displayed. The PerfTip displays the time it took for the previous line of code to execute. So the debugger that now sits on the `Thread.Sleep`, shows that the `RunFastTask()` method took 11 seconds to complete. The task is clearly not very fast:

```
RunFastTask();

Thread.Sleep(1000);    ≤11 022ms elapsed
}
```

6. Stepping in to the `RunFastTask()` method, you can place further breakpoints and step over them one by one to find the method that is causing the longest delay. As you can see, PerfTips allow developers to quickly and easily identify bottlenecks in code:

```
1 reference
public static void RunFastTask()
{
    RunLongerTask();
}

1 reference
private static void RunLongerTask()
{
    Thread.Sleep(3000);
    BottleNeck();
}

1 reference
private static void BottleNeck()
{
    Thread.Sleep(8000);
}    ≤8 001ms elapsed
```

How it works...

There are many tools on the market that do this and much more, allowing developers to view all sorts of code metrics. PerfTips, however, allow you to see issues on the fly while you are stepping through your code as per your normal debugging tasks. It is, in my opinion, an indispensable debugging tool.

13

Creating a Web Application in Azure

This chapter will introduce you to Azure. If you have never worked with Azure before, the interface might seem a bit daunting. Azure, however, is actually not all that complicated and is a tremendous benefit to any developer. In this chapter, we will have a look at doing the following:

- ▸ Creating a database in Azure for testing
- ▸ Creating a web application and hosting on Azure
- ▸ Using virtual machines on Azure

Introduction

Azure allows developers to be more productive. It is a series of cloud services that developers can use to build apps, protect data, and provide high availability to your applications irrespective of what you are building. Mobile apps, enterprise apps, web, **internet of things (IoT)**... all are welcome on Azure.

You can create apps with .NET, JavaScript, PHP, Node.js, Python, and even run Linux containers. Azure also allows you to only pay for what you actually use, allowing you to easily scale as your needs grow.

Creating a database in Azure for testing

Creating a database in Azure is really a straightforward process. A lot of work has gone into making the process really streamlined with an all-too-familiar wizard-type interface.

Getting ready

To start working with Azure, you will need to have an Azure account. You can create a free trial account. For more information on Azure pricing, have a look at the following URL: `https://azure.microsoft.com/en-us/pricing/`.

How to do it...

1. After you have logged in to your Azure account, you will be taken to your **Dashboard**. From here you can see any items you may have pinned. To the left, you will see the menu. We just want to create a SQL database, so click on the **SQL databases** menu item:

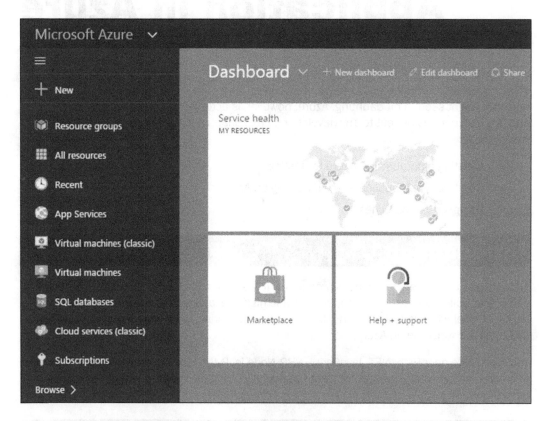

2. If this is the first time you are using Azure, you will not have any databases available in the **Default Directory**. Click on **Add** to create a new database:

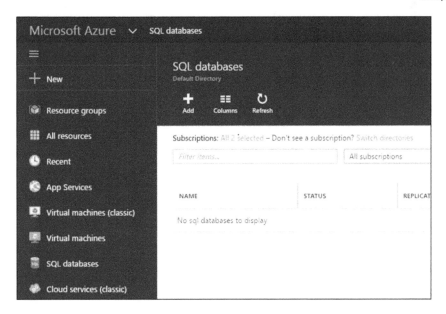

3. You will now be presented with a form that you can use to specify the database details. As you can see, you will probably not have a server selected. This is because you probably don't have one yet. Click on **Server Configure required setting**:

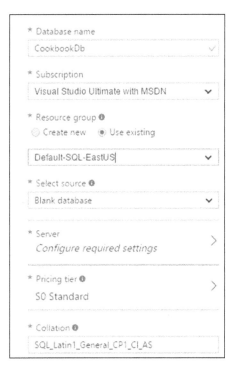

4. You will be given the option to create a new server. This is where you will also create the **Server admin login**:

5. When you have created your server, you will be taken back to the database setup screen. The server you created is now selected for you:

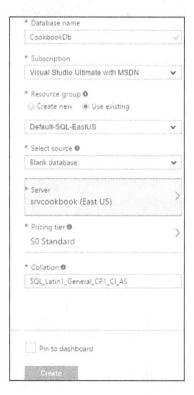

6. When you click the **Create** button, Azure will start deploying your database to the server you created:

7. This process can take a couple of minutes, so be patient while it completes. When the database deployment is completed, you will see a notification in the notifications tab at the top of the Azure portal:

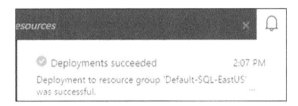

8. You might need to refresh your SQL databases screen to see the newly deployed database. In order to complete the next steps, click on the created database in the databases list:

9. The properties and settings for the created database are then displayed. Here you can see the **Resource group** you selected, along with the **Server name** and other properties. Of particular interest is the **Connection strings** property:

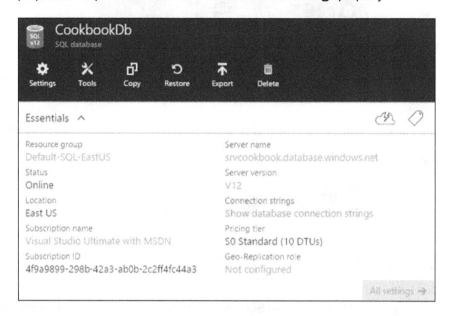

10. Clicking on the **Connection strings** will display the connection strings for the different providers for the database you created. Make a note of the **ADO.NET (SQL authentication)** string:

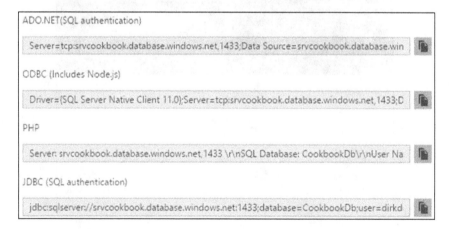

11. Going back to the previous screen, click on the **Server name** property. It is here that you will find the **Firewall** settings. You need to add a rule to the firewall to allow your computer to connect to this database:

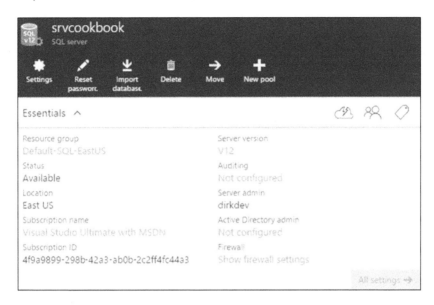

12. Clicking on the **Show firewall settings**, you will see that you can add a client IP. By default, the machine's IP address you are accessing the **Firewall settings** from is displayed in the **Client IP address** field. Click on the **Add client IP** to add your current machine's IP address to allow it through the firewall. You can change the **RULE NAME** to something more user friendly:

You can also define a different IP address here to give a colleague access to this database from their machine.

13. After you have added your firewall rules, open up SQL Server Management Studio on your local development machine. In the **Object Explorer**, click on the **Connect Object Explorer** button:

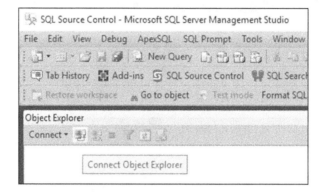

14. Have a look at the connection string you made a note of earlier. After the server portion in the connection string, I copied the server name as `tcp:srvcookbook.database.windows.net`. Paste that in the **Server name** field in the **Connect to Server** screen. Lastly, enter the **Login** and **Password** you defined when creating the server on Azure. Click on the **Connect** button:

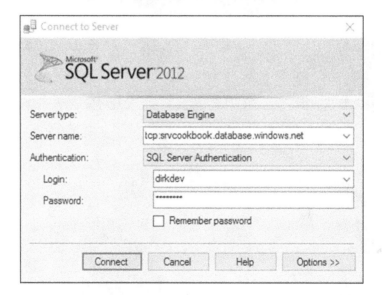

15. SQL Server Management Studio will now connect to the `CookbookDb` database on Azure:

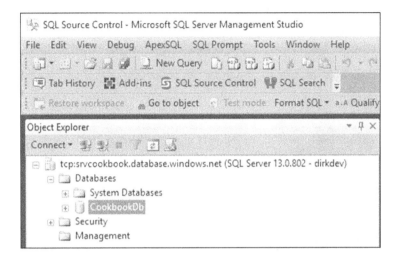

How it works...

Azure is the perfect place to store your database. It is secure and accessible to only those developers you choose. You need to be aware that if your IP address changes, you might need to reconfigure the firewall rule on your Azure database. This does, however, bode well for security, because you can be assured that your data is secure. For more information on databases in Azure, have a look at the following documentation: `https://azure.microsoft.com/en-us/documentation/services/sql-database/`.

Creating a web application and hosting on Azure

One of the things a web developer does more often than not is to deploy a web application for (**user acceptance testing**) **UAT** or developer testing purposes. Azure makes this process very convenient for you by providing a seamless publishing experience from within Visual Studio. To publish a web application or website to Azure, you first need to create a web application on Azure to publish your website to.

Getting ready

To start working with Azure, you will need to have an Azure account. You can create a free trial account. For more information on Azure pricing, have a look at the following URL: `https://azure.microsoft.com/en-us/pricing/`.

How to do it...

1. After you have logged in to your Azure account, you will be taken to your **Dashboard**. From here you can see any items you may have pinned. To the left, you will see the menu. We want to create a website, so click on the **App Services** menu item:

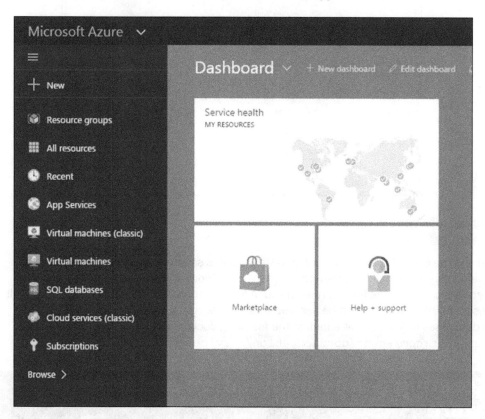

2. If this is your first time using Azure, you probably will not have any app services to display. Click on **Add** to create a new one:

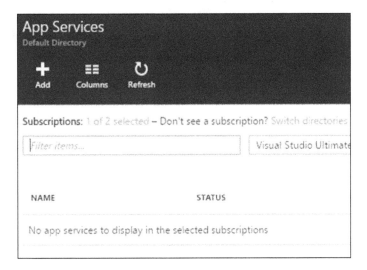

3. Give the app service a name and select or create a **Resource Group**:

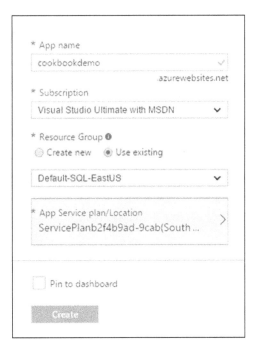

4. When you click the **Create** button, Azure starts the deployment. This process can take several minutes to complete, so go grab a cup of coffee while you wait:

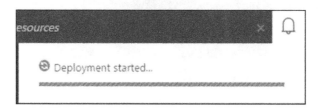

5. When the deployment is finished, you will receive a notification in the notifications menu:

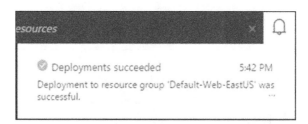

6. Refreshing the **App Services** section, you will see the **cookbookdemo** web app that we have just created. You might need to click on the **Refresh** button before the **cookbookdemo** web app becomes visible:

7. Clicking on the **cookbookdemo** web app will display the properties. Take special notice of the **URL** in the upper-right corner:

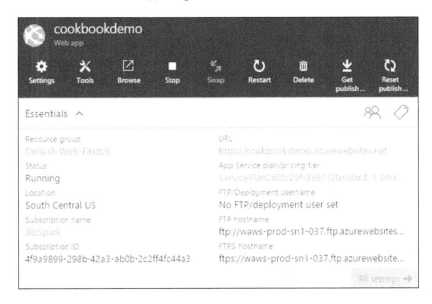

8. If you click on this URL, you will be taken to the default placeholder site for your web application. It is time to publish our website to Azure:

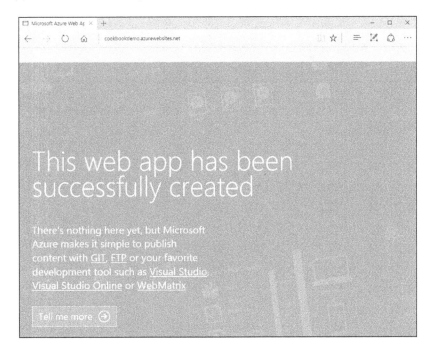

9. Start Visual Studio and create or open a website you want to publish. I have created a simple website that I want to publish:

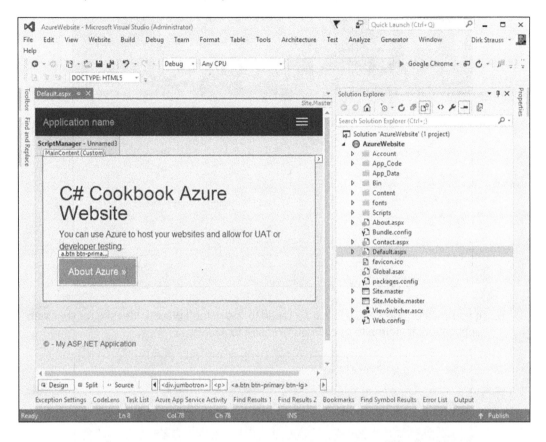

10. Right-click on your website project and click on **Publish Web App** from the context menu:

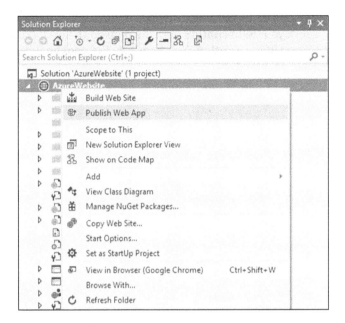

11. The **Publish Web** screen is displayed. Here you can see various publish targets available to you. We simply want to publish our application to Azure. Select **Microsoft Azure Web Apps** as a publish target:

12. Clicking on **Next** will either ask you to connect to Azure or, if you have previously connected, select your **Subscription** from the drop-down selection. Any existing web apps are displayed in the **Existing Web Apps** list. The **cookbookdemo** web app we created earlier is displayed:

13. Selecting the **cookbookdemo** web app, you now have to define your web app connection and **Publish method**. For now, we will just select **Web Deploy** as our method for publishing our web application to Azure:

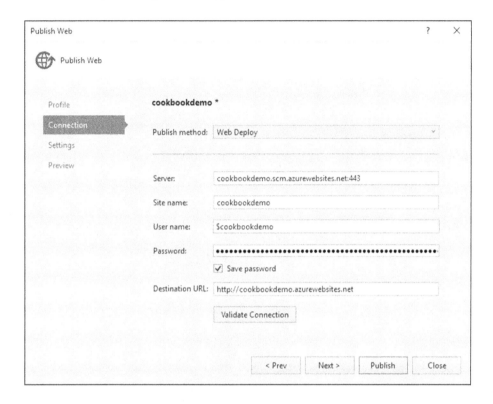

14. You can also click on the **Validate Connection** button to make sure everything is in order before continuing:

15. Clicking **Next** takes you to the **Settings** screen. Here you can select a **Configuration** to deploy, as well as define a database connection:

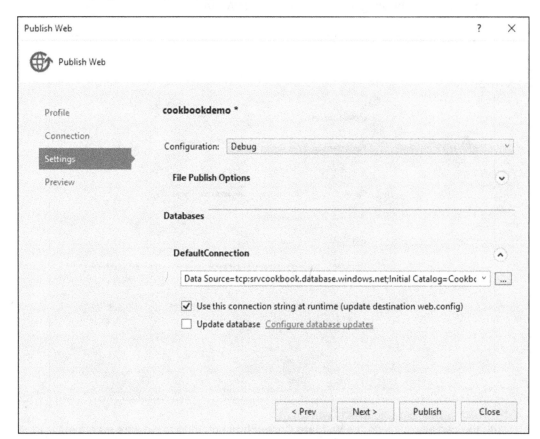

 As you will notice, the database connection I am using is the connection to the database we created in the first recipe of this chapter, *Creating a database in Azure for testing*.

16. When you click **Next**, you will see that you can preview the files that are to be published to the web application on Azure. The initial publish will obviously contain the most files, as nothing exists on the web application yet:

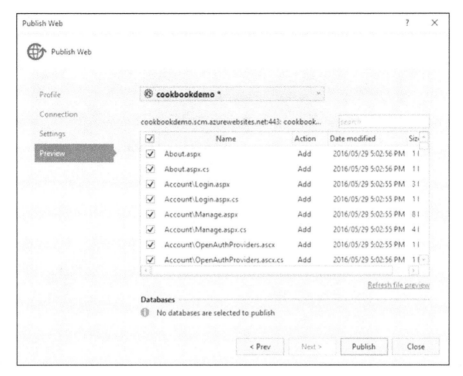

17. When you are ready, clicking on the **Publish** button will start the process of publishing your website to Azure. This can also take a few minutes to complete. When the publish has completed, Visual Studio will automatically open the published website:

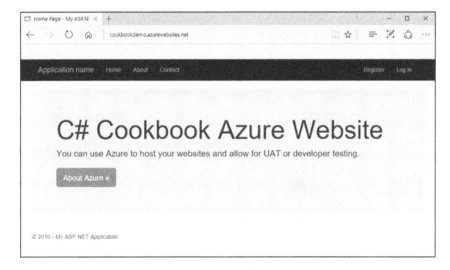

18. Back in Azure, you will see the **Monitoring** window spring to life. You can also add other sections here that will provide more information about the state of your web application:

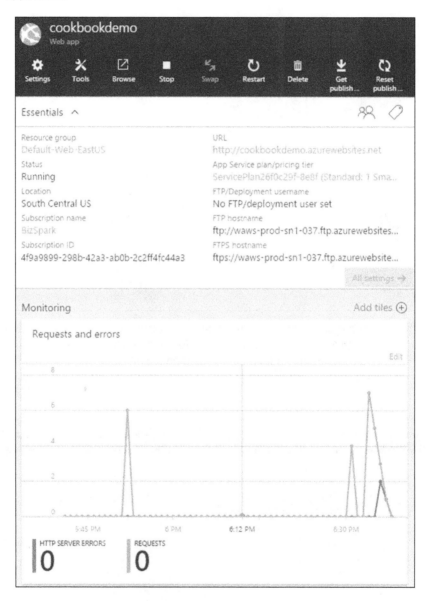

How it works...

Azure puts a lot of power into the hands of the developer when deploying to Azure. You can add additional sections that assist in the management of your web application. These are displayed to you as tiles. Some of the sections available are:

- Process Explorer
- WebJobs
- Traffic routing
- Requests and errors
- Http 4xx
- Http 5xx
- Filesystem storage
- Web tests
- Users and roles
- Performance tests
- Even your estimated Azure spend

Azure is truly a very versatile cloud solution for developers, no matter what your individual needs.

Using virtual machines on Azure

A **virtual machine** (**VM**) is indispensable to developers. I have a few myself that I use for my personal use and to try out new software. The technology behind it is quite incredible as it virtualizes a specific environment for you to accurately test your applications against. At my previous employer, we would create VMs of certain client environments in order to test application deployment and basically to see whether the application works correctly.

With Azure, developers have so many choices when deciding on a specific VM platform. You can spin up virtually (pun intended) any type of VM you need. If you want to test out the new Visual Studio, you can. A new version of Windows? You can bet there will be a VM on Azure for that. Want to play around with Linux and WordPress a bit? No problem. Azure does it all and it is incredibly easy to set up.

Consider the alternative. If VMs weren't there and you wanted to test an application on an OS such as Windows 10, you would probably have to set aside a specific machine just for testing different OS versions. That's one machine not available to you anymore for other work. Then you need to spend an hour or two setting up that PC with the correct OS. You then need to set the PC up to be available over the local network at your office. What about if you wanted to access that test machine from a remote location (at home for example)? You would need to configure it to be accessible remotely while still maintaining security. So then you set up a VPN to access the machine remotely on the off chance that the developers need to work after hours. This has to be done for a single instance of an application in development. If you have servers to spare, sure, this might not be a problem. If, however, you are a small-to-medium-sized company with limited resources, chances are you'll be reinstalling that machine soon with a different client's setup for testing.

This is where Azure is brilliant at making a difference. The setup process takes a few minutes, a moment compared to the setup required for a PC at your office. Remote access, security, event monitoring, alerts, and a whole bunch of other features are immediately available to all the developers in your team.

Getting ready

To start working with Azure, you will need to have an Azure account. You can create a free trial account. For more information on Azure pricing, have a look at the following URL: `https://azure.microsoft.com/en-us/pricing/`.

How to do it...

1. After you have logged in to your Azure account, you will be taken to your **Dashboard**. From here you can see any items you may have pinned. To the left you will see the menu. Click on the **Virtual machines** menu item:

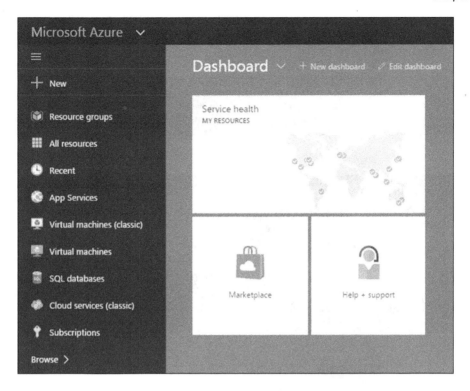

2. You will then be taken to the default directory for the virtual machines on your Azure subscription. We need to create a new virtual machine by clicking on the **Add** button:

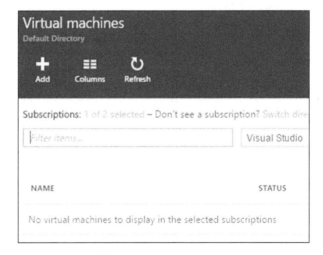

3. Azure then displays all the types of virtual machine available to you. There are quite a lot of types of machine to choose from. From Service Fabric, to Linux, to Ubuntu, the choice is vast:

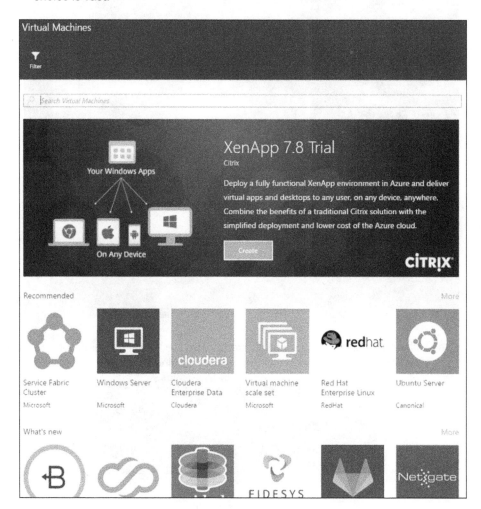

4. For our purposes, we will just create a Windows virtual machine:

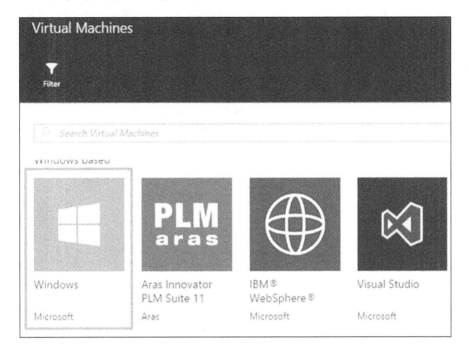

5. Clicking on the **Windows** group, you can see that we have a choice of Windows 10 Enterprise or Windows 8.1 Enterprise 64-bit VMs. We will simply select the Windows 10 VM to get started:

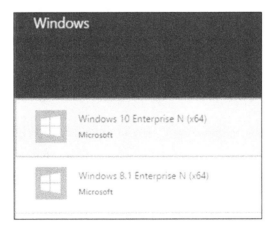

6. You will now be asked to enter various settings to configure your Windows 10 VMs. Give your VM a name and define a login user and password. The **Resource group** will allow you to select an existing one or create a new one:

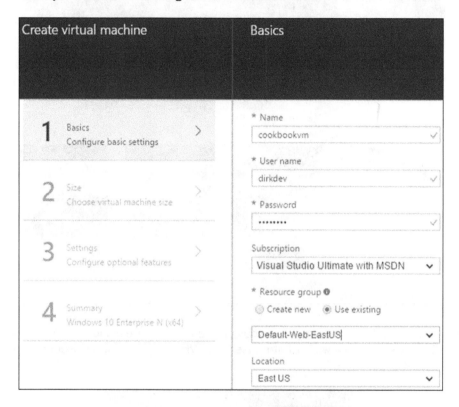

7. On the next configuration screen, you will be presented with recommended VM sizes, each with their different pricing option displayed in your local currency. Choose the option that is most suitable for you, your requirements, and/or budget.

8. The next screen allows you to configure optional features. The features available to you are the following:

    ❑ Storage account is where the disks for the VM are created.

    ❑ Virtual network acts much like a traditional network. Any VMs in the same virtual network will be able to access each other, and this is configured by default.

    ❑ Subnet allows you to isolate VM from other VMs or the Internet.

    ❑ Public IP address allows you to communicate with a machine outside the virtual network defined previously.

- Network security group is a collection of rules defined on your firewall that controls who can access your Windows 10 virtual machine.

- Extensions are quite nice. These are additional add-ons, such as antivirus packages.

- Monitoring is on by default and allows you to gather information about your VM and define alerts based on the information monitored. This keeps you in control and informed at all times.

- The diagnostics storage account is where the monitoring metrics are stored. You can then analyze these with any of your own tools if needed.

- The availability setting allows you to cluster two or more VMs together to provide a failover if one of the VMs needs to be taken offline for maintenance. This need to be configured at this step because the availability setting can't be changed after the VM is created:

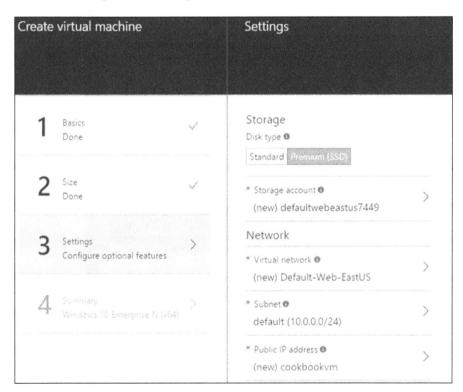

9. Once you have configured the VM, you will be presented with a summary of the configuration options you selected during setup:

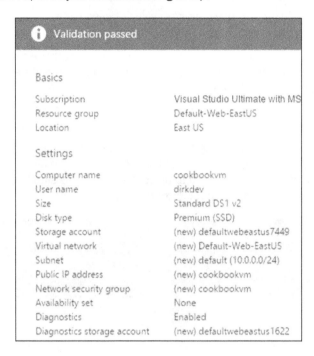

10. When you are satisfied that the VM is set up correctly, Azure will then start the deployment process:

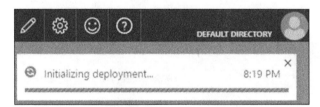

11. The progress of the deployment process is also visible on the **Dashboard** and takes a few minutes to complete:

12. After a few minutes, the VM is available and ready. You will be taken to the virtual machine page for your **cookbookvm**:

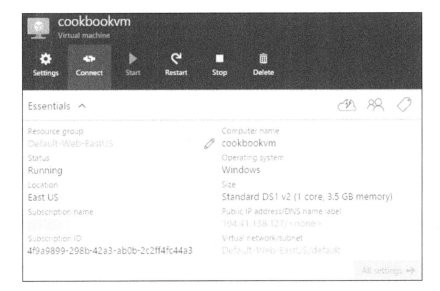

13. To connect to your VM, click on the **Connect** button:

14. An `.rdp` file is then downloaded. You can click on the file directly to start the **Remote Desktop Connection** session:

15. You will probably be asked whether you trust the publisher of the remote connection. Obviously you do, so just click on the **Connect** button:

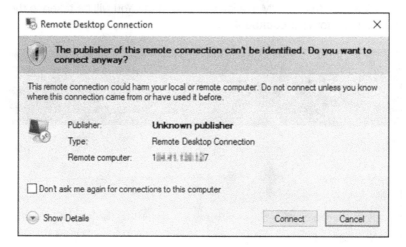

16. You will now be able to enter your login credentials, as defined earlier during the VM setup:

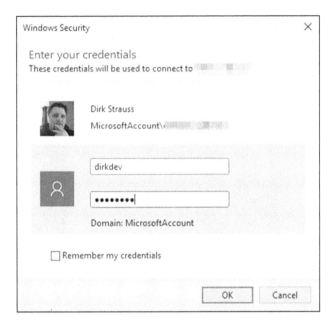

17. You will now be connected to the Windows 10 virtual machine via Remote
    Desktop Connection:

18. Back in Azure, if you selected the **Monitoring** option during the VM setup, you will see that you have a default **Monitoring** tile for **CPU percentage**. Azure allows you to add more monitoring events and create alerts for each event:

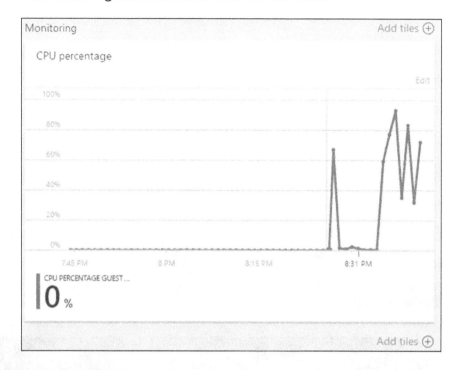

How it works...

Virtual machines are accessible via remote connections. You can use the good old Remote Desktop Connection, or something more exotic such as mRemoteNG if you have several remote machines that you need to access. The reason that Azure is so well suited for development testing is because the resource does not have to live on your own network at all. That means the overhead involved in maintaining backups of development VMs is largely avoided.

I remember the network administrator at my previous employer regularly asking what VMs we still used. Some of these VMs were used perhaps once or twice a year, so they couldn't be deleted. Having several developers access these VMs also meant that there was a lot of junk on these VMs, which made backing those up a painful process (usually run over weekends).

Azure solves many issues and problems for IT professionals. In this chapter, we have looked at only three solutions available to you as a developer. Do not be fooled, Azure is much more powerful than just being able to provide a robust testing platform for developers. Going into detail about Azure would probably require a separate book on its own.

Index

LINQ
 used, for performing queries 124-134
Liskov substitution principle (LSP) 80
lock keyword 216
low priority background thread
 aborting 200-208
 creating 200-208

M

maximum thread pool size
 increasing 208-212
microservices
 about 143
 disadvantage 144
multiple threads
 creating 213-215
 debugging 234-238

N

nameof expressions
 about 22
 using 22, 23
 working 24-27
NetBean 349
null-conditional operator
 about 11-13
 using 11-14

O

open/closed principle
 about 106-108
 working 109

P

parallel foreach loops
 cancelling 227-229
 errors, catching 230-234
 used, for running multiple threads 220-227
Parallel.Invoke
 used, for invoking parallel calls to
  methods 218-220
passwords
 encrypting 374-383
 storing 374-383

PerfTips
 used, for identifying bottlenecks in
  code 418-420
Platform as a Service (PaaS) 144
polymorphism
 about 101
 implementing 101-104

Q

queries
 performing, with LINQ 124-133
question-dot operator 11

R

Reactive Extensions. *See* **Rx**
Regular Expressions (regex)
 about 291, 292
 conditional OR 300
 start and end of string 301
 starting with 292-297
 valid digits for months and days 300
 valid separator character set 300
 year portion 300
Reliable Actors 150
Reliable Services 150
Result, code contract
 creating 268-270
return types, asynchronous functions
 task 172
 Task<TResult> 172, 185
 void 172-184
Rx
 installing 112-117
 Language-Integrated Query (LINQ) 112, 124
 observables 112, 124
 reference link 112
 schedulers 112, 124
 schedulers, using 134-139
 uses 112

S

schedulers
 reference link 134
 using, in Rx 134-139

www.ingramcontent.com/pod-product-compliance
Lightning Source LLC
Chambersburg PA
CBHW081456050326

40690CB00015B/2821